CHARLIE MIKE

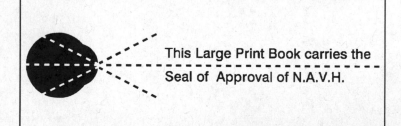

This Large Print Book carries the
Seal of Approval of N.A.V.H.

CHARLIE MIKE

A TRUE STORY OF HEROES WHO BROUGHT THEIR MISSION HOME

JOE KLEIN

THORNDIKE PRESS
A part of Gale, Cengage Learning

GALE
CENGAGE Learning®

Farmington Hills, Mich • San Francisco • New York • Waterville, Maine
Meriden, Conn • Mason, Ohio • Chicago

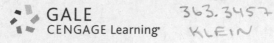
GALE
CENGAGE Learning®

Copyright © 2015 by Joseph Klein, LLC.
Thorndike Press, a part of Gale, Cengage Learning.

ALL RIGHTS RESERVED
Thorndike Press® Large Print Popular and Narrative Nonfiction.
The text of this Large Print edition is unabridged.
Other aspects of the book may vary from the original edition.
Set in 16 pt. Plantin.

LIBRARY OF CONGRESS CATALOGING-IN-PUBLICATION DATA

Names: Klein, Joe, 1946–
Title: Charlie Mike : a true story of heroes who brought their mission home / by Joe Klein.
Description: Large print edition. | Waterville, Maine : Thorndike Press, a part of Gale, Cengage Learning, [2016] | © 2015 | Series: Thorndike Press large print popular and narrative nonfiction
Identifiers: LCCN 2015040081 | ISBN 9781410486738 (large print : hbk.) | ISBN 1410486737 (large print : hbk.)
Subjects: LCSH: Mission Continues (Organization) | Disabled veterans—Services for—United States. | Volunteers—Training of—United States. | Greitens, Eric, 1974– | Wood, Jake, 1983– | Veterans—United States—Biography. | Philanthropists—United States—Biography. | Iraq War, 2003–2011—Veterans—United States. | Afghan War, 2001– —Veterans—United States. | Large type books.
Classification: LCC UB363 .K66 2016 | DDC 363.34/5763209270973—dc23
LC record available at http://lccn.loc.gov/2015040081

Published in 2016 by arrangement with Simon & Schuster, Inc.

Printed in the United States of America
1 2 3 4 5 6 7 20 19 18 17 16

FOR
ADAM WALINSKY
LESLIE H. GELB

AND IN MEMORY OF
RICHARD C. HOLBROOKE

Beloved Mentors All

Ask not what your country can do for you;
ask what you can do for your country.

— JOHN F. KENNEDY

It's hard to live a life of high moral
purpose if everyone around you thinks
you're acting like a chump.

— ADAM WALINSKY

CONTENTS

9

AUTHOR'S NOTE

The events that follow really happened. In most cases, I have used multiple sources to get as close as possible to the truth. I did make one concession: the names of a few of the characters in the story have been changed, in some instances because they continue to work downrange as special operators.

In the U.S. Military, "Charlie Mike" is shorthand for "Continue the Mission."

■ ■ ■ ■

PART I
WE HAVE A MODEL

■ ■ ■ ■

"Hey? Jake Wood? It's McNulty."

"Nick Nolte?" Jake knew full well that the voice on the other end of the line was neither old nor gravelly enough to be the actor, but goofing on people was Jake's method of interpersonal exploration.

"McNulty."

"Stop fucking with me," Jake said. "You're not Nick Nolte."

"No, asshole. Mc-Nul-ty. William Mc-Nulty. Remember we talked six months ago about doing that Somali pirate thing?"

Vaguely. Barely. "Yeah," Jake said. "What can I do for you?"

"I saw your Facebook post about Haiti," McNulty said. "I'm in."

It was January 13, 2010. A day earlier, Jake Wood had been sitting in his apartment in Burbank, glued to the news about the devastation in Haiti — the collapsed buildings, wounded civilians, the chaos in the

17

streets. There were reports of looting and banditry. It looked a lot like a war zone. He had been there before, in Iraq and Afghanistan. He realized that he missed it.

Jake had been honorably discharged from the Marines in October 2009. His plan was to make the transition to full-fledged adulthood. He was applying to business schools for an MBA. It had felt *premature* immediately after graduating from the University of Wisconsin — Jake in a suit? Jake in an office? And it didn't feel particularly wonderful now, especially after a way-too-quick rejection from Stanford Business School had detonated in his mailbox.

"Maybe I can do something in Haiti. I want to help," Jake said to his girlfriend, Indra Petersons, a meteorologist for KABC-TV in Los Angeles. They had just started living together, after dating for a year.

He knew that Indra was, at that moment, watching him think. It was amazing how clearly she saw through him, through everybody. They had met at a pickup football game, Thanksgiving of 2008. She was beautiful, Latvian — but the unexpected part was the complete absence of coy. "Oh, sure," she had said when he'd told her that one of the schools he was applying to was

Northwestern. "You can go get your MBA at Northwestern. That's a *great* place to go. But I'm not following you to Chicago. And I'm not counting on you coming back."

Jake figured Indra would go along with his Haiti excursion — she was a storm-chaser herself, after all. But he was very much on probation. The bottom line was that he was going to have to prove to her that he was serious, that he was ready to begin the rest of his life after a four-year adrenaline fiesta in the Marines. He felt a visceral pull toward Haiti. It would be for only a week or so. It was a onetime deal.

We'll see, Indra thought. Jake was, as she was, a frightening combination of brains and looks. He was six foot six, ripped — he had lost all his extraneous football weight — with soft brown eyes. But mostly he was very perceptive, in a no-nonsense way. He could think along with her; they could see the world the same.

Jake was taking some brush-up economics courses at the local community college, which weren't exactly setting his brain on fire. The MBA was something he would definitely do . . . eventually. But right now, he couldn't take his eyes off the tube. They were saying that no relief was getting into Haiti because of the general chaos and the fear of armed street gangs — but how dangerous could Port-au-Prince be? Would the gangs be an organized threat, real soldiers, like the Taliban? He doubted it. And if they *were* terrorizing the populace, all the more reason for a Marine to go in and protect the civilians. The airport was closed on account of anarchy, apparently. That was a problem. If you wanted to help, how did you get in there?

He called the Red Cross and talked to a nice lady. He told her that he was a Marine Sergeant with two combat deployments, a college graduate, and that he had experience in disaster relief after Hurricane Katrina.

"Are you a Red Cross volunteer?" she asked.

"That's why I'm calling. To volunteer."

"We're not taking spontaneous volunteers," she said. "You have to be trained. It's dangerous down there."

"I'm a . . . Marine," he said, carefully editing the f-bomb. "I can do danger. Don't you need people who can, like, protect the medical personnel?"

She was sure they did. But that would require training, too.

"How long does the training take?"

"Anywhere from a day to a week, depending on what you're going to do . . . but I'm not sure we're taking inexperienced people, in any case."

Inexperienced? He hung up. "Fuck it," he told Indra. "I'm going anyway." He posted his intentions on Facebook and started calling his friends. His best friend from the Marines, Clay Hunt, had to go to a wedding in Houston that weekend. "But I'm in," Clay said. "I'll meet you there." Yeah, sure. In the midst of all the shit and anarchy, Clay would just *find* him. He worried that Clay would only find trouble — that had happened before — but there was no time to think too much about that. He tried five other Marines; they were willing but didn't have passports. He had a better result with a Wisconsin roommate and football teammate, Jeff Lang, who was now a firefighter in Milwaukee. "Sure, dude, I'm in," Jeff said, and he'd check whether any of his fellow firefighters wanted in (one did). Later that day, McNulty called.

McNulty was also a Marine Sergeant, an intelligence specialist, but he'd spent most of his time — at the Marines' behest — as a private intelligence contractor. He had been an interrogator in Iraq and also worked for the Defense Intelligence Agency (DIA). He was trying to start an intelligence consulting firm and a film company, which he would call Title X Productions, after the section of the U.S. code that governs military conduct. "I've got to be in Istanbul at the end of the month," he said, "but I'm ready to roll right now."

Jake liked that: "Let's roll" was his generation's call to arms, made famous on September 11, 2001, when the passengers on Flight 93 decided to battle the Al Qaeda terrorists who had seized the plane. They crashed in central Pennsylvania, the first victory in the war against Al Qaeda.

McNulty had become aware of Jake a few years earlier, when a friend had turned him on to a blog called *Jake's Life,* which Jake used to tell war stories to the folks and former football teammates back home. He liked to write and was good at it; it was a way to wring out the war and to chill. He didn't dwell on the horrible stuff, although he didn't hide it either. McNulty was an obsessive consumer of war news — he read everything he could find on the net — and Jake seemed like one of those guys who had his head screwed on straight, who hadn't been addled by bloodlust or anomie.

When Jake blogged that he was leaving the military, William had called to see if he was interested in working for Title X. He was trying to get a strategic consulting contract from the U.S. government to do intelligence analysis on the Somali pirates in the Gulf of Aden. He and Jake had several phone conversations before Jake finally said thanks, but no thanks. He had a bad foot, an old football injury exacerbated by all the running he'd had to do as a Marine. He was about to have surgery on it for the sixth time. Anyway, it was time to get real, to apply for that MBA, to settle in with Indra.

And now, out of nowhere, Will McNulty was on the phone, and he had some very good ideas. Will had graduated from the University of Kansas with a dual degree in economics and communications — but his real education had been suffered at the hands of the invaluable Roman Catholic drill sergeants of learning, the Jesuits. Will knew a priest back in Chicago, who knew a Jesuit Brother down in Port-au-Prince, who was asking for help.

Within a matter of hours, Will arranged for them to meet up the *next day* with Brother Jim Boynton in Santo Domingo, the capital of the Dominican Republic, which shared the island of Hispaniola with Haiti. Brother Jim would be carrying medical supplies across the border, and McNulty offered to get letters of passage from both governments. "We're going to be carrying narcotics," he told Jake. "We should have everything in order."

"I would never have thought of that," Jake said to Indra.

So, twenty-four hours after being rejected by the Red Cross, Jake had a partner and a mission. Brother Jim was trying to get some doctors to join them. "What are we going to call this operation?" McNulty asked Jake. "We should have a name, right?"

William, in a Jesuitical frame of mind, emailed him a bunch of Latin possibilities. Jake liked "Rubicon." He knew the expression "crossing the Rubicon" but didn't know what it referred to. He googled it and told Will that it was the river Julius Caesar had crossed when he returned to Rome on his way to overturning the Republic and establishing himself as emperor. It was the point of no return.

"That's kind of cool," Jake said. "We've got to cross a river to get into Haiti, right?"

His first thought was to call it Operation Rubicon, but McNulty was wary: an "operation" suggested a lot more organization and planning than they had done. "It's just you and me, the firefighters, and Brother Jim, right?" Will said. "Let's call it Team Rubicon. You don't want to oversell."

There was one more phone call that day. McNulty had checked in with a friend in the intelligence community who told him, "Will, they've got armed gangs toting M-16s, and there's lots of looting. It's dangerous. Don't go down there and try to be a hero."

Will relayed this to Jake, who blew up: "McNulty, I've handled heavier shit than some fucking street gang in Haiti. I'm going. What I need to know from you is, are you with me or not? C'mon, we're fucking Marines. We *do* chaos."

"I'm going," Will said, noting that, like most Marines, Jake used the word "fucking" as an adjectival amplifier. "I told you I was fucking in, didn't I?"

Also that day, Jake revived his wartime blog. His first post began: "I knew I'd come out of retirement at some point."

They now had a name, they had raised enough money off Facebook for $500 plane tickets to Santo Domingo — and, remarkably, they had letters of passage that Will had secured from the Haitian and Dominican embassies in Washington. They would meet up with Brother Jim in Santo Domingo on the evening of Day 2.

25

They doubled their numbers the next day. Jeff Lang, the Milwaukee firefighter, asked the pilot to make an announcement on his flight down to Santo Domingo: Were there any doctors or nurses on board who were headed to Haiti and wanted to be part of a medical relief team? Dr. Eduardo Dolhun, an obstetrician from San Francisco with extensive disaster relief experience, raised his hand. Another doctor approached Jake at the baggage claim in Santo Domingo. "You look like you're headed to Haiti," Dave Griswell, an emergency room doc from Virginia, asked, "Can I come with you?"

"Absolutely," Jake said.

Just before he boarded his own flight to Santo Domingo, McNulty, who looked semiofficial in his Marine camouflage pants, was approached by an obvious military sort (he could always tell a comrade by his looks, his walk, his body language, his attitude). "You wouldn't be going to Haiti, by any chance?" asked Mark Hayward, an Army special forces medic. He signed on, too. Team Rubicon now had eight members.

Jake Wood and William McNulty finally met each other in Santo Domingo on the evening of January 14, 2010.

Jake saw that Will was really intense: he was about six feet tall, fit and wiry — that was good — dark Irish, clean shaven but with a heavy beard, and sharp blue eyes that almost seemed to bug out when he was talking. He'd already sensed that Will would be a perfect XO (executive officer), second in command, and organizational guy, but there was also intelligence and sensitivity, perhaps an emotional vulnerability to him. Both were enlisted men who were college graduates, who could have, and maybe should have, been officers, which infused Team Rubicon with a particular style: there wouldn't be any of that bullshit officer stiffness and formality. There would be, Jake hoped, an easy noncom pride and defiance. They would be loose and fearless. The hell with the Red Cross.

Crossing their Rubicon on Day 3 — at Jimaní, a tiny town next to a dry stream that divided the Dominican Republic from Haiti — proved to be less dramatic than expected. After hearing about the street gangs, Jake was intent on being armed for the trip. He later managed to acquire a pistol, but he would never need to use it. They piled into two vans, cross-loading the medical supplies so that a full ration of medicine would get through if one of the vans was attacked,

27

detained, or confiscated — but that proved an unnecessary precaution, too. The drive to Haiti was long, eight hours, but uneventful, and crossing the border wasn't very dramatic either. The letters of passage that Will had obtained were honored on both sides of the border; all the medical supplies got through.

The next drive, from the border to Port-au-Prince, took about an hour and a half. McNulty thought it was beautiful — the Baie de Port-au-Prince on the right and white chalk cliffs on the left. Jake was struck by the robust police presence, helicopters in the air, military on the ground. They saw none of the free-range criminality and danger that was being reported on television and by McNulty's intel friend. There were traffic snarls around gas stations as they entered Port-au-Prince from the north, but food and drink were being sold along the side of the road. This wasn't so bad.

As they moved south, though, there were more collapsed buildings, hundreds and hundreds of them, and soon, wild and utter devastation. Mark Hayward, the Army medic, told McNulty that the pervasive, gagging, rancid smell in the air came from dead bodies rotting in the tropical heat, something William had never experienced

28

before. There were crowds of people in the street as the team moved toward the Jesuit novitiate at dusk, wandering — not rioting — asking them for help. Jake was tempted to stop but decided that they had to keep moving, get to the Jesuits, and plan out their deployment from there.

The novitiate sat at the end of a winding road. It was a large compound, surrounded by an eight-foot wall topped with razor wire. There was a heavy metal gate guarded by a security team. The Team Rubicon firefighters immediately set to work assessing the structural damage to the novitiate's buildings. The damage was significant, so the team set up sleeping tents in the yard. That evening the monks fed them pumpkin soup with pasta, plus saltine crackers and pieces of goat meat. There were some refugees at the novitiate, one child with a broken leg, and Doc Griswell set it. Jake and William were daunted by the conditions they'd seen, but they were hopeful about their team. It had taken them all of four days to organize themselves, get to Haiti, and start helping out.

The next morning, they went to the Manresa refugee camp, which was well across town, on the grounds of a former Jesuit retreat. Before they left, Jake set out the logistics and gave each of the team members an assignment. He had their Jesuit translator, François, hire two tap-taps — the hallucinogenic, crazy-painted, covered pickup trucks that served as taxis — and the team hit the road.

Manresa was a hot and bare field, clogged with people. There was a single tree toward the back of the camp, and they strung a tarp from it. This would be their triage center. People immediately began to gather, hundreds of them. McNulty saw that they had crushed limbs, compound fractures, bloody and tattered bandages, open wounds. The doctors had François ask the people to line up according to the severity of their injuries, and, much to McNulty's joy and amazement, they triaged themselves, quietly, without pushing or screaming. There was, in fact, a reverent silence, punctuated by occasional sobs of pain and babies crying. The crowd parted to allow the most severely wounded to be brought in on makeshift litters — doors that had been blown off in the quake. The Team Rubicon doctors, medics, and firefighters went to work, making the most seriously injured comfortable, setting bones, cleaning and debriding wounds. McNulty didn't feel capable to do that — he had no training — so he began to break down window frames into sticks for splinting. He organized a crew to gather window frames from the Jesuit retreat and other collapsed buildings in the area.

They worked all day, snacking on protein bars, losing track of time and place, losing themselves in the effort to heal the gracious, grateful Haitians. One of their patients had a broken back and was partially paralyzed. He could move his arms, but his legs were crushed. He needed to get to a hospital. They flagged down a Haitian driving a hatchback who agreed to take their patient. He was littered on a door, which was longer than the hatch bed — the patient's lower legs were sticking out the back. They paid the driver to go to the hospital. There was no guarantee that he'd do it, but after a day of work at Manresa, their default position was that most Haitians were not only benign but also intent on helping out.

The taxis that had brought them to Manresa had promised to return at four p.m., but they didn't. As evening fell, François managed to hail a couple of tap-taps to take them back to the Jesuit novitiate. "We've got to solve the transport situation," McNulty said to Jake.

"What do you propose?"

"We can't wait for ambulances or relief

crews. Let's charter two tap-taps and over pay, to guarantee they'll be there for us."

He asked François to hire two tap-taps for $100 per day, plus $10 for every emergency run — which was ridiculously generous in Port-au-Prince, where the going rate for rides was loose change. By the end of the week, they had five dedicated tap-taps, as more teams of doctors and nurses arrived via the Jesuits back in Chicago.

Brother Jim Boynton had been a Jesuit for twenty-six years, most of them spent teaching in Detroit. A year earlier, his superiors had asked if he'd be interested in an international assignment. "Absolutely," he'd said. He asked for someplace in South America, where he could use his Spanish. They sent him to Haiti, which was close, but not Spanish-speaking; he would have to learn Creole. He was sent to Ouanaminthe, a lush, tropical town near the Haitian-Dominican border, where he became the principal of the local school.

On the afternoon of the earthquake, he was in Ouanaminthe, playing Irish jigs on his fiddle for some of the students in the street outside the Jesuit residence. The kids were dancing as the ground began to shake and tumble. And it was magical: the kids ontinued to dance as the ground heaved, as if they were playing on one of those inflated plastic bounce-house contraptions. When the temblors stopped, he surveyed the rest of the village, mostly reed and mud huts, and found everything was pretty much okay. But he soon began receiving emails about the disaster in Port-au-Prince. His Jesuit superiors asked him to go to Santo Domingo, organize a medical team, and head back to the novitiate in Haiti's capital city. He had experience with disaster relief, and he knew that these operations could take months to get organized. He didn't know where to start . . . and then, at that very moment — a sure sign of Divine Providence — the email from William McNulty popped into his mailbox.

Brother Jim's only previous experience with the military was to protest at the gates of Fort Benning against the School of the Americas, a training facility for Latin American military personnel, including those who had committed massacres against Roman Catholic priests and nuns in El Salvador. But he found himself immediately at ease when he met Wood and McNulty. "You're Jesuit-educated?" he asked Will, although he already knew the answer to that question.

"Yep," McNulty replied. "I'm a 'man for others,' " he said, citing the Jesuit motto.

Jake looked Brother Jim in the eye, from his great height. "So you're a monk?" he asked with a laugh. Brother Jim was wearing his usual — T-shirt, shorts, and a crucifix. "I'm glad you're here," Jake continued. "We probably couldn't have figured this out without you."

Boynton had been up all the previous night, securing the medical supplies and arranging logistics, and now Jake said, "You look like you could use some shut-eye. We've got a big day tomorrow," and just like that, Jim was following Jake's orders. That seemed strange: he was forty-two; Jake was twenty-seven. Over the next few days, Brother Jim would watch how Jake led — treating everyone with respect, reading situations accurately and decisively, leavening a moment with a wisecrack — and he realized that this was the first young person whose judgment he trusted more than his own.

On the road to Port-au-Prince, Mark Hayward had briefed Boynton about what to do if he got shot and how to deal with severed arteries — basic military first aid stuff and entirely terrifying — Brother Jim blanched, and Jake read that, too: "Don't worry, Jim," he said. "It's gonna be all right."

"Please God, don't let me get shot," Brother Jim prayed. But also, "Thank you, Lord, for sending me these guys." When they loaded the two pickup trucks for the trip from the border to Port-au-Prince, Boynton made sure to get into the one with Jake and William.

Brother Jim was shocked by the casualties, the number and severity of the wounds at Manresa on their first day of work. Jake and Will had told him they were shocked, too, but they didn't show it. He was amazed by how calm and well organized they were. That night, they gathered outdoors around a fire near a massive banyan tree at the novitiate for dinner and a debrief. The chow was beans and rice, comfort food, perfectly satisfying. There was beer. The debrief would become a nightly routine, as would the beer.

Jake started the proceedings, reviewing the day's deployment and explaining the next day's assignment. The Jesuits wanted them to go to an AIDS clinic run by Mother Teresa's nuns. Jake split the group into two teams and announced the new tap-tap transport arrangement. They had used up all their medicine the first day and were hoping that there would be some at the AIDS clinic. In the afternoon, McNulty would go to the airport, where two and a half tons of medical supplies and a team of doctors and nurses were supposed to be coming in on a United charter flight from Chicago, courtesy of the Jesuits. Getting the supplies to the novitiate was going to be a real headache. Every day, thousands of tons were landing at the airport, which was being run by American troops, but they were not getting out.

After going through the logistics, there was a stress debrief, which also became a nightly feature. Brother Jim led this part. The team members were encouraged to talk about the emotional impact of the things they'd seen and done, but they also talked about the strange exhilaration of being part of a military-style mission again. It was a total euphoric relief, Jake thought, being part of a Band of Brothers but not having to kill anyone.

One day during Jake's second combat deployment, as part of a scout-sniper unit in Afghanistan, his team had spotted a high-value target, surrounded by children, two hundred yards away. Jake had been the spotter; his friend and superior, Shawn Beidler, had been the shooter. The target's heart seemed to explode in a gusher of blood against a mud wall; Jake watched the chil-

..ren through his scope, their faces frozen in horror, then the screaming and running. He couldn't stop thinking about those kids after he came home. But he had been surrounded by children all day at Manresa, some of them being treated for their wounds, others asking if they could help out, others just hanging around, amazed by the presence of these giant Americans who were working nonstop to set bones and clean wounds. And Jake realized, in that moment, he was feeling healthier, too. Except for his foot, which was killing him; he was wearing combat boots again, and they truly sucked.

Brother Jim had experienced spiritual bonding before; he was, after all, part of a brotherhood. But this was different, far more intense — the spiritual unity on the team was immediate, augmented by the physical work and the potential danger. He wondered: Was this brotherhood the *real* attraction of the military? He had never really thought about it before. "I have not been the greatest supporter of our soldiers," he admitted that night during the stress debrief. "In fact, I protested against our military at Fort Benning. But you're a product of that military, and I have to say that while I'm not ashamed of protesting in the past, I can also say with a great deal of certainty that, after today, I'll never do ̶ again. You are who you are because of your military training. You are more prepared to serve humanity — to be 'a man for others' — than if you'd been in a monastery reading Thomistic philosophy for the past ten years. And, quite frankly, I'm glad you haven't been."

Brother Jim then led them in St. Ignatius of Loyola's daily prayer:

Lord, teach me to be generous.
Teach me to serve you as you deserve;
to give and not to count the cost,
to fight and not to heed the wounds,
to toil and not to seek for rest,
to labor and not to ask for reward,
save that of knowing that I do your will.

That became part of the daily ritual as well.

Jake, McNulty, and Brother Jim shared a three-man tent, and Will was the last to sleep each night. He was in charge of the blogging, which he would tap out on his BlackBerry and send to Jake's sister in Bettendorf, Iowa, who would post it. Phone calls were hard; text was easier — and, though they didn't know it, Team Rubicon's exploits were beginning to be noticed on esuit blogs and in local newspapers. Contributions were coming in, and Jake's father, Jeff Wood, was organizing transport for more medical supplies and volunteers. As the days passed, Jeff realized that he would have to take off time from his day job as the vice president of a factory in Bettendorf to coordinate Team Rubicon's stateside logistics.

The days were warm, but the nights were chilly in January. Will would slip into the tent and sleep between Jake and Brother Jim. Somehow, each morning he'd wind up with all the blankets — it was very weird — and Jake would be shivering, with none of them. Jake joked about it but never got angry.

The caseload at Mother Teresa's Sisters of Charity AIDS clinic was small compared to Manresa — only a few dozen — but nine had serious problems that required higher echelon treatment. And there was no medicine. Brother Jim offered to take several of the more seriously wounded to University — the city's main hospital — in one of the tap-taps and see if he could find some drugs, splints, and bandages.

The hospital was a white stucco building with green trim, guarded by American troops from the 82nd Airborne. Somehow it hadn't been damaged in the quake. But there was chaos inside. There were a handful of nurses and civilian volunteers trying to take care of hundreds of suffering patients. Brother Jim asked one of the nurses, "Do you have medicine that I can take to my doctors?"

"You have *doctors*?" the nurse replied. "Get them down here immediately. We have no doctors."

Brother Jim raced back to the Mother Teresa clinic. When Jake heard the news, he was boggled — the largest emergency room in town had no doctors? — and decisive: "We're going to the hospital."

Within an hour, Dr. Dave Griswell was running the emergency room at University with the rest of Team Rubicon helping out, working as they had at Manresa the day before.

That afternoon, Jake saw a middle-aged woman brought in with lesions and open sores all over her body, her legs mangled. She was barely coherent. "Be careful," Dr. Griswell said. "I think we have an advanced-stage AIDS patient here."

Jake grimaced. "Oh, God," he said. He hadn't dealt with any advanced-stage AIDS patients, and he struggled to overcome his revulsion. But he had no real choice: he was there to help. He put on an extra layer of surgical gloves.

"We've got to start taking off her clothes," said Mark Hayward — now known as "Doc Army" — and Jake pulled out his combat knife, the first time he'd used it since Afghanistan, and began slicing away her clothes from the shoulders down. Hayward worked from the bottom up, raising her skirt, and what they saw was impossible. Her pubic area, her legs and thighs and stomach were covered with purple blotches and open sores. Her entire pelvic bone was protruding through the skin on one side; the other side was crushed. Jake stopped, gasped, looked at Doc Army.

"She's expectant," Hayward said. Jake knew the term — it was Army-speak for near death, nothing more they could do.

"Okay," he said now, and moved away, thinking: Okay, let's cover her up, let her die with dignity, and go on to the next case.

About ten minutes later, Jake passed by her bed and was amazed to see Dr. Gris lying on the gurney, trying to insert a catheter to enable her to urinate. Jake stopped and watched.

Doc Army had stopped, too, and was watching Griswell reverently. "You know,

Jake," he said, "here's a weird one: if it weren't for this disaster, she'd die in the streets, alone, cold, and in pain. It took a goddamn earthquake to bring someone to this country who cares enough about her comfort to do this."

Griswell worked on her for what seemed an eternity — it was probably only ten minutes — before he conceded defeat. Her canal had withered and stiffened too much to accept the catheter, and Doc knew that his continued probing was opening lesions and causing her more pain. "I'm sorry, I can't do it," he said to her and backed away, frustrated by his failure.

She seemed to understand. She smiled weakly and nodded at him.

Jake lost it then. He rushed outside to an alley and began to weep. He was horrified by the poor woman's suffering, but he was also blown away by Dr. Gris and the dedication of the team. He didn't have much time for self-indulgence; there were other people who needed help. It was a decorous weep, brief and quiet.

McNulty also had been overwhelmed by the sight of Dr. Gris trying to care for the woman, and he took his tears to a separate alley. His cry had been explosive, the sobs erupting from a place he'd never been before. He kept his tears a secret, as Jake did — it would be years before they figured out that they'd lost it at the same moment, for precisely the same reasons.

Meanwhile, Dr. Dolhun, the obstetrician from San Francisco, was delivering babies and doing amputations. Each new baby seemed a particular triumph to McNulty, amid all the death and truncation. There were still no drugs. Amputee patients were given Motrin for their pain; they were given socks to bite on as Dr. Dolhun picked up the saw. There was terrible screaming, lacerating eardrums. Warm January breezes blew through the jalousie windows — the sort of breezes William had always associated with spring break, but now they were a blessing, a balm amid the suffering.

Brother Jim was working on a boy who had come in with his father. The boy had dirty bandages on his head, legs, and feet. Dr. Gris told Boynton to remove the bandages. One of the Milwaukee firefighters helped him . . . and the boy's skin came off with the bandage, and the cheesy smell — gangrene — almost knocked Jim down. He'd later write on Jake's blog, "As I lifted the leg for the fireman to remove more bandage, my fingers went into the flesh like I was holding canned tuna fish." The leg

43

would have to be amputated, but the boy would survive.

That afternoon, McNulty went to the airport to gather the advance guard of what he and Jake were calling Bravo Element, the medical reinforcements sent by the Chicago Jesuits. Four male nurses from Masonic Hospital in Chicago had arrived; another flight was coming the next day with the rest of the team and the medical supplies. Inside the airport, the U.S. military was running an orderly operation; outside, there was mayhem. Crowds — thousands of Haitians — banged on the gates, hoping to get at the tons of food and water sitting inside.

And now, for the first time, there *was* violence. McNulty loaded the nurses into a tap-tap and was beginning to brief them when a crowd attacked the supply truck in front of them with rocks. Apparently, the Haitians were convinced that there was food or water in the truck. Some of the rocks pelted Team Rubicon's tap-tap, which stopped. That was part of the drill, William had learned: it was called a tap-tap because you got it to stop by tapping loudly on the side panel. McNulty jumped out and yelled at the driver to keep going, then splayed himself on the hood until they'd gotten clear of the crowd. It was the only violent incident of their deployment in Haiti.

A strong aftershock — 6.1 on the Richter scale — woke them the next morning. It was Will's first earthquake, a discombobulating craziness. When they got back to University Hospital, the 82nd Airborne had moved all the patients from the emergency room, rolling their chipped enamel beds and pushing their green canvas gurneys into the courtyard. The patients were still outside, wailing and stinking, their numbers growing constantly.

Team Rubicon's firefighters did a structural check of the hospital and decided it was habitable, and the patients were brought back inside. It was now a week after the earthquake. This was TR's third full day of work. The first two had been difficult and tiring, but thrilling, too. Now they were bone-weary, and they were frustrated. Where the hell *was* everyone? Anderson Cooper from CNN was there in the emergency room, reporting on the desperate situation, there were doctors now in the operating room — but still no military doctors or medical supplies in the emergency room. The 82nd Airborne was there, but why hadn't the U.S. military sent out more medical teams — the best combat surgeons in the world? And what about the Red Cross? Jake was particularly pissed about that.

McNulty went back to the airport and was thrilled to find that the rest of the medical team included twelve doctors and nurses — and a cook. (The cook would be re-tasked as a pharmacist.) They had the troops for a real operation now. The Jesuits had also sent 150 cartons of medical supplies, arranged on pallets. McNulty went to the Command Operations Center at the airport to see if he could get the military to help transport the supplies back to the novitiate. He met with a female Major, who was in charge of coordinating the nongovernmental organizations' efforts. "How the hell did you get medical supplies?" she snapped.

William explained that they were a group of "self-deployers" who had joined together in the past week.

"That means you're an NGO and you come under my jurisdiction," she said. "And I need the medical supplies."

"No fucking way," William said. "These are dedicated supplies, sent to us by the Jesuits in Chicago."

"And what are you doing in uniform?" she asked, eyeing Will's camouflage pants. "You're not a Marine anymore. It's illegal for you to wear the uniform."

Will tried to get her name, but she refused to tell him, and her name tape was covered by her load-bearing vest. "*You* know what you're doing by wearing that uniform," she was shouting now. "You know what you're doing . . ."

He wanted to scream at her: "What I'm doing is helping people." He decided to ignore her and see if he could find a way to spirit the supplies out of the airport. He walked a quarter mile to where the medical team and supplies were waiting on the tarmac. He wanted to seem confident and in control for the doctors — he was their first impression of Team Rubicon — but he was worried. "How the fuck am I going to do this?" he asked himself aloud.

By just doing it, it turned out. He went outside the terminal, flagged down three more tap-taps, and had them back up into a secure area that was being guarded by only two U.S. soldiers. "Holy shit, this could get hairy," he thought, as the Haitian crowd, seeing the movement, surged toward the gate.

McNulty set up a human chain to move the supplies, carton by carton, from the tarmac through the cargo terminal and outside to where the tap-taps were waiting.

They stacked the boxes by the gate and — once again — the Haitians surprised him: they didn't rush the supplies. *"Mediseen . . . mediseen,"* he said, and they respected that. In fact, about ten of the Haitians joined the human chain and helped load the supplies into the tap-taps. They asked for food or water in return for their work.

"Mediseen . . . mediseen," he said, and they backed away. The local police, watching all this, offered to escort them wherever they were going. They reached the novitiate late that night.

Meanwhile, there was some good news at the hospital. A U.S. military medical team was coming to take over the emergency room. And somewhere in the middle of the afternoon, Jake heard a familiar voice. "Hey, dude. I made it."

Clay Hunt.

"Moth-er-fuck-er," Jake said, separating the term of endearment into as many syllables as possible. "How did you find us?"

"Well, you guys posted the coordinates on the blog," he said. "I got a ride on a private plane from Santo Domingo, took a taxi to the Jesuit HQ, and they told me that you were down here."

That night, around the campfire, there was a sense that a corner had been turned.

Jake laid out the assignments for the next day: there would be four FAST (Forward Area Surgical Team) units. Each would take a tap-tap loaded with supplies to separate refugee camps. Sadly, they would also be losing members of the original eight — the firefighters were heading home to Milwaukee, and Dr. Dolhun was going back to San Francisco. But Team Rubicon was moving into Bravo Element phase with a lot more knowledge, confidence, and personnel than they'd had just three days earlier.

The four FAST teams deployed successfully to remote refugee camps the next day. Doc Army noted that, finally, there were other medical teams out and about. Indeed, to his disgust, he found out that several teams of medical personnel had been locked down at the U.S. embassy, prevented from working in the field for fear of the non-existent danger in the streets.

The FAST units were far more robust than the original team, with multiple doctors and nurses and plenty of supplies per unit. Mark Hayward — Doc Army — had gone out on a FAST unit with Brother Jim, and in late afternoon, after a satisfying day's work, he looked up and saw Jim playing his fiddle with antic merriment, entertaining the children with Irish jigs. The rest of the medical team joined in, playing monster tag with the kids — Seth, a mammoth male nurse with a shaved head, was a hilarious monster. Everyone was laughing, laughing uncontrollably, laughing with relief, till the tears streamed down their cheeks. "This was a good day," Hayward told Brother Jim as they headed back to the novitiate. "I'm almost happy."

Jake was feeling pretty good that night, too. He had been out in the field with Clay Hunt — and, for the first time since the war, Clay had seemed really good. He was loading and unloading equipment, helping out where he could, playing with kids — the guy was a genius with kids — and actually smiling.

Clay was from Houston, a little guy — he and Jake would have been called Mutt and Jeff in an earlier era, but this generation of troops knew nothing about the ancient comic strip. Clay was wicked smart, but scattered. He could quote Yeats and Tennyson, but he couldn't seem to handle community college. He was a handsome guy, Jake thought, with soft, long-lashed eyes and a sweet disposition. Clay hated the war, and he let people know it when they had deployed to Afghanistan, which was not cool.

Back home, he was being treated for post-traumatic stress at the VA, but not very successfully. He was married, but that didn't seem to be working out very well either. And so it was — well, it was thrilling — to see Clay so happy and . . . *whole,* working downrange in Haiti.

"I think we may have a model here," William said that night after the meeting. His time in Haiti was coming to a close. He had those Title X business meetings scheduled in Istanbul. But he knew that this couldn't be the end of Team Rubicon.

"What do you mean a model?" Jake asked, impatient and a bit hotter than he'd intended. "For what?"

"We could do this in other places, asshole," McNulty said. "We've got skills that other relief teams don't. We go in first, right?"

There certainly was a need, Jake conceded. There were natural disasters everywhere, all the time. He'd flashed angry because he was torn. He didn't want to chuck everything and become the boss of Team Rubicon. How would he live? How would he get paid? Then again, his dad had emailed that about $150,000 in cash donations, in addition to the medical supplies and volunteers, had come in while they'd been in Haiti. Team Rubicon was all over the news, too — their blog had been linked to by military bloggers and other relief organizations. Newspaper articles had been written. There were stories on TV, featuring a rather unique angle: Iraq and Afghanistan veterans doing something good and inspiring, rather than being portrayed as basket cases, for a change. In 2010, the idea that veterans might actually be a positive force was still very much a novelty.

So, okay — McNulty had a point. If Team Rubicon could make just a small difference in the way that civilians saw veterans, and the way veterans saw themselves, in addition to helping out the Haitians of this world, well, that would be pizza with extra toppings and free drinks at the bar.

Jake was not willing to concede that to McNulty quite yet. He figured that his own fate was business school and a quiet life making lots of money. But he was willing to contemplate more missions for Team Rubicon while he pursued his MBA, keeping it small and occasional. "My dad said we had to form a 501(c)(3) — whatever that is — or pay taxes on it," he told McNulty that night, knowing that a 501(c)(3) was the preferred corporate entity for nonprofit organizations, but hating to sound like he

52

knew what that was.

"I can check that out when I get back to D.C.," Will said.

"Okay, brother," Jake said, hugging him. "This has been good."

McNulty left the next morning in a blur of bear hugs and with a lump in his throat. Within days, seven of the original eight Team Rubicon volunteers were gone — only Brother Jim remained with Bravo Element. They now had dozens of people on the ground, with a full complement of medical gear, maps, internet, and solar panels to provide energy. They had learned so much in two weeks — about medical care in chaotic conditions, about one another. Years later, Jim would think about their experiences in Port-au-Prince and feel an emotional hollow, a desire to re-create the military experience of brotherhood — the banter, the spiritual bond, the thrill of pure service.

Wood, McNulty, and Clay Hunt left Haiti exultant, firing off celebratory blog posts from Santo Domingo. Clay wrote that he and Jake were going to eat "huge chunks of cow." McNulty wrote that a Spanish relief worker had asked him out for dinner and dancing. "Problem. I can't dance, I smell like the ass of a dead rhinoceros, and all I have are dirty cammies and boots."

On the flight from Santo Domingo to Miami, Clay showed Jake a copy of *Outside* magazine, featuring a former Navy SEAL named Eric Greitens who had an organization named The Mission Continues that gave fellowships to wounded veterans who were willing to do public service. "I think people end up benefiting from serving as much as those they aim to serve," Greitens was quoted.

"That was certainly true in Haiti — for all of us, right?" Clay said. "I think I might apply for one of those fellowships."

Greitens's program was new and relatively small, but it seemed a confirmation of what Jake had experienced for real on the ground in Port-au-Prince. He had other plans, but The Mission Continues might be perfect for someone like Clay. Jake had watched his best friend do a reverse zombie in the refugee camps: Clay was fully alive again and fizzing with all sorts of ideas. He could try for The Mission Continues fellowship or maybe he could go to Loyola Marymount and take classes to become a physician's assistant. He wanted to go back to Haiti, and when he went, he wanted to be something approaching a medic like Doc Army. He was talking about this as Jake's eyes began to close.

"Okay, dude," Jake said. "I'm going to sleep." Unable to fold himself into a sleeping position in his seat, and somewhat to the dismay of his fellow passengers, he lay down in the aisle and slept there. The flight attendants, aware of what he'd been doing in Haiti, left him alone.

■ ■ ■ ■

PART II
WAR

■ ■ ■ ■

Be certain that to you too it is owed to
  suffer this
To make your life glorious after and
  through these labors.

— **SOPHOCLES**

CHAPTER 1
FRICK AND FRACK
ON AN ELEPHANT

Whoso would be a man must be a
nonconformist.
— **RALPH WALDO EMERSON**

Naval Special Warfare has an
uncomfortable relationship with the idea
of conformity.
— **ERIC GREITENS**

They called themselves the "One-Two
Punch." Their fellow Navy SEALs, with a
measure of irony and bemusement, called
them "Frick and Frack." They were fine
junior officers to be sure, smart and solid.
They were as physically tough as anyone in
the force. One, Eric Greitens, was a runner
and a boxer. The other, Kaj Larsen, was a
powerful swimmer, a super frogman. But
they were . . . different. They didn't do the
SEAL strut. They hadn't signed up because
they wanted to be the coolest, most macho

59

guys on the planet, chesting about in long hair and Oakley shades, launching themselves into the Navy bars in San Diego and on Coronado Island, dead drunk and draped with girls. They kept their hair short. They had no tattoos. Greitens didn't even drink.

Actually, Greitens's super-flashy academic record was a matter of curiosity to his peers and especially to his superiors — he was a Rhodes Scholar from Duke University who had earned a doctorate of Philosophy in Politics from Oxford. He had spent almost all of his school breaks working in refugee camps around the world. He had even spent a few weeks working for Mother Teresa in an end-of-life nursing home in Varanasi, India. His doctoral dissertation was about the treatment of unaccompanied children in war zones by nongovernmental organizations.

Larsen's résumé was less stratospheric; he was a man of the water, not the air. He had spent some time at the Naval Academy — he loved the water polo but hated the petty shine-your-belt-buckle hazing — and then left for UC Santa Cruz in his hometown, where he graduated with a degree in politics and a Nobel Prize in surfing.

The other thing was, they were both Jewish. Both had Jewish mothers and Christian fathers. Neither Greitens nor Larsen was observant in any strict sense, although each had been a bar mitzvah. They had been raised in the Jewish moral and intellectual tradition — and it certainly informed their military service. Each, at an early age, had learned about the Holocaust. Kaj's grandparents were Holocaust survivors; Eric had listened to the stories of survivors at the Jewish Community Center in St. Louis. And they'd both reacted to the stories the same way: Why the hell hadn't more Jews fought back? It was part of the reason they'd become SEALs. They would definitely fight back, if it came to that. Both joined the military before the terrorist attacks of September 11, 2001.

Their religion was largely unknown to their men. It just didn't come up, although Greitens once was asked by an enlisted SEAL, "Are you a Catholic or a Protestant, Mr. G?"

"I'm Jewish," Eric replied, and the SEAL just started to laugh, as if to say: well, of course it would be something like that.

And so it was that when Eric and Kaj were dispatched to Thailand as part of a hundred-man squadron for Operation Cobra Gold, an extended exercise with elements of the Thai Navy in May 2004, they kept away from the garish bars along Walking Street in the beach town of Pattaya. They were Lieutenants Junior Grade on their first real deployment. It wasn't Iraq or Afghanistan, but tours to the war zones would come soon enough, if they didn't screw this up. Each commanded a small boat detachment, which kept them busy. Eric's boats were a pair of sleek, fabulous 82-foot Mark Vs, loaded with firepower. They had eight twin 50-caliber machine-gun placements. They could skim the water at a blistering 50 knots; under full steam, they drafted a mere 3 feet. Kaj had a less powerful detachment of rigid-hulled inflatable boats (RHIBs). But if there was dangerous work to be done near the shoreline, the RHIBs would be doing it. Their crews were composed of Special Warfare Combatant-Craft (SWCC, pronounced *swick*) personnel, who were, in effect, elite roadies for the SEALs: they were smart and super-trained, just as the SEALs were, but they were essentially the techies who managed the equipment that enabled the rock stars to put on their show. Their senior officers believed the SWCCs suffered from something of an inferiority complex as a result. They hoped that having SEALs like

Eric and Kaj command SWCC detachments — this was a new thing — would have a positive effect on pride and morale.

In Thailand, Greitens and Larsen worked sixteen-hour days keeping the boats in shape, which was the easy part. The harder part was keeping their men out of trouble. They were billeted at the Botany Beach Resort, a fancy tourist hotel, which added to the sense that this deployment was something close to a holiday. The hotel, which was thirty minutes from downtown Pattaya, offered $5 Thai massages on the beach. But their men spent their evenings adding to their tattoo collections and hanging in the Walking Street bars, which were *not* off-limits. There was a standard twelve-hour "jigger to trigger" rule. They would have to be on duty at 0800 every morning — and therefore, theoretically, last call was 2000 hours. Eric and Kaj tried to toughen that by having their men up and out at 0600 for a rigorous session of physical training. The men called it the "dick-dragger" PT. Still, the mix of testosterone and temptation raging through the bars was worrisome. Years later, Admiral Joe Maguire, who had just taken charge of the SEALs in 2004, would wonder why on earth they were having extended exercises in the world capital of drugs and prostitution while there were wars going on in Afghanistan and Iraq.

"Hey, Kaj," Greitens said after several weeks on the ground in Pattaya. "We haven't done anything really *Thai* yet." They had a free Saturday morning, and he proposed that they go on an elephant trek — an act of surpassing FrickandFrackitude, certainly not the sort of thing real SEALs would do in their spare time. An off-the-grid tiger hunt with bow and arrow, maybe; freestyle shark-fighting with Spyderco knives, perhaps. But a slow plod along a well-worn trail with a bunch of tourists atop extremely tame pachyderms? That was not remotely the way that real SEALs rolled.

The morning of May 8, 2004, was ridiculously hot and sticky, as most mornings were in Thailand. Kaj and Eric were wearing T-shirts, shorts (for Kaj, surfer-dude board shorts, as always; for Eric, shorts with a more conservative camouflage pattern), and sneakers. The elephant trek company sent a minivan to pick them up at the hotel. There were a few tourists up front; Larsen and Greitens took the backseat.

"I got a heavy one for you, bro," Kaj said as soon as they settled in. He spoke quietly, seemed stricken — certainly not his usual self. He told Eric this story: He had been approached at his 0600 PT session that morning by two of his best men, Seaman Tom Reilly and Petty Officer Sean Galvin. They had been to the Electric Blue night-club on Friday and had bumped into Lieu-tenant Hobbs, the ranking SEAL officer in the squadron. Hobbs looked pretty strange to begin with — he had dyed his hair orange and wore brass hoop earrings like a pirate; the SEALs had flown into Pattaya weeks before the SWCC boats arrived, and the theory was that Hobbs had gone native — but Galvin noticed that Hobbs's eyes were blitzed, his pupils completely dilated. "Sir, your pupils are blown!" Galvin said.

Hobbs exploded. "What the fuck are you, a master-at-arms?" he said, referring to the Navy version of Military Police. "You better stay the fuck away from me!"

Galvin decided this was sage advice. "Let's get out of here," he said to Reilly. They needed to hit the bathroom before leaving — and were shocked in midstream when Hobbs showed up with three of his men. "Set security at the door," he told the youngest, a seaman on his first SEAL deployment. Then Hobbs pulled a baggie from his pocket and went into a toilet stall with the other two.

"Whoa," Kaj said when Galvin had told him the story. He figured that there were only two things three SEALs could do together in a toilet stall, and both would get you kicked out of the Navy in 2004. "You're sure about this?"

Reilly and Galvin were sure. Kaj told them that he would discuss it with Mr. G and then make a decision about what to do next. And now Kaj asked Greitens, "What do we do?"

"What was in the baggie?" Eric asked.

"They don't know. They think it was ecstasy or Special K." (Special K was ketamine, a horse tranquilizer.)

"I want to hear it from them first before we make any sort of move," Greitens said.

So, as they bumped along in the minivan, Kaj called Petty Officer Galvin and asked him to tell Eric the story. The details were precisely as Larsen had reported them. "So what do we do?" Kaj asked.

"We piss test everyone, the entire squadron," Greitens said without hesitation. There were two SEAL platoons, plus their two SWCC boat detachments, lashed together for this exercise. The boat detachments were making a tour of southeast Asia, but the two SEAL platoons were probably headed to Iraq or Afghanistan (where SEAL

Team One was working both sides of the Pakistani border) immediately after Pattaya. It was assumed that this would be the SEALs' last deployment before they went to war, and a certain eat-drink-snort-and-be-merry atmosphere prevailed.

There was no direct evidence of drug use yet, only rumors and suppositions. Eric believed they needed to know precisely how widespread the problem was. "What do you think about a piss test?" Greitens asked Kaj.

"Absolutely," Larsen replied. "No question." This really was a bright-line, Kaj believed. He wasn't a teetotaler like Eric; he'd go out for a beer with the guys. The SEAL protocol was different from the rest of the military: officers and enlisted men not only could fraternize, they were sort of expected to. They went through every single moment of training together, every single moment of Hell Week; it was part of the ethos that they were brothers, if not quite equals.

Kaj was ecumenical about drugs outside the military, although he had never used them. His parents were baby boomer academics. His mother, who was in charge of art projects at UC Santa Cruz, called herself a "public intellectual." An objective observer, Kaj admitted, might call her a hippie. That was another reason why he joined the SEALs after college. "How else was I going to rebel?" he told Eric. "Smoke dope?"

But this wasn't marijuana, and all drugs were absolutely forbidden by the SEALs. The squadron was doing live-fire drills with the Thais, using extremely powerful weapons. They were bobbing up and down in Pattaya Bay, firing at targets on a small island; if they weren't completely clean and clear, they could slip and do some real damage to their fellow seamen, or the Thais, or the local fishing boats, or the helicopters patrolling above. There really was no choice but to drug test Hobbs and his buddies, Larsen believed. But this would be a very big deal, if it happened.

Eric and Kaj made a flurry of emergency calls to superior officers in California, Guam, Bangkok, and Pattaya as they careened over the dirt roads into the jungle — but it was Friday night in California and Saturday morning in Thailand. No one was at work. They called Petty Officer Galvin and told him that they were intending to drug test the entire detachment.

And then there they were, at the elephant park. A languid line of ancient beasts with colorful two-seat baskets on their backs awaited them. It didn't feel right, but Eric shrugged and said, "Well, as long as we're here, we might as well do this."

Their elephant was called Sawang. Kaj was given a box of bananas to feed the animal, who had a general sense of where the bananas were and kept slinging his trunk back, searching for them as the group ambled off into the jungle on a narrow track; at one point Sawang nearly slapped Kaj's cell phone out of his hands. And then, the phone started to ring. Suddenly, they were sweating in the woolen tropical heat, taking calls from Bangkok, Guam, and Pattaya with the cell phone on speaker as they rolled along in slow motion. The most important instruction came from their immediate superior in Pattaya, Lieutenant Lawrence Bradley, who wanted to discuss the situation face-to-face ASAP. But, they explained, they were on this elephant, splashing along a stream . . .

That wasn't the worst part. Petty Officer Galvin and Seaman Reilly called again. "Sir," they said to Kaj, "you should know that if you piss test everyone, some of the guys in the Mark V team aren't going to come out so well." Eric was stunned. *His* men had been doing drugs? "And sir," Reilly said to Kaj, "one of our guys says someone laced his drink with drugs a few weeks ago."

Kaj looked at Eric and shook his head. Laced his drink? Yeah, right. But there was no escaping it — the entire squadron was now involved: the SEAL platoons, the Mark V detachment, the RHIBs. This was a steaming mess of the highest order.

Eric Greitens had been a Navy SEAL for eighteen months. He had graduated from the SEALs' notorious two-year BUD/S (Basic Underwater Demolition/SEAL) training program in late 2002. And from the start, Eric intended that his command of the twelve-man Mark V detachment — his first SEAL assignment — would be exemplary. He had inherited an office cubicle lined with pictures of near-naked women on Harleys. He took down the pictures and replaced them with quotations from Churchill and Patton and his favorite, from Thucydides: "Any nation that draws too great a distinction between its scholars and its warriors will have its thinking done by cowards and its fighting done by fools."

He knew that his men were smart; they had to be to qualify for SWCC. But they were the sort of guys who'd been bored by school. As a result, they weren't very confident about their intelligence. Eric started with a group discussion about the Thucydides quote. "What does this mean?" he asked them. There were no immediate takers. "What this means is that as warriors we have to be thoughtful fighters. We have to be people who are thoughtful about our discipline."

There was a didactic and almost condescending quality to Eric's formulation, but somehow he was able to get away with it, Kaj thought, because he was so guileless. It was a weird quality. Eric's earnestness would have been gagging if it had come from a base of moral smugness, but he wasn't at all smug. He didn't act like an Oxford hotshot or a more-righteous-than-thou humanitarian. He was a pleasant surprise, in that way, to his fellow SEAL officers, and especially to his men.

They called him Mr. G, but also, during BUD/S, they began to call him Obi-Wan after he began to perform magic on their behalf with the SEAL trainers. Somehow — and just how he did it was a serious topic of conversation — Mr. G was able to manipulate the trainers and win his men small concessions, here and there, amid the daily torture. Even Kaj saw this as a form of witchcraft. "Hey, Mr. G," they would say whenever they were scheduled to do something illogical by the trainers. "Can you go and do your Obi-Wan hand thing?" This was a reference to the *Star Wars* scene in which Luke Skywalker and his aged mentor Obi-Wan Kenobi are trying to sneak the two droids, R2-D2 and C-3PO, through a desert checkpoint. They're confronted by soldiers, and Obi-Wan mesmerizes them with a flick of his hand. "These are not the droids you're looking for," he says calmly. The troopers let them pass.

And Eric did have a weird sort of calm power over the instructors. He knew how to reason with them, respectfully. The trainers were mostly noncoms, and they understood that he had the makings of a good officer, the sort of man they'd want leading them in enemy territory. And so, if an instructor told Eric's squad to run across the training facility to the chow hall, have lunch, and be back in twenty minutes, Eric could calmly make the argument that they didn't really need to be back in twenty minutes, they'd just be hanging around the grinder — the asphalt physical training area — with nothing to do, and anyway, he had looked at the chow schedule and knew the next team wasn't due into the hall until thirty minutes later . . . and the instructor would somehow

72

succumb. "Yeah, sure, Greitens, just have them back on time." (This also meant that Eric, who ate last, would get to enjoy a full meal.)

Little things like that — having enough time to finish their meal — meant everything to the men, who were inevitably exhausted and dirty and hurting after the nonstop runs and swims and log-carrying and boat drills and killer PT that were their daily diet of pain in the first phase of BUD/S training. Eric's constant awareness of their needs and his desire to get as many of them as possible through the training had an impact. His men thought of him as sane, solid, and paranormal in their defense. Mr. G never lost his cool.

Philosophical conversations became a regular thing for Eric's SWCC team, and as time went on, they really did become conversations rather than Greitens monologues. He started a book group for his team. He chose the books. He'd gotten the idea from his own superior officer, Lieutenant Commander Charles Mellman, Jr., who had assigned him a book of Ralph Waldo Emerson's essays to read and report on at the end of Eric's two-year BUD/S training process. Mellman was, Eric believed, an exemplar of the warrior intellectual — as

73

was Master Chief Will Guild, the noncommissioned officer in charge of SEAL training who taught an ethics class during the final phase of BUD/S. Mellman enjoyed the Oxford kid. They talked about SEAL culture and how to deepen the training. Mellman asked Greitens to write, specifically, about how Emerson's philosophy applied to the SEALs.

The essay opened with a famous Emerson citation: "Whoso would be a man must be a nonconformist." To which Greitens responded: "Naval Special Warfare has an uncomfortable relationship with the idea of conformity." He then launched a direct assault on the training he had received and SEAL culture in general: "Students at BUD/S spend countless hours listening to instructors," he wrote. "The truth about this time is that an inordinately large portion of it is spent listening to stories of sex and drinking." He believed this was creating a dangerous ethos — "that what is 'special' about Naval Special Warfare is the way that Team guys party, rather than the way we go to war."

There wasn't enough time spent studying SEAL fighting traditions, the strategy and tactics of clandestine warfare. "Without this sense of tradition, it is not surprising that some men come to believe that what is 'special' about Naval Special Warfare is that they get to wear their hair a bit long, carry a Spyderco, and sport shades."

Mellman was so surprised by the candor and freshness of the document that he passed it on to Master Chief Guild, who said, "This is fucking brilliant."

It was also trouble. The Naval Special Warfare community is tight and gossipy. Word began to spread about the essay: Greitens had ratted out the instructors. In response, Guild held a meeting and distributed copies of the essay to his entire teaching staff. "I know you've heard about this. Now read it carefully," he said. When they finished, he asked, "What do you think?" Guild was an enormous man, a figure of real authority, a career SEAL, including seven years at Development Group (also known as SEAL Team Six). The instructors were wary; they didn't have much to say. Guild got to the point. "If you've got a problem with the student who wrote this, and you're intending to take retribution, I want your papers on my desk tonight because you're not working here anymore."

Mellman and Guild were exactly the sort of people Eric had hoped to find in the SEAL Teams. He wanted the SWCCs in his boat team to be able to think and make ethical judgments for themselves. He and Kaj had their men read novels that were about honor and write essays. The men hated it, but they made it through the ordeal and grew closer. One of Eric's favorites, Petty Officer Second Class Jeff Griffen, told the men, "LT [Greitens] has a different way of doing things. And you know what, it's the right way."

But if members of his boat team were doing drugs, Eric's way had been a failure.

As Lieutenant Lawrence Bradley saw it, he was looking at a story told by two relatively junior SWCC crewmen implicating Hobbs, the highest-rated officer in the last SEAL Team One evaluation cycle. Before he did anything, he wanted to talk to Kaj's storytellers — and, with great courage, they told him the same story they had told Greitens and Larsen. He then called in the young SEAL who had established "security" at the bathroom door in the Electric Blue club. He denied everything. "Everything's fine," he said. "I don't know what you're talking about. Those [SWCC] guys must have been drunk." This became the operative narrative in the SEAL platoons: the SWCC boat crews had screwed up. *They* were the ones,

76

not the SEALs, being investigated for drugs. Greitens and Larsen were lousy leaders.

"Do you know what's going on?" Hobbs warned Greitens back at the hotel. "You gotta watch out for your guys, because something's going down."

"Are you talking about drugs?" Greitens asked.

And Hobbs said, "Yeah, so if you've got any of your guys that you're worried about, you might want to let them know."

"Thanks," Greitens replied. "I got it."

That night — it was still Saturday, an endless day — Greitens contacted his highest-ranking enlisted man, Chief Petty Officer Don Curtis, and said, "Hey, Don, we've got a problem here." Eric could see that Curtis was thinking about the usual hassles: one of the engines was down again, or the Thais had changed the time of the exercises. "We've got a drug problem in the detachment."

Curtis was stunned, distraught. He was responsible for unit discipline. He didn't want to have to deal with drugs — but he knew he had to. It was the worst part of his job. And this was a crucial moment. Later, when the story came out, more than a few SEALs believed that the Oxford boy should have handed the problem to Curtis and told him to take care of it, with the assumption that Curtis would issue a quiet warning and the whole thing would go away. But Eric simply could not do that; it would run counter to everything he believed about honor and responsibility. And the most serious problem was not in his boat crew. It was Hobbs, who was distributing the stuff. "Kaj and I have put our detachments on lockdown," he told Curtis. "No one leaves the hotel. Everyone stays in their rooms. We don't want them congregating. Tomorrow we're going to question them."

The confessions came easily enough. "I'll talk to you," said one of Eric's crewmen, "but I only want to talk to LT." When the others left the room, the young crewman began to cry. "Yeah, I've been doing drugs," he said, and he proceeded to implicate Hobbs and another member of Greitens's crew who was the intermediary between Hobbs and the boat teams, distributing the ecstasy and ketamine.

That Monday, Hobbs and five of his SEALs, plus the three SWCCs who'd been implicated, were sent to Bangkok for urinalyses. Hobbs tested positive for cocaine and was immediately relieved of duty. He would spend the summer in the brig and be court-martialed that fall. He was charged with using cocaine and ecstasy, distributing ketamine, and conduct unbecoming an officer.

All the men involved were relieved of duty. The two SEAL platoons were sent back to Coronado, their chances of an immediate deployment to Iraq or Afghanistan obliterated. One of the SEALs convicted of drug use later committed suicide.

Greitens was mostly infuriated with Hobbs, who was the alpha dog, the ranking SEAL in a squadron of very young men, many of them out on their first deployment. Hobbs had set the example; the others might never have considered using drugs if they hadn't seen a SEAL platoon leader not only wasted, but also dealing. Eric felt terrible for the members of his boat team who had admitted to drug use and were cashiered; they were good men. They would always have to live with this. But most of his team had been better men — they had resisted the temptation, had not been led astray. He thought back to his Emerson paper: if they'd been trained properly, this might never have happened. "If you had told them," Eric mused later, "what happens when we go to Thailand is that every night, everybody goes out . . . and we *play chess,* they would have gone out and played chess."

Perhaps, but after their nightly game of chess, they would have gravitated toward the tattoo parlors and nightclubs on Walking Street — they were, after all, men in their early twenties, men who could be facing crazy-dangerous deployments downrange before too long. Eric knew that sailors had been drawn to the fleshpots since before the Greek fleet destroyed the Persians at Salamis. He assumed his crew understood the rules, but he blamed himself for not sending the message more directly.

There would be ramifications across the SEAL and SWCC communities. Rear Admiral Maguire knew that he had a major mess on his hands; Thailand was just a symptom of a much larger problem. SEALs were coming home from their seven-month deployments in Iraq and Afghanistan hooked on adrenaline and unable to figure out how to decompress. The work they were doing in the field was stellar, but there were all sorts of fights and craziness in the bars back home. After Thailand, Maguire ordered a urinalysis across the Naval Special Warfare community and a hair analysis in Development Group because he'd heard rumors of a major problem in the super-qualified secret unit that eventually became a bit *too* well-known as SEAL Team Six. The results were devastating. There was significant use of methamphetamines in SEAL Team Six; an investigation revealed that SEALs were not only using but also dealing the drugs. The news dribbled into the *Navy Times* on September 4, 2004: Chief Aviation Boatswain Mate John F. Holcombe was arrested by the local police in Virginia and charged with possession of methamphetamine with the intention to sell. The story was hushed up quickly; Seal Team Six, like its Army equivalent Delta Force, didn't officially exist.

There were repercussions for Eric as well. When his Mark V boats moved on to their next deployment in the Philippines, the first question his new superior officer SEAL Commander Pete Stonecraft asked was, "What the fuck happened in Thailand?" He asked it harshly, like a slap in the face. "Why the fuck did you do that? You've created this huge mess. You don't know Hobbs, you don't know these guys — those were SEAL platoons. You're not even *operating* as a SEAL on this deployment. You're a SWCC. Why didn't you have your Chief handle it? Tell them to quit it or there would be hell to pay. That's how it's done."

"Sir," Greitens replied evenly, "guys can't

do drugs and shoot bullets past other guys' heads." But now he knew. Stonecraft was a SEAL's SEAL. His judgment on Thailand would be the final verdict — not with the brass, perhaps, but within the more macho sectors of the brotherhood. Eric would never be considered a real SEAL by those guys.

He reacted to his ostracism stoically. He knew he hadn't done anything wrong. Ever since high school there had been people who considered him a goody-goody, but he'd always had a strong circle of friends and supporters. This was the first time he'd tried to walk his talk in the real world — or at least in a world, the military, that allegedly lived with a strict code of honor. He had stood his ground but lost altitude among some of his peers.

He was intent on living a life of consequence. He would not change who he was. But he was beginning to realize how tough a road he had chosen. He was an American anachronism, a credulous outlier in a society drifting toward cynicism.

CHAPTER 2
THE UPHILLS

Eric's Obi-Wan act didn't come naturally.
He had a flip side, equally intense. He was
a wild physical creature. He'd amazed his
mother by flipping himself over a week after
he was born. He walked and talked early.
And then he ran. He would go down to the
basement, turn on the radio, and just run in
circles, listening to music. Becky Greitens
was a prekindergarten teacher who worked
with special needs children, and she sometimes wondered if Eric had Attention Deficit
Hyperactivity Disorder (ADHD). But then
she'd think: Nope. Not possible. It was
more like Attention Surplus Disorder. He
had full-throttle ADHD energy, but there
was no deficit of attention. By the age of
two, he seemed — to Becky, at least —
observant, thinking, thoughtful. He looked
at you strong and hard with ardent blue
eyes; he seemed to be listening hard, too.

"You think maybe we brought the wrong

kid home from the hospital?" she would ask her husband, Rob, an accountant at the U.S. Department of Agriculture, whose very mild manner camouflaged a sharp, inquiring mind. Rob was a devotee of Eric Hoffer, the longshoreman philosopher of the 1950s, and of Michel de Montaigne, the sixteenth-century French essayist. He and Becky were thrilled by their son, but also a little frightened by him. Becky worried that his physicality slipped too easily into violence, especially after his brother, Marc, was born. Very early on, Eric grabbed Marc by the throat and flipped him like a rag doll in the bassinet; Marc survived intact and Eric got a lecture, but it didn't have much impact on his subsequent behavior. Eric spent his elementary school years banging on his younger brothers. There were times when he seemed on the brink of being out of control: during a snowball fight Marc broke Eric's sunglasses, and Eric pinned him down and was just pummeling him. When Aaron was born three years after Marc, he'd join in the mayhem, using weapons like wooden blocks to make up for his lack of size.

There was a fair amount of tension in the house. Eric certainly provided his share, setting the warp-speed tone for his brothers.

Becky seemed to be on the phone 24/7, talking to the frightened parents of her needy students. She worried that she wasn't doing enough for her own kids, that she wouldn't get the laundry done on time — and the amount of dirty laundry produced by her sons was prodigious, an Everest of soil. Rob helped by jiggering his hours at the USDA, starting at six a.m. and ending at three p.m. so that he could come home to be a coach and scout leader for his boys in the afternoon. Meals were often chaos, hot dogs or tacos eaten on the run, as Rob took the boys to sports practice. And the times when they did sit down as a family — like Friday nights, for Banquet fried chicken — were a zoo, the boys often stumbling in from the yard filthy and noisy, bloody and sometimes shirtless. "Do you think," Rob would ask, terminally wry, "you might consider putting on a shirt for dinner?" It was, he believed, like eating with a pack of wolves.

Eric's aggressiveness was balanced and, ultimately, conquered by his inner Obi-Wan — and here his attention surplus served him well: he had a reflexive respect for his elders, especially those who appealed to his heart and mind. He was easily socialized. His Obi-Wan education began with Bruce Carl, who taught Sunday school at the B'Nai El synagogue in suburban St. Louis. Carl was tall and curly-haired, a college basketball player, a dynamo, a classic "Ask Not" Kennedy liberal who believed his mission was to teach the protected middle-class kids of the B'Nai El congregation about the desperate lives being lived in the St. Louis ghettos and in the developing world. He taught *tikkun olam* — repair the world — as *the* core Jewish value, the place where your soul flourished, or not.

Eric was Carl's most enthusiastic student. He always had his hand up, always had an opinion or a question about everything. He dominated the class. Eventually, Bruce took him aside and said, "I read this story recently about how American and Japanese executives behave when they have joint meetings. The American executives do all the talking. So, Eric, what's the consequence of that?"

They were sitting on the grass outside the synagogue. Carl was speaking softly, casually. Eric didn't know where he was going. "The consequence," Carl continued, "is that after the meeting, the Japanese know everything the Americans know — but the Americans only know what they knew at the start of the meeting. You should keep that in mind."

Eric would never forget it. He worked on it, honed it over the years. The outer calm became the brake against his inner Maserati; it was, in its way, as intense and relentless as other teenage boys' need to flash their hormones. Later, after he became a Rhodes Scholar and Navy SEAL, he would use this skill to charm the people who expected him to be a self-righteous braggart. He refused to megaphone his résumé or drop names or talk about the important things he'd done. He'd ask the people he met about their lives — real questions, not perfunctory ones — and then run with their interests. He had a tendency toward pedagogy when it came to issues, especially ethical issues, but he would not talk about himself, or use himself as an example, unless it was unavoidable.

Deep in the Reagan era, he followed Bruce Carl to a program called Youth Leadership St. Louis, which attracted overachieving high school kids from all over the city. Carl began to take them out into the world — to a landfill, to learn about the solid waste disposal problem, to work in soup kitchens. At one point, they spent a night in a homeless shelter, much to Becky's dismay.

Carl gave the Youth Leadership St. Louis

kids whistles. He told them to blow the whistles every time they were in a meeting and someone said something that was racist or bigoted. One of the girls in the program took that extremely literally and blew the whistle on the mayor of East St. Louis, a black man who was going on about how the reporters and editors at the *St. Louis Post-Dispatch* were all against him and didn't pay attention to East St. Louis because they were racist. "I don't believe that," the whistle-blower said to the mayor's amazement. "There are a lot of sensitive journalists at the *Post-Dispatch* and they've written some really good stories about the problems in East St. Louis."

That became part of Eric's nature as well: he was a whistle-blower from an early age. He was afflicted by a slightly goofy literalism at times, the sort of kid who actually *said* that he wanted to be President of the United States. He said it in third or fourth grade, when a teacher asked him what he wanted to be when he grew up. "I want to be President," he said, "because I want to help people, and the President gets to help the most people."

Fair enough. But he was still saying it early in high school, when one of his favorite teachers, Bill Jenkins, had to set him straight. Jenkins was short, barrel-chested, African American, with a church bass Voice of God. He was faculty adviser on several of Eric's extracurricular programs — and he thought one of his best students was acting foolishly. "Eric, I keep hearing from all of these people that you want to be President," he said one day. "You can't *want* to be president. That doesn't make any sense. You have to want to *do* something. What do you want to do?"

Eric responded with political boilerplate. He wanted to create better schools and more jobs and . . .

"That's not good enough," Jenkins said, "and I don't want to hear you talking that nonsense ever again."

In the second semester of junior year, Eric's honors English teacher, Barbara Osburg, opened her Trends in American Literature class with a summary course description she had written about the life and death of the American dream. This would be the core theme of the class. She was a passionate teacher and liked to challenge her students' assumptions. But Osburg also had some assumptions of her own, nurtured in the 1960s: she believed the American dream had collapsed into a rubble of tinsel materialism.

The students took the summary paper home to read, and the next day Eric raised his hand and asked, "Who wrote this paper?"

"Well, I gave it to you and there's no name on it," she said, "so you can assume I wrote it."

"Well, I just don't think what you're saying is true."

"Why not?" she asked, amazed by the kid's maturity and confidence. This was not a teenage boy showing off. She had landed herself, she realized, in a serious intellectual dispute with an adolescent. And she was on shaky ground.

"There's a Mexican American immigrant family who lives across the street from us," Eric said. "The father — his name is Sergio — told me about how hard he worked to make it in America. When he first came here, he only learned how to speak English by listening to the radio." Now Sergio had a job and a house in the suburbs and was able to put food on the table for his three kids. "Those are important things for people," Eric continued. "They're not hollow and materialistic, the way you argued in that paper. Eric Hoffer says, 'America still offers more raw opportunity than any other country on earth.' I agree with that. That's the

American dream."

Eric Hoffer?

After their American dream confrontation — the kid was right, dammit — Barb Osburg would do anything she could to help Eric Greitens succeed. His goals were stratospheric. He wanted to go to Harvard, Stanford, or Duke, or nowhere at all. His family didn't have the money to afford those sorts of schools — they lived in a modest three-bedroom ranch in Maryland Heights — and he would need a full scholarship if he got into any of them. He asked if he could do an independent study with Osburg for senior year so that he could work on writing the application essays, both for college and for a pile of scholarships, which he'd researched in the guidance counselor's office.

He was accepted at Duke, where he received a full-tuition A.B. Duke scholarship. He also won a national Mars Milky Way scholarship competition to pay for his living expenses.

At Duke, his goals remained ambitious, but they became more personal: He wanted to live a life of service. He wanted real intellectual stimulation. He knew his body needed an athletic outlet. And he wanted to see the world. It would take a while — all of freshman year, in fact — before the components fell into place. But when they did, there was a surprisingly heterodox quality to his new obsessions, most of which — except the academic part — involved Duke University only peripherally. He became a Big Man Off Campus.

One lingering impulse from high school worked very much to Eric's advantage at Duke — the constant search for fellowships, scholarships, awards, and prizes. He wanted to travel, but he didn't have the money for it. He soon found that the Trent Foundation for International Studies offered a grant to Duke freshmen who'd never been out of the country before. It was a research grant and, with the help of his uncle Don Leventhal, who was part-owner of a broom factory in Beijing, Eric put together a proposal to study working conditions in joint Sino-American business ventures in the industrial city of Changchun, where Uncle Don had a friend with a factory.

The China trip, which took place in the summer of 1993, established many of the protocols for his future travels. He traveled light, and alone. He arrived in Changchun and was overwhelmed by the place, the din of it, the crowds, people pushing their way toward their destinations in a manner that would seem brazen and impolite in St. Louis, bicycles threading the streets lazily but sometimes unpredictably, with wild abandon, the smell of spices frying in oil mixed with the stench of open sewage, the coal dust pollution so intense that the air was a physical presence, the pigs and goats grazing next to brand-new factories. He found the people friendly and curious about him — reddish-brown hair and freckles were major events in China. They would approach him on the street, ask who he was, ask to touch his hair; sometimes they spoke a bit of English.

Changchun was a tough, industrial town, not fitted out for tourists. If he was hungry and his hotel's restaurant was closed, he would go out to the street vendors and point or make hand motions to secure some food for himself. Alone, and looking for friends, he decided to take some kung fu classes — his first real experience with martial arts — which he enjoyed immensely. He also tossed aside standard tourist conventions. He'd brought a convection coil to boil water for drinking but soon grew tired of the hassle and began drinking from the tap. He ate the local food and drank the local water; he was sick once in China but never afterward in any of his travels.

One of his first meals in Changchun was a banquet with some young Chinese joint venture executives. He was still learning how to negotiate the food without offending his hosts — the dishes spinning around the traditional lazy Susan were lovingly described, in detail, and often involved improbable animal organs not entirely overwhelmed by heavy sauces; he was required to sample each, which required a fair amount of furtive concentration, as he took the smallest possible portion and shoved it deep into his rice bowl and hoped no one would notice. And then the host said, "Mr. Eric, now you will sing?" Sing? His mind went blank. He couldn't remember the words to any song; he was even boggled by "The Star-Spangled Banner" as he tried to rehearse it. Of course, there was always "Row, Row, Row Your Boat" . . . He began to sing and made rowing motions with his arms, trying to get the others to sing along. They just sat there. It was awful — and became more painful when his host stood up and sang a traditional Chinese song with surpassing seriousness and beauty. As the years passed, and his exotic travel intensified, Eric realized that moments of awkwardness were the times he learned most about the cultures he had parachuted into, the times he remembered best.

Traveling alone, he was also a mark. The night before he was to return to Beijing, the hotel manager brought him his bill, and the rate was far higher than had been agreed upon. The manager said it was tourist season, which was transparently absurd. There *were* no tourists in Changchun. Afterward, Eric realized that he should have simply said, "We agreed to the lower rate," handed the man his traveler's checks, and headed for the train station. But he paid the bill and arrived back in Beijing nearly broke — and with three more weeks remaining in his trip.

He was greeted at the station by one of Uncle Don's associates, who suggested that he come and live in the broom factory dorm and make some money teaching English to the workers. He had no idea how to teach English, but there were no other options. His students had varying levels of fluency. Conversations were possible with some of them, though, and he soon learned that a few had participated in the Tiananmen Square demonstrations four years earlier. They were starving for news of the outside world. They wanted to know about the American reaction to Tiananmen. They asked him questions about the Constitution, especially the Bill of Rights. The conversations became animated, passionate, as they got to know and trust one another — and, Eric noticed, every time they began to talk about politics, one of the students would get up and close the door. Sometimes their classes spilled over into dinner; they would ride their bikes to a local restaurant and eat dumplings. Eric found that he was envious of these young people. They had made history. He wanted to find his way into history, too.

It was inevitable that an American having conversations about Tiananmen and the U.S. Constitution with former demonstrators would eventually draw the attention of the Chinese security services, and one Friday night, just before he was due to return home, two policemen came to the factory dorm and took Eric to the local police station. He was deposited in a bare room with a table and two chairs and made to wait. Then he was questioned for two hours. After the questioning was over, the police interrogator, who spoke halting English, said that Eric had broken Chinese law and must be punished. This was true: he'd been teaching without a license, although there was no way of knowing if that was the nature of his crime. Eric tried to Obi-Wan his way through the panic and politely asked to call the U.S. embassy but was told, "We can call the U.S. embassy only if you are hit."

Hit? He asked for a drink of water and tried to assess his situation. He was nineteen years old and clearly not a spy; he didn't think the Chinese would risk an international incident with an American college student — but they weren't allowing him to call his embassy either. He asked again to make the call and was told again that he could do that only if he was hit; this time, he realized that the policeman — and it was becoming clear that this guy was only a policeman — was probably citing a manual that said that if an American was injured ("hit") in Beijing, they had to call the U.S. embassy. The interrogator was chain-smoking, sweating, and getting flustered; he seemed as confused about the situation as Eric was. Eventually, Eric was allowed to go, but the police kept his passport. They said that it would be available Monday for retrieval.

Eric returned to the station after a nervous weekend and was told that he could get his passport if he signed some papers he didn't understand and paid a fine of approximately

$9 for a crime that was never made clear to him. He did what he was told, secured the passport, and left the country soon after. It had been a terrifying experience, but it had been an *experience* — a potential moment of peril, in which he had to think clearly, in which he hadn't been in control, and he'd made it through without losing his composure.

When Eric returned to Duke for sophomore year, he chose a new major and a new sport. The new major was an independent study, a blend of philosophy and public policy, supervised by Bruce Payne, who was another "Ask Not" Kennedy liberal like Bruce Carl.

The sport was boxing.

Eric's grandfather Harold Jacobs had grown up at the gyms on the south side of Chicago and regaled him with stories about the characters he'd met and the fights he'd fought. There was an elaborate mythology to the sport, created by intellectual devotees like A. J. Liebling, who called it the "sweet science," as well as Norman Mailer, David Remnick, and Joyce Carol Oates, whose reflections on the spectacle was one of Eric's favorite books. It seemed a noble challenge, mano a mano, a far more primal affair than the usual run of sporting possibilities. Eric's journey to the E. D. Mickle gym at the beginning of sophomore year was almost as exotic as his trip to China. He was the only white person in the place.

His first action came the very first day when a bantamweight asked him if he wanted to spar. "No, thanks," Eric said. He didn't know how to throw a punch yet.

"How you gonna learn to box if you don't spar?" The bantamweight asked. Eric got into the ring and exited a few minutes later with a black eye and a split lip. The other boxers assumed that was it for the white boy — they'd seen the phenomenon before — but Eric was back the next night, doing push-ups and sit-ups, working the heavy bag. He came back every night for the next three weeks.

Eventually the gym manager, a former welterweight named Bob Pugh, took pity on Eric as he worked the heavy bag one night. "You're telegraphing your right," he said.

"How do I fix that?"

Pugh gave him the phone number of a fighter named Derrick Humphrey, who trained with a man named Earl Blair — in fact, Derrick was one of the few fighters around who was willing to put up with Earl's physical and moral rigor, a matter of personal loyalty after Earl had saved him from the streets. Humphrey told Eric to come to his apartment complex and there, in the parking lot, they met Earl, who told Eric to start running in place with Derrick, fast and then faster, which they did until Eric's legs were burning. After more exercises, Earl asked Eric to lie flat on his back, his legs six inches in the air, and he punched Eric hard in the stomach. Eric reached for his gut — what on earth? — but Earl said, "You can do this," and he proceeded to demonstrate with Derrick, who took Earl's left and right and left without a wince.

Earl was short, dark, sixty-six years old. He had the barrel-chested build and the commanding style of Eric's high school teacher Bill Jenkins, and he shared the same philosophy: the only way to save poor teenagers from the streets — the only way to turn boys into men — was to work them as hard as possible and build a granite determination and toughness that was impermeable.

He was an Army veteran whose nickname was Bebop because he walked with a bounce and had a big smile. He had his sayings, mostly about the Lord, and he had his ways, which were entirely stubborn. He had gotten kicked out of the Mickle gym after an argument with the owners and was training Derrick Humphrey out on the track at North Carolina Central University, a historically black college. "If you really want to do this," Earl told Eric when he finished the parking lot workout, "you pay twenty-five dollars a week whether you show up or not. Everyone wants to box, but nobody lasts. They hang out for a week or two, and then Derrick cracks them in the face and they leave. Or they start to feel sore and they don't show up again. Lots of 'em come and go," he said. "I'm always here."

A few weeks later, Derrick cracked Eric in the face for the first time, and Eric showed up the next day. Earl worked Eric like a beast, and he showed up every day. The trainer began to suspect that this white boy was different — diligent, respectful, able to withstand pain, stubborn as a rock. The real test came on a monsoon November day, the cold rain pelting so hard that Eric could barely see the road as he drove from Duke to North Carolina Central, even though his wipers were on high. Eric figured that there was no way Earl could be out at the track in this weather, but the man had said *every day* and *I'm always here.* Eric had to show up and find out for sure. He certainly didn't want to disappoint Earl. He pulled up to the North Carolina Central track but couldn't see the dirt patch where they trained from the road, so he began walking down the hill — and there was Earl, sitting in his lonely, dark blue plastic classroom chair without an umbrella or rain gear, wearing a baseball cap that read, REAL MEN PRAY and a zip-up Windbreaker. As he saw Eric walking down the hill in his workout gear, Earl stood, smiled, and started walking — bebopping — toward his fighter and gave him a huge hug in the lashing rain. Nobody else had shown up that day, not even Derrick. There was a quiet appreciation in Earl's eyes, as if to say: the Lord has sent me a solid white boy. "The Lord don't always give you what you want," Earl would often say, embellishing the Rolling Stones a little bit, "but he'll give you what you need."

The Lord had not given Earl a natural boxer, just a very persistent one. Eric had been a baseball and soccer player in high school, but his favorite sport was long-distance running. His father was a runner, and one day when he was in elementary school, Eric rode his bike alongside Rob, who was training for a 5K race. "Do you know where you pass people in the road races?" Rob asked his son.

"Yeah, it's on the downhills, because that's

when you can run really fast," Eric replied.

"No, it's on the uphills," Rob said, "because that's when it's hard."

Eric came to love the uphills. He loved all the tough, unglamorous things about sports. He loved training; the pain in his legs when he pushed himself past previous points of endurance was entirely satisfying. He won his first race, the junior division of the St. Louis marathon, at the age of sixteen. He was never the fastest runner — although he eventually would run marathons in less than three hours — but he could go on and on. He graduated to running double marathons and triathlons. When the time came, the regular five-mile run in the sand in full uniform at SEAL training was a piece of cake.

Eric trained with Earl five nights a week for the next three years. He fulfilled every pathetic white-boy stereotype: he had no flow, no rhythm, no smoothness. He even had trouble skipping rope at first. Eric found comfort within the rituals of the sport — he would learn to jump rope, and he would happily train to the point of exhaustion, and he would work the corner when Derrick had a fight, and he would watch carefully as Earl taped Derrick's hands and laced on his gloves. He kept his own gloves in pristine condition, especially the laces, which had to be spotless if you wanted to train with Earl.

He also enjoyed the violence. Getting cracked by Derrick was painful, but educational. Derrick could have decked him at any moment he chose, but he used their sparring sessions to keep in shape and to help Earl teach Eric how to move. They worked in tandem, Earl shouting instructions and Derrick making Eric pay if he didn't follow them. "Keep your hands up," Earl would say and if Eric dropped them, Derrick would shoot a jab and bloody his mouth or his nose. "Move to your right!" And if Eric didn't, Derrick would throw a right cross to get him going.

Early on, after an especially tough sparring and heavy-bag session, Eric unwrapped his hands and saw that his knuckles were bloody. He looked into the mirror above the sink and saw that his lip was cut. He dipped his hands into the soapy water and saw the blood ooze out. He would develop scar tissue there; it would be a painful process. But that wasn't a bad thing. There was a difference between pain and injury; the pain would make him tougher and enable him to give a little more tomorrow. He wasn't close to reaching his physical limits yet. He looked in the mirror, and he was hurting, but he felt very good.

Earl began calling Derrick and Eric "my babies."

That fall, Eric learned that one of his professors, Neil Boothby, was organizing a group of students to work in Bosnian refugee camps during the summer of 1994. Their job would be to help out where they could, observe, and write a report about how the orphaned children were being treated in each camp. Eric also decided to document the conditions in the camps with photos, so he took a class at Duke with the accomplished professional Margaret Sartor. He fell in love with the Walker Evans photographs that accompanied James Agee's magnificent account of Mississippi sharecropper life, *Let Us Now Praise Famous Men*. He loved the strength and dignity that Evans accorded his subjects.

The first camp Eric visited that summer confounded his dire expectations. It was called Puntizela — and it was gorgeous, set in a public park overlooking the Adriatic in the ancient city of Pula. The kids were well-clothed and -fed, and they seemed happy. "Welcome to paradise," the aid worker who ran the program for children said when Eric arrived. Well, not exactly paradise; these children had seen things that no one should ever see. Eric wasn't in Puntizela long enough to get to know them well, but he found that he really loved being with the kids. He organized soccer teams and then matches, which the adults in the camp would come and watch. He worked in the kindergarten and hung out in the common room, playing chess (badly, compared to teenagers who had grown up with the game) and watching the older adolescents and adults drink beer and dance. This was good and satisfying work, but it didn't seem the real refugee camp experience — the desperation he'd seen on television.

After a few weeks, he was transferred to Gasinci, a much larger camp where conditions were much worse. Gasinci was a dull compound of prefab shelters set in straight lines near the Croatian city of Osijek, patrolled by a not very friendly unit of the Croatian Army. On Eric's second day there, Croat soldiers shot and killed two puppies, the beloved mascots of the kids in the kindergarten. The camp was in an uproar and the UN workers who supervised the operation had a meeting about how to respond to the outrage. They decided to write a letter of protest. They were powerless to do anything more, Eric realized — just as the Europeans and the UN had been powerless to do anything to prevent the mass rape and slaughter that was forcing the Bosnians into these camps.

As he walked through Gasinci one morning, Eric was approached by a man in his late thirties. He spoke pretty good English and invited Eric into his prefab trailer, his young children playing in the corner. They sat on folding chairs as the man told Eric his story, about the terror that had caused him to flee his home in Bosnia. He lifted his shirt and showed Eric the shrapnel scars he'd received in a grenade blast. Eric had heard many similar stories, but what set this man apart was a question he asked: "Why aren't you *doing* anything?"

Eric knew the man was talking about the American government, which was dithering over how to respond to the human disaster in Bosnia. But he took the question personally. He knew he was doing valuable work with the kids, and he was learning a lot from the experience. He wasn't making much of a sacrifice, though. The conditions in the camp were tolerable except for the food, which often featured a tasteless cornmeal mush served along with an apple. He lived simply in a prefab bunkhouse with other volunteers from around the world. He had his backpack, a couple pairs of pants, a pair of shorts, some underwear and T-shirts, plus his camera and his notebooks. It was not a life of privation; he had suffered worse training with Earl. He was serving others, but was this sort of service enough?

Another insight came through the lens of his camera. He wore it around his neck and snapped casually, refusing to pose the children or make a big deal of what he was doing. His intent was to show them as they were. The photos were beautiful, well-composed, and emotionally resonant, but without the perfect sheen and depth that a professional might have brought to the shot. They were inspired nonprofessionalism, unadorned, humane, and therefore very moving. More important, Eric began to understand that they told a story: there was pain in many of them, but also joy. Happiness was a part of the daily experience for most children in the camps. He photographed them looking up to their elders with love and respect — and, especially, looking directly at his lens, but not really at the camera. They were looking *at Eric,* their friend, with love and puckish humor and a certain dignity. It was as if his snaps were part of the conversation, a demonstration of affection for these kids. The things he saw through his lens were, Eric realized, very different from the photographs of children in refugee camps he had seen back home. Those showed only one kind of child — pitiful, haunted, desperate, and dirty, holding a crust of bread, perhaps, with a perfectly located tear on her cheek. Eric captured some of that desperation, too, but he knew there was more to life in the camps. There were families who took care of most of these children, even the ones who had lost their parents. There was love and a rude form of security.

One day, the director of one of the charities working in the camp asked Eric to gather all the children together outside. A major donor was coming to visit and wanted to hand out gum to the children. The director asked Eric to record this beneficence for posterity. "Why doesn't he sit down and talk with them?" Eric asked. "Why doesn't he come to the kindergarten and look at the artwork they've done?"

But no, the donor wanted the traditional charity shot — and Eric began to wonder if this fetishizing of refugee children worked against their best interests. There were charities that ran pity ads on television back home, encouraging Westerners to "Adopt a

Child." It bordered on exploitation, Eric thought, enabling Westerners to feel less guilty about their comforts. It raised money for the charities, but what was it doing for the vast majority of kids — or for their families?

He spent the next summer in Rwanda, and the summer after that in Bolivia, and then his Oxford school breaks in Cambodia and Mexico and Albania and Gaza and India, in one of Mother Teresa's end-of-life homes. He would spend every school break for the next five years in refugee camps. He figured that he had found his life's work.

One day, early on during his stay in Rwanda, Eric stopped at a roadside church with several aid workers. It was a rudimentary building with brown mud walls and a simple cross. He went to the door, opened it — and saw a sea of human skeletons, skulls and rib cages and arms and legs, scattered across the floor. He had heard about places like this. People had gathered in the churches during the genocide. Marauding Hutus had punched holes in the mud walls and tossed grenades into the church, then charged in and raped and murdered the survivors. He had heard about it but couldn't really imagine it until that moment. He tried to visualize the screams and the panic, the carnage. Then he turned his back on the room, stared out into the dusty sunlight glare, and imagined that he was holding an assault rifle, a brutish, angry-looking instrument, holding off the Hutus. There was a visceral click: he desperately wanted to take on the killers, to protect the people in the church. It was the ultimate test, he realized, the real thing — especially for a humanitarian. Now *that* was counter-intuitive. But it was true: the innocent of the world needed heavily armed moral protection. Maybe the best way to save lives was to go to war.

CHAPTER 3
AT THE CORNER OF
ANGELS AND PIRATES

It was a running play, nothing special. Jake Wood propelled himself forward into the Bettendorf High School lineman, pushing him back and down — and then a devastating force crashed into his left foot. It was friendly fire: one of his Pleasant Valley teammates pushing into the pile. Jake heard his foot crack — not a snap or a twist, not a broken toe — it sounded as if his entire foot had cracked in two. But he didn't feel anything. He disentangled himself from the pile, stood up, and started to walk back to the huddle, thinking: "It doesn't hurt yet, but I know it's going to fucking kill me pretty soon." The quarterback called the play, and Jake started walking back to the line of scrimmage. With each step, he heard a series of smaller cracks — metatarsals snapping off from his tarsus, the main bone in his arch, all five of his toes. His arch collapsed, and now the pain came on. He managed to get down into his three-point stance, but the agony was overwhelming and he fell over, drifting away from consciousness. The quarterback thought he'd had a heart attack.

Jake had spent his adolescence growing into serious plausibility as a football player. As he grew, and then grew some more, he'd been moved from fullback to tight end and, finally, to the trenches — he was, in fact, an offensive line coach's dream, a huge kid, strong not fat, who loved to work and had bulked himself up to nearly 270 pounds, with a minuscule amount of body fat and a maximal amount of brains. You had to be clever to be a good offensive lineman; you had to figure out ways to jujitsu the bull-rushing defensive linemen, stand them off, or fake them into an overreaction. Jake sneered at defensive linemen; he considered them a reflexive, Neanderthal life-form. Jake also sneered at his coaches at Pleasant Valley High School, who didn't take things, especially the rivalry with Bettendorf, seriously enough. Pleasant Valley was too well-named. Jake wanted a major league strength and training program — he had to bulk up if he was going to be a blue-chip college lineman — but the weight room was open only on Mondays, Wednesdays, and Fridays.

The coaches had ordered a perfunctory "Bigger, Faster, Stronger" training program off the internet, but Jake didn't think it was enough. He did his own research, found a more elaborate physical training regime, and convinced his teammates to join him.

By the middle of his junior year, it was clear that Jake had real talent, and the college recruiters were out in force. The fact that he was riding a 3.8 grade average in advanced placement classes, with a 32 (out of 36) on the ACT college aptitude exam and was class president and very active in community service projects made him an irresistible prospect. He was recruited by Harvard, but they didn't send many ballplayers to the pros. He received full-ride scholarship offers from prestigious schools like Stanford and many of the Big Ten football factories.

Those were all at risk now. At home that night, he lay on the couch in the family room. His mom and dad, Jeff and Christy, and his two sisters were bawling. The Iowa State coach called and said, "Don't worry. We still love you, Jake." But no other coaches called, even though the word of his injury was flashing around the internet. The high school football prospect network was hot-wired, and Jake's left foot was a national story. The Woods' next-door neighbor was an orthopedic surgeon who came over that night and said, "I need you in my office first thing tomorrow."

The X-rays showed a podiatric disaster. "I've got to tell you, Jake, this is a very serious Lisfranc injury and very rare for football — it's more like a rodeo injury, like someone getting their foot twisted in the stirrup. A lot of people don't recover from this."

Jake had five surgeries his senior year. He suffered two staph infections in the foot, which forced two of the operations, and another when one of the screws holding his arch together broke. Still, he continued to work out — no running, but plenty of lifting — to get ready for college football. Many of the schools that had been chasing him pulled their offers after Jake was hurt, but Stanford, Wisconsin, and Iowa State were still interested. (Jake would remain infuriated in perpetuity that the University of Iowa, his local Big Ten school, pulled its offer.) His father wanted him to go to Stanford; his mother wanted him to stay as close to home as possible. Christy Wood called Jake the "President of the Mama's Boy Gang" — a family joke, but it was true: he adored her.

Christy and Jeff were worried about their

son. He had never faced any real adversity before. He had always been sunny, unflappable. Jeff was an expert in the scientific management of manufacturing processes. When Jake was six, the family had moved to a small town in Austria, near Graz, for several years. There were no international schools nearby; Jake had to go to the local public elementary and take all his classes in German. Jeff and Christy hired a tutor for their three kids, but Jake was the one who really excelled — he just dived into it, became Jakob Wood, not only fluent in German but also earning the highest grades in his class.

When they moved back to the States — to Danville, Illinois, for a few years — they put Jake and his sisters into a Lutheran school, and once again, Jake dived into it. He had always been interested in Jesus — at the age of four, he had "creeped out" his father by sitting at the dining room table for hours with a scroll of computer paper, drawing pictures of Jesus on the cross, and now, at the age of ten, he dived into the Bible, really studied it, and had serious conversations with Christy's brother, a Lutheran minister, about faith and service. The family assumption was that he was going to be a minister — although that wasn't a certainty: he was serious, but not in a righteous way. When he received an errant B in high school and Jeff bawled him out, Jake said, "Forget it, Dad. I'm going to enjoy myself in high school."

Even when he was obnoxious, he was fun. When he scored his 32 on the ACT, he danced into the family room with his arms over his head, singing, "32 . . . Ba-bee, 32 . . . Ba-bee."

"Jake, that's just not fair," moaned his older sister Sarah, who had managed a pretty impressive 30 herself. "I'm supposed to be the smart one. You're supposed to be the charming one. Megan is supposed to be the athlete."

The truth was, he had it all. And he was easy with it — even after the injury, when nothing was as easy as it had been. He was in a wheelchair with his leg extended for two months. He was on crutches for months after that.

He decided to go to the University of Wisconsin. "It's just so beautiful," he told his mom. And it was even more beautiful when Wisconsin stayed with him after his injury. It also didn't hurt that the Badgers' offensive line coach, Jim Hueber, had a remarkable track record of getting his start-ers drafted into the National Football

League. When Jake arrived in 2001, the Badgers were a Big Ten powerhouse, winners of the previous two Rose Bowls.

Jake was back on the field, and running, the summer after he graduated from high school. He excelled in freshman camp, at first. Then the rest of the team arrived. In his second serious practice, playing with the freshmen against the starters, he was tossed aside by Wendell Bryant, an all-American defensive tackle who went on to play in the National Football League with the Arizona Cardinals. He landed hard on his shoulder. Jake knew it was dislocated, which was not the end of the world. The trainers simply snapped it back into place. What Jake didn't know, but soon found out, was that he had torn his labrum, the tendon that holds the shoulder in place. He tried to play on — dislocating his shoulder several more times — before the coaches decided that he had to have season-ending surgery.

He still dreamed of playing in the NFL, but he knew he was falling behind. His natural position was left tackle, but Wisconsin successfully recruited Joe Thomas — a major stud who would go on to become an All-Pro tackle with the Cleveland Browns. The coaches moved Jake inside to left guard, and he had just about won the starting job in his junior year when he dislocated his *other* shoulder. "I am fucking made of glass," he lamented to his friends. He continued to work hard to stay in shape, but it wasn't easy. Varsity football was a forty-hour workweek, beginning at five a.m. every day. He worked out relentlessly and then watched film in the mornings; he practiced every afternoon. All that muscle required feeding, or it would begin to wither. He had to stuff himself at mealtimes and scarf down ten thousand calories of protein shakes every day to stay at 295 pounds — and the coaches wanted him at 310. The prodigious effort to turn an ectomorph into an endomorph played havoc with his body. His growing assortment of injuries limited the amount of time he could stay on the field; he lived in the land of whirlpools, liniment, ice packs, and bandages. By senior year, he knew that the NFL wasn't going to happen. Which raised the question: What was?

Even with all the football, Jake had made the dean's list several times and was carrying a 3.5 grade-point average. He was double-majoring in business and political science; he loved the politics but figured that business was his fate. There was, however, another option, to his parents' dismay: he had always been interested in the military.

It started when he was a boy in Austria, on a trip to the Mauthausen Concentration Camp Memorial. The camp was situated in a quarry, the inmates worked to death. There were pictures of the haunted survivors, all eyes and bones. It was the U.S. Army, his dad told him, who liberated those people. He and Jeff spent the next few years in Europe collecting World War II memorabilia. He grilled his grandfathers for every detail of their service in the war. Before Jake became a football stud in his junior year of high school, he had given serious thought to applying to West Point. He researched the physical requirements and began to work at them. And then, when the September 11 terrorist attacks happened during his first weeks at Wisconsin, Jeff Wood said to Christy, "I just hope Jake doesn't do something stupid and sign up."

He *wanted* to sign up. He almost signed up. And it nagged at him when the Arizona Cardinals' safety Pat Tillman quit his team and joined the Army to fight Al Qaeda in Afghanistan. Jake figured that if he had any guts, he would do what Tillman had done. We had been attacked; he had skipped weeks of classes, watching cable news after

120

September 11. But if he quit school and went to war, he would have to kiss the NFL good-bye, and he just couldn't bring himself to do that.

The military wasn't very popular in Madison, a notoriously liberal redoubt, and, as George W. Bush began to shove the nation toward war in Iraq, the atmosphere on campus became toxic. Jake hated the anti-American rhetoric; he hadn't really studied the situation in Iraq — and he was too young to know much about Vietnam — but he figured that Saddam Hussein was certainly part of the problem in that region. There were large antiwar demonstrations on campus now, so Jake tried to organize a pro-America demonstration after the Iraq invasion. About twenty supporters showed up, as did a handful of opponents, one of whom spat on him.

Then, in Jake's senior year, Pat Tillman was killed in action in Afghanistan. Jake saw the news and began to cry. It was a blub that had been a long time coming after the frustrations of the past four years, a mixture of sadness about Tillman and shame that he hadn't had the guts to quit school and enlist. It ended with resolve: he was going to join the military.

But that turned out to be ridiculously

complicated, too. He figured he would join the Marines or the Army. Those were the two services actually fighting the wars on the ground. He wanted the real deal; he wanted to lead men in combat. The Marines were the mythic way to do that; it didn't hurt that a few years earlier he had read an article in *Inc.* magazine arguing that Marine officer training was better than an MBA: "Preparing for Business Battles? Learn Some Lessons from the Marines."

Jake played his last football game, a loss to the Georgia Bulldogs in the Outback Bowl in Tampa, Florida, on January 1, 2005. He visited a Marine recruiter a few weeks later, still bulked up, which — the recruiter told him — was not the Marine way. "I don't know if you can hack it. How many pull-ups can you do?"

Pull-ups were not part of his PT program. They were the opposite of what he had been training to do. "Fourteen, last time I checked," Jake said.

"A Marine officer needs to be able to do twenty," the recruiter said. "Have you had any serious injuries?"

Jake cataloged his woes. He felt as if he were trying to sell a used car.

"Whoa!" the recruiter said. "That's an awful lot of paperwork. Why don't you call me back in a month?"

Jake did, having shed twenty pounds and reached twenty pull-ups. He left a message; the recruiter never called him back. He shed another twenty pounds without effort — the muscle bulk was just burning off naturally. Meanwhile, the war was intensifying. A year earlier, four American contractors had been incinerated and hung from a bridge in Fallujah; a big battle was under way. Jake tried the Army recruiter, hoping for a special forces or Ranger contract. But once again he was told he would need a medical waiver for his foot. He continued to research his choices: Did he actually have to become an officer? Everything he read, everyone he spoke with, pointed in the same direction: this was a squad-level war. That was where the real action was. Squads were led by Corporals or Sergeants. All he had to do was enlist.

But even *that* wasn't easy. His foot, again. At the end of June 2005, however, he lucked into a Marine recruiter who desperately needed to make his monthly quota. Somehow he was able to get expedited waivers for Jake's foot and shoulder — and Jake Wood was a Marine, bound for Camp Pendleton.

He starred in boot camp and the School of Infantry — first in his class in both — and found himself ticketed for the Marine Air Ground Combat Center at 29 Palms in the middle of the Mojave Desert, a notoriously dreadful place. Jake was now at the bottom of the ladder again: a newbie or, more commonly in the Marines, a *boot* — and also something of a zoo show. Word got around the camp that there was a boot who'd actually played football for Wisconsin. People sidled by just to look at him. Marines are tough, as advertised, but they tend to have a larger cohort of little guys than big guys — historically, the Corps has been the most direct path for a little guy with something to prove to prove it. Among those who were curious about the Jake Zoo Show was Corporal Jeff Muir of the First Platoon of Golf Company, of the second battalion of the 7th Marine regiment (2/7, for short). Muir was the son of a Peoria police officer and an average-sized Marine, just short of six feet tall. He had just returned from a combat deployment in Fallujah, which gave him street cred with the new recruits. He therefore had the credentials to amble over and check out the new guy with some of his friends. "Some boot here play football for Wisconsin?"

"Hey, Wood . . ."

Jake stood. Jaws dropped. "Uh . . . okay," they said. "Good to meet you." And slunk away. "Dude's large," Muir's Sergeant said.

"A big target," Jeff said.

"You want to get close to him downrange. They won't even *see* you."

A few weeks later, Muir was transferred into Third Platoon, and he found that he wanted to get close to Jake, but not because he was a big target. Jake wasn't your normal, pimply eighteen-year-old boot; he was Jeff's age, twenty-three, and seemed to have his act together. When they went out on maneuvers, Jake always had his gear in good order — he could produce his knife, his compass, an extra canteen without even looking for it. He listened carefully, followed orders well. He had studied the field manual, and he knew stuff. When Muir would ask, "What's the proper response to an L-shaped ambush?" Jake would know. A fair number of the guys with whom Muir had deployed couldn't do that.

Quietly, Jake was dismayed by the quality of his fellow boots — they were slow, incompetent. These were Marines, the toughest fighting force in the world? How could he entrust his life to all these fools? But he kept it to himself. Indeed, in the field, Jeff Muir began to notice other things about Wood. When guys in their squad were lagging on a hike, Jake picked up their gear and carried it. He didn't advertise it, didn't say, "Here, let me help you with your gear!" so that everyone would notice. He quietly said, "I got it," and carried on. So Muir and Wood became friends, and even there, Jake had all the nuances covered. He called Jeff "Lance Corporal," respectfully when other people were around; he stood at parade rest when Jeff spoke to him in the presence of others. He did neither of those things, however, when he and Jeff drove the three hours to Hermosa Beach on weekends. They got drunk, chased girls, watched insane amounts of college football at an apartment owned by some of Jake's friends who weren't in the military.

They were joined by a third amigo — Clay Hunt — who was also older and smarter than most of the other recruits, and a solid guy. Jeff noticed that Clay would never bitch, even when they had to do something crappy, like go on patrol at 0300. "Let's do it!" Clay said, always cheery, entirely dependable.

Clay wasn't as easy as Jake, though. He had been kicked out of recon school, the Marines' equivalent of the Green Berets — kicked out in spectacular fashion during his *very last* exercise, an ocean swim with full gear. The Sergeant had been ragging him, making fun of him, telling him he was fucking up. It was all bullshit. Clay stopped in the water and gave him the finger. And that was it. He was out.

It was an utter disaster in a mythic Marine fuckup sort of way. Clay, of course, didn't see the humor in it. He was back to *boot,* back to the regular infantry, and his superiors would hassle him about it — and Clay would turn red and get angry, which made them rag him all the more. He was a little guy, about five eight, and given his closeness to Jake, his littleness seemed all the smaller. So it was: "Hey, tiny." "Hey, recon dropout." And when he responded, they'd say, "Hey, emo."

When Clay talked about playing football in high school, they would go, "That's bullshit dude — you're too small to play football." Actually, Clay was a fine athlete — especially when it came to individual sports like hunting, skiing, and biking — and he was tough, a total gym rat, a PT fanatic, which he and Muir had in common.

But that counted for nothing. His fellow Marines had found a target of opportunity. They even ragged him when he got a Marine Corps tattoo: a Ka-Bar knife with the words "Death Before Dishonor."

Jake and Jeff tried to help Clay through the hazing. Ignore those assholes. It's part of the game. They do it to everyone. But Clay wasn't buying. One day, Jeff Muir found Clay in a screaming fight with his team leader, Oscar Garza, who was tossing Clay's stuff — his sleeping bag, his clothes, his helmet — around the barracks. Clay picked up his helmet and tossed it in the general direction of Garza, not quite at him, but close enough. Muir stepped in and stopped it, which was not a good thing to do: he had intervened to help a boot. It hurt Jeff's standing with the senior noncoms, but he didn't care — Clay and Jake were his brothers now. Seniority was important, but not that important.

Jake arrived in Iraq a newly minted lance corporal and leader of a four-man fire team. His first impression was filth. There was garbage everywhere, especially those little plastic shopping bags and shreds of bags, swirling in the wind. It also stank to high heaven. There was open sewage. The people were poor in the countryside; most had no running water or electricity. Most of them hated the Americans after four years of occupation. But they also hated the Al Qaeda fanatics who wouldn't let them smoke or watch TV and forced marriages with their daughters. A change was coming — the Sunni tribes would switch sides that spring — but the members of Third Platoon, Golf Company, couldn't sense it yet.

Three weeks into their deployment, on February 18, 2007, word came to headquarters at FOB (Forward Operating Base) Viking, where they were stationed, that a Humvee convoy had gotten stuck in the mud, outside the wire but near them, and needed security while it waited for a tow. Jake's squad saddled up and headed out at sunset, hoping to get back to Viking in time for dinner. They drove along the main highway, MSR Mobile, looking for Route Reds (all the local roads were named after baseball teams) as it grew dark and cold — as it does in winter in Iraq — with Jake and his fire team in the third Humvee. They made a turn onto a darkened route, which should have been Reds but wasn't — there was a big bridge over a canal on Reds — and the convoy stopped and tried to figure it out.

Jake unfolded himself from the Humvee and stepped into ankle-deep mud. "I thought this was supposed to be a fucking desert," he said and squished his way over to Sergeant Rosenberger in the lead vehicle, which was driven by Blake Howey, a friend of Clay's. They consulted maps. Jake had a pretty good sense of where they had gone wrong and volunteered to turn around and take the lead; Rosenberger told him it wasn't necessary. He'd stay in the lead, with Howey driving . . . but now Howey's Humvee was stuck in the mud. Jake and three others got in back and pushed, mud splattering their faces, their jumpsuits, everything. The mud tasted like shit. Iraq was a field of shit. "I don't see how this night could get any worse," someone said.

"Don't. Fucking. Say. That," Jake said. "Don't ever say that."

They traced back to Reds and saw the bridge and then a white puff of smoke. Jake realized he was suddenly near-deaf; he could barely hear a thing. From a very great distance, someone — Bullard, up in the turret — was yelling, "IED . . . Howey hit an IED."

Jake was out of the Humvee quickly, pulling Doc Campanili with him. The IED had been placed under the bridge — the lead

Humvee should have stopped to check it out, but they were already late, and so they had breezed through. Now the bridge was on fire, a gagging reek of gunpowder, gasoline, and burning rubber in the air. Jake saw Sergeant Rosenberger limping toward him; a big piece of shrapnel had gashed through his calf. Jake began to run toward the bridge. He saw Latcher pull himself out of the turret, and then he saw Latcher and Sergeant Payne pulling Howey from the driver's side. Jake was on the bridge now, skipping through puddles of burning gasoline. He reached the Humvee and started giving orders. He told Latcher to set up security about fifteen meters farther down the road — it was entirely possible that the IED was the beginning of a complex ambush. He told Sergeant Payne to go twenty-five meters down the road that ran along the canal. He didn't stop to think that he was giving a superior noncom orders, and Payne, a very good guy, didn't seem to mind. "I'm on it," he said.

And then he looked down at Howey.

His legs were covered in blood, missing flesh. Jake would later write in an unpublished memoir, "His right arm lay at an impossible angle, mangled and charred and bloody. His flak jacket was torn open and scorched black, revealing a chest peppered with shrapnel. But all that still looked vaguely human. It was his face, Howey's face, which no longer bore resemblance to the carefree California kid we all knew. The blast had warped the size and shape of his entire skull, cruelly leaving his features intact, so that what remained looked humanoid, but not human."

The Humvee was engulfed in flames now, and ammunition began cooking off. Jake and Doc Camp moved Howey off the bridge and into a nearby field. They called in a medevac, and Jake stood in the field, half-warmed by the fires, half-chilled by the air, twirling a string of red warning lights over his head, a signal for the choppers. His shoulder ached, but he kept twirling until the birds came in a gush of wind and another splatter of mud. He got on the medevac with Sergeant Payne, Latcher, Doc Camp, and several others who'd been stranded on the far side of the bridge. He fingered his dog tag, thinking, "If they'd let me lead the convoy back to Reds, that would have been me."

Back at FOB Viking, word of the attack was cascading and distorting through the camp. There were five KIA. No, there were two KIA, six WIA. Wood had burns over 90 percent of his body. Wood? Jeff Muir ran over to the operations center (TOC) and asked, "Who got hurt?" No one knew. Muir began praying, "Please don't let it be Jake or Nick Roberts." And then he thought, "How fucked is it that I'm praying that someone other than Jake or Roberts got hurt?" But he couldn't stop praying. And he thought about Clay, who was out on a three-day dwell op with his squad: How would Clay handle it if Jake had bought the farm?

By the next afternoon, Muir had assembled the details — Jake was fine, but he was still at al-Taqaddum air base and wouldn't be coming back to Viking for a couple of days. Muir was walking back to his hooch when Clay's squad came in, and he told them what happened. The news was greeted by torrents of shits and fucks, but Clay didn't say anything. He just stared straight ahead as if, Muir thought, he were trying to work his way through a complicated math equation.

Two days later, Muir found Clay sitting on his bunk, staring across at Howey's empty rack — again, just staring at it. "Dude, you okay?" he asked.

"Yeah," Clay said. "Fine." But he didn't sound fine.

That night Clay had moved down into Howey's bunk. "I just want to be close to him," he said.

It was that night or maybe the next that Clay called his dad, Stacy Hunt, back in Houston. "Dad, we lost a couple of guys a few days ago," he said. Stacy couldn't make out much of what Clay was saying; the connection was awful, and the call didn't last very long. But Stacy heard a quality in his son's voice that he'd never heard before. The boy was scared.

"This is hard, Dad," Clay said. "Really hard."

Ten days later, Jake and Clay's platoon hit a village market at the corner of Routes Angels and Pirates. There was supposed to be a significant ammunition cache in the market warehouse; there was bound to be AQI (Al Qaeda in Iraq) security and resistance. But the mission turned out to be a dud at first, another false alarm, Iraq as usual.

Jake blew the lock on the warehouse door with his Benelli shotgun. There were no weapons inside, no AQI security. The other squads began to collect and interrogate the men in the market to see if any useful information could be gleaned from the wasted morning.

Lieutenant Clevenger told Jake to deploy his five-man team atop a house about two hundred yards above and behind the market. It was a standard Iraqi structure, cinder block, one story with the hope of two, rusted steel rods poking up from a flat roof, with a staircase leading to the top. It was amazing how everything looked unfinished or partially destroyed in Iraq. On the roof, Jake had his radio operator, Cartwright, set up a communications line with HQ and then sat there, sweating like a banshee in the stupefying dust-sauna, watching the heat ripple across the field to Route Pirates and beyond, past the ancient irrigation canal on the other side of the road, which brought water from the Euphrates River. The area was thick with reeds and bulrushes, biblical stuff: these lands between the Tigris and Euphrates had once, in legend, been the Garden of Eden. It wasn't exactly how Jake had pictured it in Sunday school.

The heat seemed to intensify, radiating off the black tar roof. The dust raised by their convoy hadn't yet settled, or maybe it had; everything in Iraq was sepia-toned. Communications were hard, too — his radio on the rooftop was the only connection with HQ. Jake could raise Lieutenant Clevenger by unit intercom, but that connection was sketchy at best. So his team was it, the only contact with the rest of the world.

He heard children singing and laughing. He looked down from the roof and saw two little girls — the children of the house — playing and eating the candy that his squad had given them, their innocence blatant, egregious. The intercom was scratching on and off with orders and info. Jake heard that one of the prisoners collected in the market was talking; Clevenger wanted a gunshot residue (GSR) test kit to check if the guy had recently used a weapon. Jake watched a Marine get out of one of the Humvees, two hundred yards away, and struggle to open the rear hatch in search of the kit.

The Marine — Jake couldn't tell who it was — jerked suddenly, a marionette panto-mime, he would later write, "as if an unseen string attached to his right shoulder had been violently pulled."

Then, instantaneously, *crack* — the sound of the rifle shot. The Marine seemed to crumple in slow motion. He was still stand-ing upright, but as he brought his hands up to his neck, his knees began to fold, and blood geysered through his fingers. And now there was gunfire everywhere. The noise was hellacious, ear-crushing, as if someone had just turned on the car stereo, full volume, to AC/DC at its most suicidally stupid loud. Jake saw three, maybe four enemy machine-gun positions across the road, camouflaged by the heavy vegetation. He saw the four turret machine gunners in the Marine Humvees turn in unison and begin firing back into the reeds. Then, to his right, he saw a white sedan pull up on Pirates facing the convoy; the doors swung open, and two men began firing.

He ordered Cartwright, the radio man, to call in a 9-line medevac request* and told Bullard, who carried the M-249 SAW machine gun on the northeastern corner of the roof, to light up the sedan. There were machine-gun rounds flying over their heads, punctuated by gorgeous, luminescent red and green tracers — and he ordered Arguello to go to the back of the house and make sure there wasn't fire coming from their six, from behind.

* The nine lines were location, radio frequency (call sign), urgency, special equipment needs, number of patients by type (litter or ambulatory), security of pickup site, method of marking the pickup site, nationality and military status of patient(s), and presence of nuclear, chemical, or biological agents at the landing zone.

Jake had always wondered about actual combat. He was surprised that, in the noise and chaos, everything seemed to be moving in slow motion — and in good order. He was jazzed, but clear. He felt great.

Bullard wiped out the sedan with his SAW. Jake, staring at the disintegrating spiderweb tracery that used to be the windshield, ordered him to cease fire.

Cartwright called in the medevac.

The helicopters were on their way to the intersection of Pirates and MSR Mobile. But there was a problem.

They couldn't raise Clevenger to tell him about the medevac.

Well, Jake thought, we're going to have to go down there and tell them ourselves. They were going to have to get down there eventually, anyway, to get out of Dodge.

He organized his team into two groups. He ordered them to bound the two hundred yards down to the convoy. He and Cartwright would lead on the left flank; the other two men would follow on his right.

"Moving!" he yelled. And he was racing across the field of fire. Eight-step bounds: left-right, left-right, left-right, left-right, down. "Set!" he yelled.

"Moving!" the right flank yelled and bounded past him.

"Set!" They dropped.

"Moving!" Jake yelled.

Machine-gun rounds were snapping the air above Jake's head. When he got closer to the convoy, there were machine-gun rounds skipping through the dirt beneath him. This was it: actual combat, like in the movies. The sort of thing that almost never happened in Iraq. He wasn't panicked. He was flying with each bound.

His foot didn't hurt. He wasn't even aware of it, which, after five surgeries, was a rare blessing. For six years now, his foot had defined his level of physical competence, which was central to Jake's life as a football player — and as a human being — and then as a Marine. It made him a mediocrity in close order drill, which was important but not that important — he had been named Guide, the top recruit in boot camp and then, again, in the School of Infantry. Mesmerized by the constant pain, he had even screwed up handing off the damn guidon at his graduation ceremony. But he wasn't thinking about his foot at all now; combat was liberation from that particular ball and chain.

He had no idea how long it took to bound the field. Minutes, certainly; it could have been five or fifteen. Finally they reached their destination, the berm that rose up to the elevated road. They dropped down and began firing their weapons at the unseen enemy through the ground level crevices of the convoy. Jake and Bullard looked at each other and smiled guiltily with the same thought: that shit was fun.

The firefight was still very much *on,* but Jake knew the convoy would be leaving soon to move the wounded Marine to the med-evac. He led his squad down the convoy, back to the truck that had brought them, an armored deuce and a half. They sat in the truck, giddy, swapping stories as bullets pinged off the outer armor. Jake's doubts about the quality of his fellow Marines had evaporated in combat. His fire team had done everything right. They had been fabulous, perfect. He totally loved them.

But, he realized, the convoy wasn't moving. The medevac helicopters were going to arrive down the road, at Pirates and MSR Mobile, the main highway between Fallujah and Ramadi, and they wouldn't hang around for very long. Jake got out of the truck and ran up to the front of the convoy, where Lieutenant Clevenger was with the wounded Marine who was being worked on by two medics. There was still heavy fire incoming. He looked down at the wounded man — the Humvee had been turned around to protect him from the incoming — and it was Nathan Windsor, face white, lips blue, a gurgling sound coming through the hole in his neck.

He told the Lieutenant they had to get out of there; the birds were on their way. Clevenger said Windsor had to be stabilized before they could move. They were still under intense fire. Jake dropped down and studied the field across the canal, trying to figure out where the machine-gun nests were. He saw movement in the reeds on the right . . . and, using the passenger-side seat of the Humvee as a vault, climbed up and slapped Wherry, the turret gunner, on the helmet and directed him, "Move your sector to the right." Wherry couldn't hear him. Jake cupped his hands and yelled, "Right flank!" Wherry got the message and moved his sector to the right, and Jake clambered down, missing a step, stumbling and falling to the ground, his hand landing in something wet. Windsor's blood. He looked at his bloody glove and wiped it on his camouflage tunic. Then he took it off and threw it away.

"I think I have him stabilized," Lacea, the medic, yelled over the machine-gun fire. Windsor could now be evacuated. But,

Lacea warned, they had to lay him flat, or the wound would rip open again. They had a highback Humvee with a flatbed and up-armored sidewalls farther back in the convoy. They tried to contact Little, who was in the highback, but the coms were just not working very well — and Jake decided to run back and commandeer the vehicle. More running. But he flew and jumped into the driver's seat — into the most insanely refreshing air-conditioned chill — and drove through a tracer-beaded curtain of bullets to the front of the convoy, where he helped get Windsor on board. Then he sped to the LZ — praying that AQI hadn't planted IEDs in the road as part of the ambush — just in time to meet the medevac.

Windsor was still alive. The medic was holding his hand and saying, "Hang in there, Windsor." They loaded him onto the Chinook, but he died in the air.

CHAPTER 4
THE COMPLETE WARRIOR

"They don't want you back in Seal Team One," Eric Greitens's SWCC commander Michael Lumpkin told him when he returned to Coronado from the Philippines in the fall of 2004.

"Why not?" Eric asked, stunned. This was a gut punch.

"You're considered a distraction," Lumpkin told him. ST-1 was having drug and behavior problems back home, as many of the other teams were. Eric's superiors believed he had done the right thing in Thailand, but too many of his fellow SEALs thought he was a snitch who might call them out for untoward behavior. "It's a tough situation and Sam Russell considers you an 'irritant.' "

"What can I do?" Eric asked. He respected Lumpkin. He was one of the honorable guys.

"Well, you can spend the last six months

of your tour here as a SWCC," Lumpkin began. "Then you're going to have to re-up and join another team. If you really want to lead SEALs in combat, you're going to have to be patient."

Eric was thirty; his four-year commitment was almost over. Kaj Larsen had already decided to leave the SEALs; he was going off to do a master's at Harvard's Kennedy School of Politics. Eric had options, too: he had applied and was soon accepted as a White House fellow.

He and Kaj left the SEALs frustrated, but there would be a second act for Eric as a SEAL reservist. He began to arrange his next deployment even before he started his year as a White House fellow. Lumpkin agreed to help him, as did several of the superior officers who had been impressed by his skills.

As soon as his year in Washington ended, he was headed to Iraq.

He would not go there as the leader of a SEAL unit; he would never command men in combat. That possibility had been fore-closed when he chose not to reenlist. He was going as an intelligence officer; in effect, he was a human switching station, operating out of the air base at Balad, sending the latest intel on the whereabouts of high-value Al Qaeda targets to special operators in the field, and forwarding their requests for help to the proper commands. It was important work, but it still wasn't combat, and when an opening came in January 2007 to run an Al Qaeda targeting cell in the embattled city of Fallujah, he leaped at the chance.

Fallujah was an ancient place dating back to Babylonian times — it had been a center of Babylonian Jewry and of Jewish Talmudic academies until 1000 AD. It had a population of approximately 300,000, which made it the second largest city in al-Anbar province, the heart of the so-called Sunni triangle — Ramadi, with 500,000, was largest — but Fallujah had achieved legendary status since 2003 as a place of unparalleled hostility to the American invaders. Indeed, it could be said that the full-fledged Sunni rebellion began with an unforgettable act of brutality, the hanging and torching of four Blackwater Security contractors from a bridge over the Euphrates River in 2004. Two major battles had been fought for control of the city after that, in 2004 and 2005. By the time Eric arrived in 2007 — about the same time that Jake Wood and Clay Hunt arrived at FOB Viking on the outskirts of town — Fallujah was occupied by American troops, Marines mostly, but it was still difficult to control.

Major Joel Poudrier, the ranking Marine intelligence officer in Fallujah, considered Greitens a godsend. Intelligence was notoriously stovepiped; special operations forces didn't share their sources, and the Marines either got the scraps or were left to patrol blindfolded through the rubble of the blasted city. Lieutenant Commander Greitens — he had been boosted a rank for this operation and was the Naval equivalent of a Marine Major — was different. He was happy to share targets with Poudrier, though not the top secret high-value ones, which were reserved for the SEALs. He was very professional, Poudrier thought, very smart but also friendly and, unlike some of the other SEALs he'd met, not at all full of himself. They began to roll up some pretty bad actors together.

Eric thought Poudrier was a hoot, always easy with a laugh, a storehouse of snacks sent from home by his wife — and, more seriously, a creative officer who was willing to try new things. Most days, Poudrier stayed at his desk in the depressingly dusty warren of Camp Fallujah, sorting through the intel streams that came his way. Greitens

146

could have done that as well, but he was finally on the front lines, and he wanted to see what the war was all about. He began to go out on patrols in order to understand the operational restraints and opportunities, and he advised his team in the targeting cell to do the same. Early on, Eric went on patrol in Ramadi with Army Rangers, a very well-trained and capable force, but none of them spoke Iraqi-dialect Arabic (their one translator spoke a Lebanese dialect, which the locals struggled to understand). They barged into a house where they believed Al Qaeda operatives were hiding and forced the family members down on their knees with their hands behind their backs and their foreheads against the wall, while the translator questioned the kneeling head of household. Eric understood that these procedures had been developed for the safety of the troops, but they seemed brutal and counterproductive all the same.

He was, for the first time, under fire now — nothing very sustained, an occasional rocket-propelled grenade or *bap-bap-bap* potshots at the American convoys passing through. He began to notice something very odd: from time to time, Iraqi men — much older men, sometimes — would come out from under cover, stand tall, and start shooting at the convoys. It seemed suicidal. Why on earth were they doing that? Eric figured that the public display of courage was essential. These were people whose homes had been violated by the Americans. They were defending the honor of their families.

There was a Marine battalion operating in Fallujah, but Eric found that the most effective units were the ten- to fifteen-member Marine MiTT teams (Military Transition Teams) that were serving as trainers for Iraq army and police units. He especially liked patrolling with a young Lieutenant named Travis Manion, who seemed — both Greitens and Joel Poudrier believed — a poster boy for everything an American military officer should be: smart, fit, principled, and creative. Manion was an Annapolis graduate and had served in Fallujah before as part of a Marine Force Recon unit. Poudrier gave him the toughest part of the city — an area called the Pizza Slice — to secure.

The regular Marines were skeptical about MiTT teams. They wanted no part of patrolling with the Iraqis. Who could trust them? But a strong bond had developed between Manion's team and its Iraqi army unit. The Iraqis went to war, courageously, in unarmored pickup trucks and with half the body armor that the Americans had. Manion's team and the Iraqis patrolled together at night, using the intel that Eric's targeting cell provided, and Eric often went along. The Iraqis would knock on the door and explain the situation to the head of household. "Where's your cousin Abu Mohammed? We were here two weeks ago and you said he was with your cousin Ahmed. You gave us an address. He wasn't there. We've heard that he's back here. So here's what we're going to do: we're going to look through the rest of your house. We'd like you to come with us and show us around."

The Iraqis spoke quietly to the head of household. They didn't force him to his knees or embarrass him in front of his family. They made it seem as if he were giving his guests a tour of his home. This seemed far less intrusive than the tactics that Eric had seen the U.S. forces use in Ramadi.

One day, Eric and Major Poudrier brought a photo of a suspected sniper to an Iraqi unit. "We're looking for this guy," Poudrier said.

"That guy?" The Iraqi Lieutenant said. "He's down at the barbershop."

"Now?" Poudrier asked.

"Now," the Iraqi replied. And sure

enough, he was. They arrested him there.

The Iraqis were not perfect allies; they didn't have much discipline. They were careless with their weapons and the way they organized their patrols. Their Army was mostly composed of Shiites who had no love for Fallujah's Sunnis.

One afternoon in late March, Eric was out on patrol with Manion's MiTT team — another team was riding in a convoy along a parallel route — when he heard an IED and several grenades go off. The other team had been hit.

A Marine Humvee had been jolted by a rocket-propelled grenade, but the Iraqis had been hit far worse: one of their pickup trucks had been blown up by an IED; several of their men had been killed. They brought three suspects who had been loitering in the area back to their command outpost.

When Eric returned to base, he heard a major commotion in the common room. He ran down the hallway, along with Manion and Poudrier, and found Iraqi soldiers pummeling the suspects they'd brought in after the explosion. Both the prisoners *and* the Iraqi soldiers were screaming and crying. One of the suspects was on the ground, getting kicked by the Iraqis; another was still standing, getting punched and throttled by his captors, then knocked to the ground. The Americans tried to separate the combatants, but the screaming and stomping seemed only to intensify with their efforts to stanch it. The Iraqi soldiers were furious about the deaths of their comrades, terrified by how close they all had come to getting killed.

Eric had never seen wild rage like this before. He was wearing his sidearm; indeed, everyone in the room was armed — and someone could start shooting at any minute, a possibility that became more immediate when Colonel Ali, the commander of the Iraqi troops, stormed into the room screaming as loudly as his men and brandishing an AK-47.

Poudrier considered Ali to be a very good soldier — certainly far better than Ali's predecessor, who had been pocketing his soldiers' pay — and the Colonel proved it now. He went after the loudest, most passionate of his men, who was still trying to get at one of the prisoners, jammed the AK-47 in his sternum, and, in a drill sergeant's bellow, told him to shut up. That calmed things down very quickly. In the evening, the Americans ate together with the Iraqis and then watched the James Bond movie *Casino Royale;* somehow the incident had drawn them closer. They were fighting the same enemy, the same war, and experiencing the same rage when their comrades were hurt.

This, Eric realized, was what the *individual* experience of war was all about. It wasn't about some great cause: it was about the protection of your friends, your family, your tribe — and the gut hatred of those who would do them harm. It didn't matter if the war was misguided, as Eric believed this one to be. It was all about the love and muscular bonding that comes with brotherhood under fire. For the overwhelming majority of the men and women at war in Iraq — Americans and Iraqis alike — these relationships would be the most intense of their lives.

The next day began with a mortar attack, which was not unusual. "Here's our morning wake-up call," said Poudrier, who could find the humor in just about anything. "Damn. I was hoping to sleep in."

But Eric sensed that there was something purposeful about these mortars. The explosions seemed to be marching in an orderly fashion toward the barracks. Usually a mortar attack was a hit-and-run affair, the perpetrators dashing off before they could be located and obliterated.

He and Joel had bunks next to each other, and they stood and began to get dressed.

Then Eric was down.

He may have lost consciousness for a moment, or perhaps not — the explosion so loud that no one could hear — and he found himself on the floor, tucked into the SEAL incoming artillery position with his hands over his ears and his mouth open.

A truck had somehow gotten past — or been allowed past — the checkpoints, through the switchback entrance between blast walls and Hesco barriers into FOB Fallujah. It had sidled up next to the old administrative building that served as the Marine barracks, and then it had detonated. The front of the building had been blown away. Inside, it was dark, the electricity blown, and the air was filled with choking dust — and another chemical smell: chlorine. The bomb had been laced with chlorine. Eric picked himself up, too stunned to ache. The Marines began to call out to one another: "Hey Maurice, you all right?" "Joel? Francis?" People were saying, "Yeah, I'm okay," but Eric's ears were ringing, and it was hard to keep track. A Marine Lieutenant Colonel found his way to them in the tangled darkness. He had a flashlight, and Eric could see the clogging dust in the air. He was having trouble breathing and his eyes were burning, but he grabbed hold of Staff Sergeant Francis and they followed the flashlight, stumbling out of there.

They made it out to the rear of the barracks, where Eric fell to his hands and knees, coughing furiously. His body wanted to retch — people around him were vomiting — but he could only spit. He stood up and tried to figure out who had gotten out and who hadn't. Joel Poudrier hadn't. Eric could swear that Joel had said, "Yeah, I'm fine," but he hadn't come out. The Lieutenant Colonel and some of the men went back in and found Poudrier, who was bleeding severely from the back of his head.

Eric realized that there was a pretty fierce firefight going on, and he and Staff Sergeant Francis ran up five stories to the roof of the building to reconnoiter. When he emerged on the roof, there was a rip of small-arms fire, and he dived to the ground and low-crawled to the front of the building. He took the northwest corner, and Francis took the southwest. In Eric's corner, an Iraqi soldier was firing his rifle out toward the attackers. But Eric couldn't see any attackers below, just people running around. He got out his scope and took a closer look — there were Iraqi police running about in the distance. There didn't seem to be any attackers left. The Iraqi soldier was laying friendly fire on the Iraqi police. Eric had him stop.

Travis Manion and some other Marines arrived on the roof a few minutes later with a medic who asked if Eric was okay. "I'm fine," he said. "Good to go."

But he was bleeding and stunned, and they insisted that he go to Fallujah medical. A convoy of Humvees rolled up below; by the time Eric got down from the roof, they were all full. There was one open-bed truck, and Eric got in with a young Marine and they rolled through Fallujah on their backs, staring up at the blasted buildings as the sun rose in the sky and the day became impossibly hot.

Eric was diagnosed with a mild concussion. He had taken some shrapnel in his head — twenty splinters, fragments from the building. He told the medics he was fine, but his head was still ringing, and he couldn't hear or breathe very well. He asked about Poudrier, who'd already been medevaced to the hospital in Balad, which meant his wound was probably pretty serious.

Eric called Kaj as soon as he could.

"You're going to hear about this truck bomb in Fallujah," he said. "I'm fine, but I need you to call my parents and tell them not to worry."

It took Eric nearly a month to recover from the blast. He would wake at night, coughing, and it was hard to do his usual workouts — his lungs had obviously been damaged by the chlorine. But he kept pushing himself, and his lungs regained capacity, and within weeks after he got home, he was running as strong as he ever had. His vision came back to normal after several weeks of tremendous irritation and constant blinking. His hearing took longer, but eventually that returned as well.

His deployment ended on April 5, 2007, a week after the blast. His return home was almost like an experiment in dive physics, experiencing the bends — not physically, but psychologically. One moment he was in Fallujah, preparing his last target list alongside his successor, and then he was choppered to Balad, and then he was flying home, and then he was in Dam Neck, Virginia, retrieving his white Ford Ranger pickup truck in the parking lot and driving through the gates . . .

There was a Wendy's just outside the base,

and there was a line of people waiting at the drive-through, and suddenly Eric was infuriated. He wanted to stop his truck, storm the drive-through line, and shout at them, "You have no idea! You don't know anything!"

They were just sitting there in the cars, annoyed, perhaps, by the length of the line, while young men like Travis Manion were off on the other side of the world, doing a night raid in a Humvee that might be blown to bits by an IED, or being targeted by a sniper in that vulnerable moment when they contorted themselves out of the Humvee and surveyed the street, or shot in the face while entering a house. And these burger-and-fries people were just sitting there, in extraordinary comfort, not even getting out of their cars to get a fast-food meal, *cocooned* in their cars, listening to their music, living their lives, ordering Frostys.

Eric realized he was being irrational. He was in Dam Neck, Virginia. The people on that line were Navy families, as likely as not. That was probably a chief petty officer ordering that Frosty. But his anger — so unlike him — reinforced by a sense of loss, and a sudden loss of purpose, continued in intermittent fashion for the next several months. He would see something or hear

some civilian complaining about the stupid-
est thing, and he'd want to wring someone's
neck.

The other thing was, he wasn't quite sure
what he was going to do now, what he
wanted to do with his life. He wanted to do
something useful. He still wanted to lead;
he still wanted to help refugees . . . Or
maybe, he proposed to Kaj, they could train
to become astronauts, or maybe climb
Mount Everest. "Eric," Kaj reminded him,
"it's cold up there. We're water people,
warm weather people."

This was part of the bends, too: for the
moment, there just wasn't anything he *had*
to do. In Iraq, his life had been a rigor of
necessary tasks — an all-day, all-night
proposition. Even chow was crucial: he had
to keep his energy up. But now, life spooled
out in a leisurely fashion. He could actually
sit and talk and savor a meal. He had a
girlfriend, a woman he'd met during his
White House fellowship, who was also in
the service, and they went on vacation
together. Summer was coming. He had just
turned thirty-three years old. His war was
over.

CHAPTER 5
CAN YOU GET ME A BEER?

Jake Wood's platoon was given a day off after Nathan Windsor was killed at the intersection of Angels and Pirates, just outside Fallujah, in February 2007. The next day was to be a light one, too — one of the squads would go out on a routine patrol. A coin was flipped. Clay Hunt's squad lost; Jeff Muir and Jake Wood got to spend another day hanging around FOB Viking. Jeff, Jake, and Clay were watching a season of *24,* the Kiefer Sutherland spy series, and Jeff told Clay, "Don't worry, bro, we'll hold the next episode until you get back."

An hour or so later, Jeff went to take a shower. He had just finished brushing his teeth and was walking back to his hooch when a Marine he barely knew came walking in the opposite direction and said, "Hey, Muir, you know anyone named Hunt?"

"Yeah. Why?"

"He got shot."

Muir grabbed the guy. "How bad?" He didn't know. Jeff ran back toward his hooch and saw that everyone was getting their stuff together, mounting up, going out to Route Lincoln where the attack had taken place. He ran to his bunk and was gathering his gear when Jake came in and said, "Hey, Clay got shot."

"How bad?" Jeff asked, knowing from the tone of Jake's voice that it wasn't terrible.

"He got shot in the wrist . . . He's out there, over by the CP. He wants to see you."

Jeff dropped everything and ran to the command post, where Clay was sitting on the front of his Humvee, all bandaged up and high as a kite on morphine. "Hey, man," he said when Muir approached. "Can you get me a beer?"

There was no beer downrange, no drugs or alcoholic beverages permitted. Muir began to laugh.

"C'mon, bro, get me a beer. I love you, man."

Ahhh, the morphine, Jeff thought: everybody loves everybody on morphine.

"You'll be drinking beer before I will," Jeff said. "You're out of here. What happened?"

"I was prone, on the SAW," he said. "Fucker shot me through the wrist. He missed me by six inches."

"You okay?"

Clay shrugged. And then they took him to the hospital in Fallujah. Within a week, he was back in California.

"Mom, I should have been dead," Clay said, when his parents visited him at the Naval Medical Center in San Diego. "Two seconds earlier, I would have been dead. I was prone, with the machine gun, but I lifted up. I used my left arm to lift up, so my left wrist was down where my head had just been."

There had been an AQI sniper in their area of operations, a magic sniper, very talented. The theory was that he had nailed Windsor in the neck, which was a great shot. He'd also nailed another Marine they didn't know, from a moving car, and that guy had been *walking* — it was nearly impossible to make that shot. Clay believed the magic sniper had shot him, too. (Back in Iraq, Jake and Jeff came to the same conclusion.) Clay had certainly been lucky: the round had gone straight through, with minimal damage. Still, his wrist would never be quite the same. He would no longer be able to push open a door with his flat palm — he could only use his fist. He would have to do push-ups with his left fist and right palm on the ground in perpetuity. It wasn't so bad.

"Well, that's over now," Clay's dad said. "You've got a million-dollar wound. You don't have to go back."

"I'm going back," Clay said.

"They might not let you."

"I *need* to go back," Clay said. "They need me."

Stacy Hunt knew better than to argue with his son. When Clay got an idea in his head, that was pretty much it. The boy ran at two speeds, obsessed or scattered. There had been an official diagnosis for this: Attention Deficit Hyperactivity Disorder.

Clay had been born early, tiny. He had always been . . . a *challenge,* different, a bundle of real talents and vexing deficits. Stacy didn't always handle this as well as he could have — certainly not as well as Clay's mother, Susan, who had more patience and more time for her son and could express her love for him far more easily than Stacy could. Susan seemed focused on Clay's strengths; Stacy worried about his weaknesses.

The Hunts had met at the University of Texas and done very well for themselves. Stacy was in a boom market in Houston, a city that exploded in the last twenty-five years of the twentieth century. They weren't exactly wealthy, but they were certainly comfortable, living in the western suburbs in a development called Rustling Pines. Their older child, a daughter, was a straight-ahead success in high school. She was a cheerleader with very good grades, a real go-getter. Clay had the makings to be all that, too — a normal kid, a *better* than normal kid. He was very smart, ticketed for the Advanced Placement track in school and — to Stacy's delight — a fine athlete, even though he was small; in football, he made up for his size with toughness. He was a very good kid, too, in his way: he loved going on church service projects, thought hard about the deep things — like God — and never was mischievous in an evil way. But he sometimes would drift into trouble — a knack for being in the wrong place at the wrong time, Stacy believed. Or he was just oblivious, off in his own world.

When Clay was four years old, Stacy took him to the country club and began to teach him golf, which, along with football, was an iconic Texas sport. Much to his delight, the kid wasn't bad. He bought Clay a mini-set of golf clubs, and Clay was knocking the ball around — hitting it very well for his size — by age five. Stacy knew that Clay didn't have the patience for more than four or five holes, but he expected that limit would expand over time. No doubt they'd be playing full rounds before long — but the opposite happened. The golf course featured several water hazards, and on sunny days turtles would bask on the banks. Clay was far more interested in the turtles than he was in golf. He would abandon his clubs mid-hole, run down to the water, and try to capture the turtles. Stacy couldn't pull him away. There were times Clay would arrive home in tears. He desperately wanted to please his father, but the turtles . . . He couldn't stay away from them.

Soon Clay was organizing his friends to go over to a nearby bayou on turtle-hunting expeditions. He brought his captures home, and Susan set out a washtub on the back patio — within weeks, the washtub was crammed with seventeen red-eared slider turtles, which stank to high heaven. But Susan tolerated it because Clay had taken his obsession to his fourth grade classroom. He read everything he could about turtles and was going to write a report. But he just couldn't get it out. He had physical trouble writing — he'd had, from birth, a fine-motor-skills deficit. And now it was driving him crazy. "Mom, I know everything there is to know about turtles. Why can't I write it all down?" So Susan negotiated a deal with the teacher. Clay would tape-record his paper, and Susan would write it out.

Not all of Clay's classroom problems were so easily solved, especially as he moved into middle school, where the teachers weren't as interested in nurturing a rambunctious kid, no matter how intelligent. He would bounce and chatter in the classroom, disturbing the other students. If he was interested in something — anything that involved the natural world, for example — he would be intense to the point of disruption; if he was bored by a subject, he would make that obvious, too. The Hunts were told that their son would have to be medicated. Ritalin helped, and Adderall helped more, but sometimes Clay seemed dulled to the point of witlessness. Stacy had very mixed feelings about this: drugs for a kid so young? It wasn't until Clay went off to summer camp in central Texas without his medication — the doctor had said Ritalin wasn't required in the summer — that Stacy was entirely convinced that all this stuff was necessary.

Four days after Clay left home, the Hunts received a call from his camp counselor. "Listen," he said, "I'm not sure this is going to work for another three weeks for Clay. He's bouncing all over the place."

Susan said, "Okay, we'll get his medicine to you as soon as possible," and she began to cry. Stacy felt terrible, but he didn't know what to say. There was no way of escaping this thing.

Life was no easier when Clay returned from camp. His football jersey read "C. Hunt" on the back, and some of the other players made the "H" silent; that would be his nickname. He hated being picked on; he internalized every harsh judgment and was unable to distinguish between good-natured ribbing and serious personal attack. Even when he knew the teasing was benign, he found it hard to come up with the quick riposte. Any sort of jibe was like oil-spill petroleum on a duck's back.

He was a good little football player, but again, prone to screw up. In one junior high school game, Clay's team was leading a local rival 7–6 late in the fourth quarter. Their opponents were driving toward the goal line. Clay, playing defensive back, intercepted a pass in the end zone. If he had just dropped down and taken a knee, the ball game would have been over. But he decided to run the ball out and fumbled it to the other team on the 4-yard line. Clay's team

166

won, so it wasn't a total disaster, but Stacy wondered: Why were things like that always happening to Clay? Why couldn't he make clear decisions? He knew rationally that the ADHD had something to do with it, but he was — and this was hard to admit — worried about his son at times. Susan, watching Clay struggle for his father's approval, was growing impatient with Stacy, drifting away.

There was one respite, one thing that not only seemed to calm Clay down but made him feel pretty good: he loved smoking marijuana. Somehow, he had a very good freshman year in high school, but things began to fall apart when he became a sophomore. He got his driver's license and a certain amount of freedom — but freedom was the last thing he needed. And by spring break that year, Clay told his mom, "I need to get out of here. I've got to change schools." Preempting her Why? he added, "I can't go back to Stratford and stay away from the things I need to stay away from."

Stacy's reaction, privately, was negative. Why was Clay tossing this monkey wrench into the middle of a school year? Would he lose his credits? All his friends sent their kids to Stratford; it meant something in Houston.

"At a certain point, with a kid like this,

you've got to quit worrying about what people think and just do what's right for your kid," Susan said.

In fact, she was proud of Clay. He knew he was in trouble and wanted to save himself. That took real guts. Susan and Clay visited Houston Christian High School, which was smaller and more structured than Stratford. They met with the principal and walked the grounds, and Clay said, "This feels good. This will work."

It did work. Because it was a smaller school, he got to play a lot more football than at Stratford. He stayed on his meds and did well academically. He scored an impressive 1380 on the SAT and, just like Jake Wood, 32 on the ACT. He decided that he was strong enough to go back to Stratford for his senior year and graduate with his class.

To keep himself disciplined, Clay joined a church drug treatment program in Katy, Texas, which was about an hour west of Houston. The program — which met every Wednesday night and Saturday morning — had a family component, which Stacy found uncomfortable. Clay would go for group counseling, and the parents were expected to go to a group session of their own. Some of the other parents were rough, uneducated. They talked about their demolition-derby lives with an unembarrassed candor that seemed intrusive and undignified. "I can't do this," Stacy said after several sessions. His life wasn't a demolition derby; he had a kid with a learning problem. "I just cannot relate to these people."

One evening, around dinnertime, Clay received a phone call from one of his friends in the treatment program. He raced back into the dining room, a man on a mission. "Robbie's in trouble out in Sealy," he said. "He needs me to come help."

"What about his parents?" Stacy asked. Susan was off at a meeting somewhere; he and Clay were alone.

"His parents suck. He wants *me.*"

"You've got school tomorrow," Stacy said. "Sealy's fifty miles away. You need to do your homework."

"*You* need to move your car," Clay said, resolute. Stacy had come in late and parked behind Clay's pickup.

"Clay . . ."

"I need you to move your fucking car." Clay was angry now, but Stacy wouldn't budge, and soon they were toe-to-toe, Clay screaming, Stacy telling him to get a handle and do his homework . . . and Clay took a swing at him, hard, a right to Stacy's left temple.

Stacy staggered, but he didn't fall and didn't swing back. He was stunned, furious, but mostly just shocked by the sudden violence. He wasn't a violent man; he simply gathered himself and left the house. He took a long walk around the neighborhood, giving Clay time to calm down and himself time to think. This was pretty scary, and the worst thing, he realized, was that this was who Clay really was. He'd been desperate to help a friend, a fine impulse — Susan would be proud — but it was out of all proportion, out of all reason. Stacy now began to understand that all the usual upper-middle-class restraints — the need to study, go to college, control his impulses — were plastic Bubble Wrap to Clay. He would rip through and destroy it all, if it prevented him from doing the things he felt were important. Helping others was very important; loyalty to his friends was sacrosanct. But restlessness, disorganization, avoiding the hard work in subjects that bored him, and — this was now undeniable — lashing out, sometimes violently, when he was frustrated, those were part of the package, too.

■ ■ ■ ■

Clay meandered around for the next three years. He went to Blinn Junior College, a Texas A&M feeder school, but he didn't last there for very long. He went to the University of North Carolina at Asheville but he joined a fraternity, majored in partying, and didn't last very long there either. He became a snowboarding bum and spent a season working at Winter Park, Colorado.

His parents separated, divorced, married other people. Susan Hunt was Susan Selke now, living near Lexington, Kentucky, married to a kind man who had ditched real estate to become a minister. And then one day, as she was shopping in Walmart, her phone rang.

"Hey, Mom, whatcha doin'?" Clay asked.

"Buying groceries, getting ready to head home," she replied. "What's up?"

"Well, Mom, I wanted you to know that I just joined the Marines," Clay said. She was in the kitchen and bath aisle. She sat down on a pile of towels.

"You know they'll send you to Iraq," she told her son.

"I know," Clay replied. He sounded calm, he sounded . . . good. There had been enough blood under the bridge by now that Susan knew not to trust that completely.

She asked him to check in with a trusted psychologist who knew Clay before he did anything drastic, like actually *join* the Marines — but a part of her also was thinking: maybe the military would be good for Clay, maybe it would help him to organize himself. A few days later, the counselor called her in Kentucky. "I talked to Clay, and he really has thought it through," he said. "I think Clay was made to do this."

Stacy was surprised, but proud as well. He took Clay back to the recruiter to discuss what his MOS (military occupational specialty) would be. Clay was excellent at taking apart cars and putting them back together — it was one of the things he loved doing — and Stacy hoped that he'd get a billet in a tech specialty like aircraft mechanics. But Clay wanted the infantry.

"Well, if that's what you want," he said, frustrated. Yet again, Clay was going his own way.

Two months later, Stacy and Clay woke up well before dawn and went down to the central post office in Houston to meet the four thirty a.m. military van that would take Clay to the airport. Clay gave his father a big hug — Stacy was near tears — and said, with utter discipline and clarity, "Dad, this is what I want to do. Thanks for letting me get to this point."

And he was an excellent Marine, honored as the second-best recruit in his boot camp class. Both Stacy and Susan attended Clay's boot camp graduation at Camp Pendleton in California, and they saw a stunning transformation: he had put on some muscle, and Susan was struck by what a physical *presence* he seemed to be. More than that, he had lost his nervous, desperate edge. He was confident now, quietly confident, and he was calm. He had been selected for re-con school — the Marine equivalent of special forces — which was a major achievement. He was very proud of himself, Stacy saw, and in a manly way. Susan had the exact same feeling. "My little boy is now a young man."

Except that he was a young man going to war.

Clay survived his brief time in Iraq, but something about him had definitely changed. Both Jake and Jeff noticed it from the emails Clay sent after he was shot. They came in bunches, scorching the screen, fierce and desperate:

"I miss you guys so much."

"Can't wait for you to come home, so we can have a beer."

"What's happening? Has anyone been hurt?"

"I miss you guys so much."

"I should be there with you."

"I should be there with you."

Jeff thought he understood Clay's frustration. Blake Howey had been killed — and Clay hadn't been there for him. Howey's best friend, Nathan Windsor, had been shot by the magic sniper — and Clay had been stuck in his truck. There was real humiliation to that: The Humvee driver's job was to stay behind the wheel, no matter what was going on outside — which was why drivers, in most cases, tended to be the guys you couldn't trust to be outside in the fight. Or they were the guys you wanted to punish for mouthing off or generally being uncooperative, which was why Clay was driving. He had a big mouth and took orders reluctantly, if at all, from people he considered jerks.

And then three days after Windsor's death, Clay had been shot — and before he came off his morphine high, he was gone: Baghdad, Germany, San Diego in a blur. His war was over, and he had barely fought it. And now he had to sit home — a REMF, a rear echelon motherfucker, doing REMFy crap back on post at 29 Palms — while Jeff and Jake went through all sorts of hairy shit. Jake was the best friend he'd ever had, he told his mom; Jeff was a brother. Nobody else in Third Platoon was killed during the five months that Clay wasn't there, but plenty had been wounded — the spring of 2007 was the bloodiest period of the war in Iraq — and Clay felt like a slacker. He should have been there for them. And yet, when he'd been there, he'd been trapped, unable to help Howey, unable to help Windsor.

When Jake and Jeff came home from Iraq, Clay was waiting for them at the airport with their families. The three amigos, reunited, went on a mammoth road trip to Vegas and a Wisconsin football game. Clay seemed great at first, but it gradually became clear that something was off. It was especially clear to Jeff, who roomed with Clay at 29 Palms (Jake had been selected for a scout-sniper course and was being trained at Camp Pendleton). Clay seemed all tangled up in himself. He was trying to fight it, for sure. He had gone for help and been diagnosed with post-traumatic stress disorder. The VA gave him its usual cocktail: Lexapro for anxiety, Valium for panic, and

Ambien to get to sleep. But the drugs seemed to work at the wrong times or in the wrong ways, or perhaps they weren't working at all. Clay would be up and hyper-hyper at eleven p.m. and then totally exhausted, unable to get off the couch at midday.

There were times, many times, when he was good old Clay — he had a girlfriend named Robin Becker, and they spent most weekends together — but he was kerblooey often enough to worry Jeff a lot.

Clay was intent on going back for another deployment, and he wanted to be with Jake. "That's crazy," Jeff told Jake. "I love Clay, but there's something wrong with him. Believe me, I'm living with the dude. He can't get to sleep. He can't stay awake. Do you really think he can make it through sniper school?"

Jake wasn't sure. Sniper school required fabulous discipline; the physical requirements were much tougher than boot camp had been — Jake was worried about his own ability to make it through, given the amount of running involved. The sand hills surrounding Camp Pendleton were brutal, especially without the benefit of combat adrenaline. There were days when Jake wanted to cut his foot off; the pain was constant, withering. But he also felt responsible for Clay. He had a choice: he could go back to Golf Company and be a squad leader in Third Platoon, or he could bring Clay along to snipers.

"You can't bring him along," Jeff said. "He has P-T-S-fucking-D."

"But he's a good Marine," Jake said. "You know that. He's fit, he can run and swim, and you know he's a PT nut. For Christ-fucking-sake, he would have made it through *recon* school, if he hadn't screwed up." This was a good argument: recon school was the toughest training there was.

"I don't know, Jake," Jeff said. "Do you really need this burden?"

No, he didn't. But he had no choice: cutting off Clay would be like cutting off his arm — and a lot worse than amputating his foot.

"Will you vouch for him?" his scout-sniper platoon Sergeant had asked.

"Yes," Jake said. "Absolutely."

"Then he's your responsibility. If he doesn't make it, you don't either."

And Clay did, indeed, make it. He handled all the physical parts easily; he'd always been an excellent shot. He had some tough moments — especially when he was being hazed, which was part of the drill — but everyone had their moments in sniper school. Jake had nearly gotten kicked out when his superiors found that he was still blogging; *Jake's Life* had to be stowed for the next seven months. But this was Clay's proudest time as a Marine; he was finally one of the elite.

Shawn Beidler, the Sergeant who had recruited Jake into snipers, thought this six-man sniper team was the best he'd ever had. Shawn was older, like Jake and Clay, and had been to college. He had worked with Jake in Iraq and loved the guy. He'd been skeptical about Clay — but found, as the training progressed, that he loved him, too. Shawn fell in easily with the three amigos when it came to partying in Manhattan Beach. He and Clay would have long, deep political conversations. They'd disagree at times, but that was okay. Clay knew stuff; he read a lot. He had real doubts about Iraq, but Afghanistan was supposed to be the good war — and they were all happy to learn in February 2008 that they were not going back to the sandbox, but heading to Afghanistan.

Their sniper team would be attached to Echo, Fox, and Golf companies of the 2/7 Marines, and that felt good, too. Golf had been their old company; as scout-snipers, they'd be out protecting their guys. They were ticketed for Helmand province, a dreadful, empty place in the far southwest of the country on the Pakistan border. The area would have been a complete wasteland if the Americans hadn't built an elaborate irrigation system off the Helmand River in the 1950s. Wheat had been grown there in the past, but now the cash crop was poppies. It was the source of 90 percent of the world's opium.

There were those who believed the Marines should never have gone to Helmand. They were needed elsewhere, especially in the mountainous east, where there was some tough fighting against the Taliban — or perhaps in Kandahar province, a major population center just east of Helmand, which was Taliban central, Mullah Omar's home turf. But the Marine brass wanted their own area of operations — and the Brits, who'd been holding the fort in Helmand, needed help. Afghanistan was heating up; the Taliban had become a serious fighting force again after being nearly wiped out in 2001. The "good war" was becoming an issue in the 2008 presidential campaign, and those poppies were funding the Taliban insurgency (as well as the corruption of Afghan President Hamid Karzai's regime).

So in the spring of 2008, Jake and Clay's sniper platoon was deployed to Helmand province.

It was a mess from the start. They were stuck at Kandahar Air Field for a month. Then they were moved to Camp Bastion, a British fort near Lashkar Gah, the capital of Helmand. They sat at Bastion, too, even as Echo, Fox, and Golf deployed. "What the hell is going on?" Jake asked Beidler. "They don't have enough ammo for us?"

"Helicopters, I think," Shawn said. In truth, the Marines were still trying to figure out where everyone should go.

"We should be out there, protecting our guys," Jake said.

Which was prescient: a few days later, word came back that Third Platoon of Golf Company — their old platoon — had been hit. A Humvee had been blown up by an IED; four had been killed. Jake and Clay were berserk, trying to find out the names, experiencing a combination of guilt, disgust, and anger.

The names were awful. Clay lost a fire-team buddy, Layton Crass. Jake thought, at first, that he'd also lost a beloved member of his fire-team, Kevin Colbert, a Choctaw Indian from Oklahoma. It turned out that Colbert was still alive, but he had been seriously injured in the blast, with burns over 90 percent of his body. But the worst loss was Sergeant Mike Washington, Jr., the squad leader who had been given the job that Jake had been asked to take. Jake loved Washington. He had come to the Marines directly from high school in Seattle, but somehow Mike could bridge the gap with the older guys like Jake and Clay. He was a tall, handsome black guy, an excellent Marine, smart and funny, able to handle the physical challenges with ease.

Jake had felt good when he learned that Washington had been selected for the squad leader's job that he'd rejected; Mike would take care of the guys. He'd bring them home. And now, for the second time in two deployments, Jake was thinking: that should have been me in that fucking Humvee. When he heard the news, he rushed out to the edge of Camp Bastion, over to the sandblasted Hesco barriers, and wept. He gathered himself and went back to Beidler. "I want a fucking transfer," he said. "If we're not going to be in the fight, I want to go back to my squad and take Mike's place."

Shawn calmed him down. The sniper team was a unit; removing Jake would be like pulling the carburetor from an engine. "I know it's fucked," Beidler said. "But we'll be out there soon enough."

Jake and Clay talked about it that night. They wanted to get out there *now*. "I would really like to get out there and waste some of those assholes," Jake said. He looked at Clay, at the calm fury in his eyes, and thought: my brother is right there with me.

They were deployed about a week later to the heavily contested town of Sangin, which sat on the east side of the Helmand River in the north of the province. Jake was amazed by how primitive it was compared to Iraq: there was no infrastructure, no literacy. The Afghan government had zero presence there; the local tribes provided what order there was — and there wasn't very much. The Taliban were everywhere; IEDs were everywhere. Their battalion would suffer thirty amputations during the deployment.

The conditions for the sniper team were rudimentary as well. They lived in a corner of the British FOB, in tents, in the midst of a sea of gravel. There were no shower trailers, no Porta-Jons. The hygiene was atrocious. They bathed in the river, dumped in Wag Bags, and peed wherever. Jake contracted a MRSA staph infection there.

Much of their work was at night. They would go out in the darkness, establish an oversight position in advance of an American troop movement, and wait for the Taliban to come and try to plant IEDs. It was boring, frustrating work. Clay fell asleep on security watch in the field one night, a near-unpardonable offense. "It was my medications, man," he said to Beidler.

That didn't wash at all. "If you can't handle your medications, bro, you shouldn't be here," Shawn said.

"I'll be okay," Clay said. "I promise."

But he wasn't okay. He wasn't reliable. He had come to the conclusion that the whole deployment, the whole war, was bullshit. He would complain constantly — and while Jake and some of the other snipers thought Clay's complaints were valid, he was bumming out the team, cratering morale. Beidler pulled Jake aside. "What's going on with Clay?"

"He's got some personal shit he's working through," Jake said. "He'll be all right."

"You've got to talk to Clay, bro. He's got to get his act together."

Jake tried to appeal to Clay's sense of duty and integrity. "You've got a job to do," he told Clay after the sleeping incident. "You signed up for this. You have to do it — because if you don't, if you're not out there doing your job well, some of your brothers *are not going to make it home.* Clay, you do

183

not want to be responsible for that. You do not want to live with that."

Clay knew Jake was right. He promised to get his shit together. "I definitely do *not* want to be the guy who gets someone killed."

And he did try, very hard. That was one of the toughest things for Jake, watching Clay trying so hard and sometimes struggling. Clay was never asked to be a shooter when they were out on a mission, but he held positions of great responsibility. He was integral to the team's first coordinated shot. Two shooters were trained on two men in a group of Taliban, several hundred yards away. Clay counted down: "I have control," he said calmly. "I have control. Stand by. Firing on the T of two. Five . . . four . . . three . . . t" — two Taliban dropped in their tracks — "two." There was immense technical satisfaction in this, and there was vengeance for all their comrades who'd been blown up by IEDs, but Clay remained troubled. What were they *doing* out there in Sangin? What was the point?

There were rumors that they were going to be pulled out of Sangin and moved into a major battalion-sized set-piece battle for control of the town of Nowzad. That would make sense: taking territory, rather than just sweeping it and watching the Taliban leak back in like dirty water. But it never happened.

As the weeks passed, there were days that Clay simply did not want to go out on missions. "I cannot fight this war," he told Jake. The reaction from their superiors was sympathetic at first. Everyone was exhausted. It was high summer, scorching, damp from all the irrigation water and yet dusty, with no amenities. No computers, no electricity for nonessential business, like watching DVDs. So, sure, it made sense that Clay really did need a break — you certainly didn't want him in the field if *he* thought he would be a liability. But the days Clay stayed in began to increase, and finally the platoon Sergeant said to him, "Hunt, you're on tent watch until further notice." And he spent several weeks hanging out at the FOB, while the rest of the team went out on an extended mission.

Jake continued to protect him as best he could; he remained loyal, defended Clay to the others — and the rest of his teammates understood what Jake was doing and why. Shawn Beidler felt terrible about it — he really liked Clay, and they would remain friends when they got home — but the guy just couldn't hack it downrange.

On one of their last patrols, the sniper team took an overwatch position in an old stone house, one of the more prodigious structures in the area, providing security for an Echo Company sweep through the adjoining farmland. They stashed the owner and his family in the basement and, situated on the second floor, tried to pick off the Taliban who were attempting to pick off Echo. As the sun rose and a hot day began, they saw children running out to the Taliban positions, carrying things — ammo, food, water, it was hard to tell. It seemed an organized operation, and they tried to put eyes on the organizer. Wheeler went downstairs and thought he saw the guy, a religious sort with a long beard, wearing a dark djellaba (or "man dress," as the Marines called it). But it was impossible to get a shot at him without blowing their position. There was some debate about shooting one of the kids, a girl with an RPG tube running out toward the Taliban, but nobody was really up for that either.

As the sun arced toward midday, the Taliban called it quits and retired from the field. Beidler's sniper team received a radio message that it was cool to pack up and leave. Normally they would have waited till nightfall, but there was a Cobra gunship in the air, ready to escort them out.

Jake walked point. He took two steps out of the compound, with Beidler just behind him. "Wood, hold," Shawn said. "Is that the motherfucker?" Jake followed the line of Beidler's sniper rifle and saw a man with a long beard standing in front of a rude mud hut, proselytizing vehemently, waving his arms in front of five children. Wheeler confirmed it was the guy he'd seen before.

Jake looked at the man, who seemed to be angry with a very young boy, gesturing out to the field and then back to the mud hut and out to the field again. He didn't feel good about shooting the guy in the midst of the kids, but he told Shawn, "If this is the guy, let's smoke him."

Jake would later write, "The man jerked as if punched in the chest, and behind him the drab wall exploded in color as his heart erupted out his back. In an instant the man dropped to the ground . . . the splotch of red slowly dripping down the tan mud wall. Nothingness was replaced with screaming, the terrified shrieks of five children who, after a moment of disbelief, fled in every direction from the confines of my scope. I blinked, and suddenly my scope was empty."

Eric Greitens *(right)* at his BUD/S graduation. *(Courtesy of Eric Greitens)*

Eric in Iraq in 2007. *(Courtesy of Eric Greitens)*

Jake Wood in Afghanistan in 2008 after an overnight operation searching for IED emplacers. *(Courtesy of Jake Wood)*

Jake's sniper team (*left to right*): Jake, CJ Wheeler, Stephan Thenn, Jon Davis, Josh Kernan, and Shawn Beidler. *(Courtesy of Jake Wood)*

Jake with Mike Washington, Jr. and Sr. *(Courtesy of Jake Wood)*

Jake (*far left*) leading Team Rubicon's first mission in Haiti after the earthquake in 2010. (*Courtesy of William McNulty*)

William McNulty (*center*) and other members of the first Team Rubicon mission in Haiti. (*Courtesy of William McNulty*)

Left to right: Brother Jim Boynton, Jake Wood, and Clay Hunt in Haiti in 2010. (*Courtesy of William McNulty*)

Clay Hunt with a Haitian mother and child. *(Courtesy of William McNulty)*

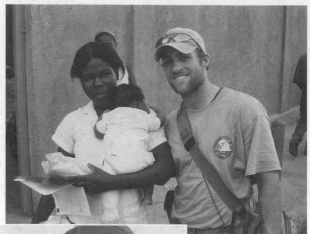

Clay and Jake during Team Rubicon's second relief mission, in Chile after the earthquake in February 2010. *(Courtesy of Jake Wood)*

Jake, Clay, and McNulty with a Chilean soldier. *(Courtesy of Jake Wood)*

Eric Greitens leading orientation for The Mission Continues at the Dream Center in Los Angeles in January 2013. *(Courtesy of Eric Greitens)*

Left to right: Mike Pereira with Jake Wood and Clay Hunt on the day they met in California. *(Courtesy of Jake Wood)*

Natasha Young at The League School in Brooklyn during a Mission Continues orientation in May 2013. *(Courtesy of Natasha Young)*

Natasha Young and Tiffany Garcia, both former fellows and staff members for The Mission Continues. *(Courtesy of Natasha Young)*

The wrist tattoos that Tiffany *(left)* and Natasha *(right)* got together in memory of another Mission Continues fellow, Mark Weber. *(Courtesy of Natasha Young)*

McNulty on his cell phone, coordinating Team Rubicon's Sandy relief efforts. *(Photo by Kyle Murphy)*

McNulty in New York City after Hurricane Sandy hit the area in 2012. *(Photo by Kyle Murphy)*

Team Rubicon at their Annual Leadership Conference in October 2014 in Dallas, Texas. *(Photo by Kirk Jackson)*

The Mission Continues. *(Courtesy of Eric Greitens)*

■ ■ ■ ■

PART III
FINDING HOME

■ ■ ■ ■

Be strong, saith my heart; I am a soldier
I have seen worse sights than this.

— **THE ILIAD**

CHAPTER 1
THE DIAMOND STANDARD

On the last day of April 2007, Eric Greitens parked his pickup near his apartment in Washington, D.C., and was just stepping out of it when his phone rang. It was Joel Poudrier, who was back home in North Carolina, recovering from his head wound. "Eric, I got some bad news," he said. "Travis was killed in Fallujah yesterday. A sniper."

Eric went numb. "No," he said softly. Everything seemed to be moving in slow motion on the street. A taxi pulled up, stopped, emptied out laughing passengers, and took off. People sleepwalked their daily lives, doing errands. Eric was distracted, then disturbed by the normality: Was there anyone for blocks around — anyone in this capital city — thinking, *at that moment,* about the men and women like Travis who were, *at that moment,* in mortal danger in Iraq and Afghanistan?

Joel thought he'd lost Eric. "Hey, you okay?"

"I'm okay," Eric said, but he didn't seem okay to Joel.

"Hey look, Eric, I'm going back in a few weeks."

"You're going back?"

His wound was healed. He needed to be back with his men. "But I was thinking that I really want to visit the Manions before I go. They live up in Pennsylvania. You want to come with me?"

"Absolutely," Eric said. "Of course."

Eric had rented a Capitol Hill flat during his year as a White House fellow. He'd sublet it during his tour in Iraq to Mike Lumpkin, who was serving as a Naval Special Warfare liaison to the Congress. It was a small, sparsely furnished place. Joel Poudrier thought it was like a starving artist setup. "Hey, I've got something to show you," Eric said when Joel arrived to drive him up to Pennsylvania. He opened one of his Navy gear bags and pulled out his body armor. There was blood all over it. "Your blood," Eric said with a smile.

"You think I could have some of that back?" Joel asked.

"Too late," Eric said. "You forgot to duck."

Tom and Janet Manion lived in a beautiful home in Doylestown, Pennsylvania. He was a retired Marine lieutenant colonel, now an executive with Johnson & Johnson, and every bit as rectitudinous as his son, who had been buried a few weeks earlier at Arlington National Cemetery. The Manions had been too stunned to talk with Travis's Marine buddies who'd attended the funeral. But now they were curious about what Fallujah had been like and how Travis had been regarded. Joel and Eric were the first of Travis's comrades to sit down with them and really talk about their son.

Joel, who knew Travis better than Eric did, took the lead. Tom Manion had maps of Fallujah, and they went down to his office to look at them — Janet Manion wanted no part of this. Joel showed Tom the Pizza Slice and talked about how the patrols operated, how well Travis had worked with the Iraqis; Eric talked about being out on patrol with Travis, how strong he'd been. Joel had brought some photos from Travis's MiTT team.

"Tell me about them," Tom asked Joel, pointing to a picture of the team. He wanted to know about each one, individually.

"And who's that?" Tom asked, pointing to an imposing Iraqi officer.

"That's Colonel Ali," Joel said. "He's a

really great leader. The guy never took a cut for himself when he paid his men, which is saying something for the Iraqis. He actually" — and here Joel hesitated — "he insisted on saying a few words at the memorial service they had for Travis in Fallujah. You would have loved it, sir. All the Iraqis who worked with Travis's MiTT team were there. They all respected him, sir," Joel concluded. "He showed them what a true warrior and a true leader looked like."

Travis's sister, Ryan, who owned several clothing stores, joined them for dinner. Janet had prepared a wonderful meal — and Eric was deeply moved by their graciousness. He realized that he and Joel had taken Travis's place at the table; the Manions felt the same way. After dinner, they went downstairs to a covered patio, where the real conversation began.

Tom and Janet were angry — Janet, particularly — about how the war was being portrayed in the media. "Travis called us once a week and he didn't sound anything like the news reports we've been hearing," Janet said. "He was *optimistic.* He said things were getting *better.* What do you guys think? Was Travis right?"

They assured Janet that Travis's team had been doing very effective work. Eric knew that it was too soon to tell if Fallujah was really calming down, but he wanted to reassure these lovely, shattered people. As it happened, Travis was prescient: a little more than a month after his death, in June 2007, al-Anbar province quieted considerably; there were days, then weeks, when no shots were fired — not just in Fallujah, but throughout the province. The local tribes had turned against Al Qaeda; General Petraeus was signing up their young men to become Sons of Iraq, a paid militia force.

The Manions asked Joel why he was going back to Iraq. "My guys are there," Joel said. "I've got to complete my mission." Ryan would remember her mother saying that she wished Travis's mission could continue as well.

"What do you think Travis's legacy should be?" Eric asked.

Janet said that Travis's friends had encouraged them to put an ad in the local paper advertising the creation of a Travis Manion Memorial Fund. Somehow the ad had gone viral in the online military community, and $200,000 had come in from all over the country. She and Eric began to talk about how that money should be spent. She was thinking about providing Travis Manion college scholarships for students at his alma mater, La Salle High School.

Eric was struck by this. He hadn't given much thought to how his generation of veterans would be remembered. He and Joel talked about it all the way back to Washington. He remembered the quote from Thucydides' account of Pericles' funeral oration: "What you leave behind is not what is engraved in stone monuments, but what is woven into the lives of others."

Eventually, Ryan Manion would sell the two clothing stores she owned and take charge of the Travis Manion Foundation. It seemed more important work than worrying if she had enough size 8 jeans in stock. Eventually, the Travis Manion Foundation would provide funding for eighteen Mission Continues fellows, including four of the first five — and then annually award a Travis Manion fellowship to one of the more promising TMC candidates. One of the first would go to Jake Wood of Team Rubicon.

For the moment, though, Eric drove through the darkness, back to Washington, overwhelmed by the realization that his generation of warriors — fighters of two forlorn wars — was about to take its place in history. The active duty military represented a tiny portion of the American population, and the actual warriors a fragment of that. Eric thought about the admirable qualities, the moral and mental discipline that Travis Manion brought to Fallujah and would have brought home. Somehow — he wasn't sure how — those qualities had to be leveraged and, as Pericles suggested, woven into the lives of others.

Eric had served his White House fellowship at the Department of Housing and Urban Development. He wasn't thrilled by the assignment at first. HUD was a sleepy backwater in the George W. Bush administration. Eric was hoping for Treasury or the National Security Council — but the HUD Secretary, Alphonso Jackson, took a personal interest in the White House fellows program, interviewed Eric himself, and gave him an office right down the hall from his own. And then on August 29, 2005, the week before Eric was to begin his fellowship, Hurricane Katrina demolished New Orleans and HUD wasn't so sleepy anymore.

On Eric's first day in the job, Secretary Jackson's special assistant Kim Kendrick handed him a piece of paper and said, "Take a look at this and see what you can do with it."

It was a message from the Auburn University College of Architecture offering to help with the planning and rebuilding of New Orleans. Eric called the dean of the school, who didn't have any specific ideas but said, "We've got a whole bunch of students and faculty who want to help in some way." He then called several other schools of architecture, all of whom wanted to help but weren't sure how. He wrote a brisk, five-point military action memo proposing a program — the Universities Rebuilding America Partnership (URAP) — that would give federal grants to schools of architecture that joined with local community development agencies to plan and build new housing in the battered neighborhoods of New Orleans. He handed it to Kim Kendrick that night.

"You don't even have a phone yet," she laughed, "and already you're proposing new programs?" But she liked the idea and passed it along to Secretary Jackson, who called Eric into his office the next day. "You did this on your first day on the job?" he asked.

"Well, I'm not sure if it's a great idea or not, but I did get to talk to some of these deans and . . ."

"It's a really good idea," Jackson said. "I'm going to take it to the President." By the end of the week, they had Bush's approval and rearranged the HUD budget to provide $6.2 million in funding for the program.

Eric found the work at HUD satisfying, but the best part of the White House fellowship program was the opportunity to meet people who had real experience in government — not just the guest speakers in the weekly fellowship seminar meetings, but also people he sought out — and in the process, he gained two new Kennedy-era mentors, Harris Wofford and Adam Walinsky.

The relationship with Walinsky was immediate and intense — all relationships with Walinsky were immediate and intense, or they didn't happen at all. He was a tough-looking guy, a former Marine, shaved head, gravelly voice, still physically fit in his seventies, always wearing his PT-109 tie clasp when he wore a tie. He had been a top aide to Robert Kennedy, a young Turk trying to push Kennedy to publicly oppose the war in Vietnam. He adored Kennedy, who was fierce, emotional, and tough — the President's hatchet man — and compassionate enough to burst into tears in an Appalachian sharecropper's shack. After the Detroit riots, in which 43 residents were killed by the police and 1,189 wounded, Walinsky and the senator tried to think their way through the disaster.

The Detroit police had gone berserk; they weren't very well trained and they weren't very well educated. There was a need to lift the quality of policing in America, to make it a profession rather than just a job. It would be a good thing, Kennedy and Walinsky agreed, if you could begin to inoculate American police forces with the functional equivalent of West Point cadets — recent graduates from Harvard and Princeton and Georgetown who could be trained, rigorously, as police officers.

The idea consumed Walinsky, especially after Kennedy's assassination. He formally proposed the Police Corps in the early 1980s and introduced a brilliant lure to bring the best young people to serve in the poorest communities: if they agreed to spend four years serving as cops, they would receive scholarship money for graduate school — and more, he was able to get some of the most prestigious law schools, like Harvard and Yale and Stanford, to promise special preference for Police Corps graduates. He formed a board of directors — Bill Clinton was chair — and he kept pushing, but nothing happened.

Clinton appropriated Walinsky's idea of service for scholarships when he ran for

President. His audiences loved it, and when he was elected President, he launched AmeriCorps — and eventually he delivered on the Police Corps as well, over the objections of some on his staff and assorted liberals who thought that training college kids to become cops was probably sort of dangerous.

But the Police Corps worked. Brilliantly. Some states wanted no part of it, but cities like Baltimore; Portland, Oregon; and Charleston, South Carolina — and states like Utah, Missouri, and Mississippi — took advantage of the federal funds. The centerpiece of the program was a residential boot camp, which featured intense physical training, firearms exercises, and courses in sociology, ethics, and arrest and control. The training was, in effect, not much different from the way the military trained special operators. And it made a difference on the streets: Ed Norris, the Baltimore police commissioner, said that he could tell which of his cops were Police Corps graduates simply by the way they stood and looked and carried themselves. They were fit, which meant they could run down fleeing felons rather than shoot them; they were trained by Lew Hicks, a Navy SEAL, in the most efficient and least violent ways to arrest and control suspects. They became integral to the communities they policed, just as Travis Manion's MiTT team had become part of the landscape in Fallujah's Pizza Slice.

But George W. Bush killed the Police Corps. It was a program that fell through the cracks, unloved by liberals, not loved nearly enough by conservatives, for whom cost-cutting was more important than national service, even if that service promoted the values that conservatives claimed as their own. Walinsky, who never suffered fools even a tiny bit, was isolated politically and increasingly embittered, but he was brilliant in his bitterness, a scorching Old Testament prophet with a great deal to offer if you could stand the heat of his never-ending fire.

Walinsky met Greitens over dinner at The Monocle restaurant, a Senate hangout on Capitol Hill. Eric was accompanied by several of the other White House fellows, but he took the lead: Walinsky noticed that Greitens asked questions that took the conversation to the next level, both up and down — abstract questions about the largest ethical and policy questions out there, but also detailed questions about the intricacies of policy. He was fascinated by Walinsky's work with the police, which raised issues that sounded very similar to the problems he'd seen in the Navy SEALs, though he never told Walinsky that. They had several more dinners. As Eric was about to leave for Iraq, Adam gave him a copy of Vali Nasr's *The Shia Revival,* a look at the larger forces at work in the region — the real fault lines, which were not the straight-line borders drawn by the Europeans after World War I, but the ethnic and sectarian divisions that had been unleashed by the American invasion of Iraq.

When Eric returned from Iraq a year later, Walinsky made him an offer. Fred Bealefeld, the Baltimore police commissioner, had asked Adam to retrain the entire Baltimore police department in the manner of the Police Corps. "I got two thousand five hundred guys out there on the street who are acting like they're completely un-trained," Bealefeld said to Walinsky. "What am I going to do about them?"

Walinsky then explained his training plan to Eric. "You go with the macho stuff first in order to establish credibility. Give them amped-up situational firing sessions with paintball guns, taught by military trainers, rather than the one-dimensional target range sessions." Then they would have Lew Hicks teach them arrest and control. But they also needed to learn how to behave in the community — this was the tough part — and that was where Eric came in. "I need a trained killer," Adam concluded. "Someone they have to respect, to teach them how to talk to kids and how to be a moral presence, respected on the streets."

"Oh," Eric said, "I've got that."

When he'd returned from the debacle in Thailand, Eric had been asked by his superior officer Michael Lumpkin to sketch out a code of ethics for the SWCCs. He produced, in consultation with Kaj Larsen, a 47-slide PowerPoint called *The Complete Warrior.* The slides were dense with anthropology, sociology, and aperçus:

SWCCs are warriors.

Warriors are servants.

Servants are humble.

Lumpkin thought the effort was potentially valuable for both SWCCs and SEALs and passed it up the line of command, where it died. It was the right message, but Greitens was considered the wrong messenger.

Now he and Walinsky began to adapt *The Complete Warrior* for the Baltimore police. Eric came up with a mnemonic device to make it indelible for the cops: the Diamond Standard. The top and bottom of the diamond came from a slogan the Marines used in Fallujah: "No Better Friend, No Worse Enemy."

" 'No Worse Enemy' means that if somebody pulls a gun on you, you're going to kill them," Eric would tell the cops. "You're going to be so well-trained, so proficient with your firearms, that you can defend your fellow citizens. If someone makes the choice that they're going to engage in a violent confrontation, you're going to win that confrontation every single time."

But "No Better Friend" was just as important. "It means you are someone who people in your district can count on," Eric would tell them. "Your fellow police officers need to be able to count on you, the community needs to be able to count on you. You have to be there for people."

The left-hand point of the diamond was "No Better Diplomat," and here Eric would talk about *The Odyssey*. Homer always called his hero "clever" Odysseus. "This is his virtue," Eric would say. "Odysseus is clever because he knows how to speak to everyone in his world. He knows how to talk to a potential enemy. He knows how to talk to his allies. He knows how to talk to his stable boy and to the grieving widows of his soldiers." Eric would give examples of what he'd seen Travis Manion's MiTT team do in Fallujah. "The point is, don't create enemies," he would conclude. "This is not necessarily going to make you friends, but you have to be a diplomat."

The final point of the diamond was "No Better Role Model." "You are working in a lot of environments in Baltimore where you may be the *only* adult with a responsible job and a respected position in the community these kids see. You have to be an example."

Both Walinsky and the Baltimore police commissioner were in the audience when Eric delivered the Diamond Standard lecture for the first time. He was a strong speaker, simple and direct. He knew how to weave in SEAL stories that engaged the cops. Fred Bealefeld was impressed, and he hired Eric to give the Diamond Standard lecture once a month to each new training class — which was very satisfying for Eric, not just because it brought in some money, but also because he had found someone, in Adam, who saw the world the same way he did.

Eric wasn't very interested in money; his apartment was famous for its lack of . . . almost everything. He did buy a stately, and very used, brown leather couch from craigslist, and most of his life took place on or near it. The one luxury he afforded himself, using his trove of combat pay, was to hire an assistant who would help organize his refugee camp photos — they had won awards at Duke — into a possible coffee-table book. A friend from Duke recommended a recent graduate named Rachel Wald, and Eric hired her.

Wald was smart and fast, but she was blitzed by the speed and intensity of Eric's world. That summer Eric and his best friend from Duke, Ken Harbaugh — a former military pilot now at Yale Law School and, like Eric, a human protean shake — decided to create their own public service organization, which they christened, with great sobriety and mind-crushing blandness, the Center for Citizen Leadership. They wanted to give scholarships to college students who were willing to do public service work. They weren't sure where the money would come from or how the students would be chosen or what the program would entail. But they were absolutely confident — and this was astonishing to Rachel — that something essential would emerge.

Her first task was to organize the photos for the book. "Make them beautiful," Eric told her. But that soon took a backseat to

207

Eric's desire to start a career on the lecture circuit, which had been inspired by the Diamond Standard speech. He had been invited to address Boys Nation — the American Legion's leadership program for high school students, famous for having been the venue for Bill Clinton's handshake with John F. Kennedy — and Eric figured that he could use that speech as a way to sell himself to lecture agencies. He spent weeks writing and practicing it. Rachel had a theater arts background and tried to help him with his delivery — he was too straight, too remote, too serious. She suggested that they buy a video camera so that Eric could see for himself.

"You've got to lighten up, tell some self-deprecating jokes," she told him. "You've got to be human." Rachel soon realized that Eric wasn't like most other confident guys: when she made a suggestion, he listened very carefully; if he thought it made sense, he acted on it. He became addicted to video practice.

The speech, delivered on July 26, 2007, was called "The Next Generation of American Leadership" — and Rachel sensed an immediate, hushed bond with the audience of idealistic, straight-arrow high school leaders from across the country and their chaperones. The content was *Tikkun Olam* 101, a plea for their generation to engage in public service and repair the world.

He started funny. He talked about the Christmas cards he'd gotten in Iraq from children across America. He described two unusual examples. "Have a Good War," one read, and the other: "Try not to die."

But that was it for humor. Within a paragraph, he was marching his argument forward. It was a young man's idea of what an "important" speech should sound like, formal and worthy, bedizened with orotund Kennedyesque flourishes. But the argument was sound. He challenged his audience directly: they had to serve their country in some way. It was difficult to become full-fledged men and women, true *citizens,* unless they served their country and sacrificed their comfort. This didn't necessarily mean military service — he mentioned programs like Teach For America, AmeriCorps, and the Peace Corps.

Eric had been circling this idea since college: citizenship wasn't just a passive thing. It required action. If people didn't feel part of something larger than themselves, if they were devoted only to their immediate material self-interest, society would begin to crumble. There were signs that it was crumbling in America — a coarsening of standards, the common good subsumed beneath a tide of rampant individualism — but Eric was, already, enough of a politician not to say that.

When he finished, the students stood and roared. Eric was thrilled by the reaction; it was confirmation that he was on track to do something important with his life. But the truth was, he still had no idea of what that would be.

He was back in touch with Harris Wofford, the other Kennedy-era mentor he'd met during his White House fellowship. Wofford was as gentle as Walinsky was tough. He had secured himself a place in history as the staffer who had pushed John F. Kennedy to call Coretta Scott King just before the 1960 election, when her husband was facing serious jail time in Georgia. The call established Kennedy as a supporter of civil rights in a Democratic Party that had long been a bastion of segregation in the South. Wofford went on to have a major role in almost every significant national service program of the Kennedy era and after: he was a founder of the Peace Corps, active in VISTA, and later, president of the Corporation for National and Community Service, which ran Ameri-

Corps. He was elected to the Senate from Pennsylvania in 1991, a harbinger of Bill Clinton's 1992 victory, and was promptly defeated on his next try by the archconservative Rick Santorum, a harbinger of the radicalization of the Republican Party.

The summer of the Boys Nation speech, Greitens and Wofford had dinner with Steve Culbertson, who had just been named the CEO of a private organization called Youth Service America, which promoted community and national service for young people, rather optimistically, "from 5 to 25."

Eric and Culbertson hit it off and arranged another dinner meeting at a Mexican restaurant near Eric's apartment on Capitol Hill. Eric wanted to know more about the national service community, what was being done and what wasn't, and what *he* might do. Afterward, they continued the conversation at Eric's apartment, sipping green tea — Steve was disappointed there wasn't a drop of alcohol in the place.

"What do you really worry about?" Eric asked.

"I worry about those kids coming back from the wars with no arms and no legs, and even more about the ones coming home with significant brain injuries and post-traumatic stress disorder," Steve said. "What do they do next? They're the same age as the kids that I work with in high schools and colleges, and yet there's something about them that is so different because they've had this military experience."

"Do you want to meet some of them?" Eric asked — and as he said it, he realized, with no small amount of guilt, that he hadn't visited the wounded at Bethesda Naval Hospital.

"Could we do that?" Steve asked.

"Absolutely," Eric said.

In a matter of days, Rachel arranged the visit. Eric wore his khaki uniform, SEAL pin prominent. He seemed a different person to Rachel, even more serious than usual. They went to the amputee ward and she was just stunned. Afterward, she couldn't remember how many men they'd visited or what had been said. She just shut down, terrified that she'd lose control. Everything was white, the doctors wore white, the patients were swaddled in white bandages. There were men whose entire heads were covered by bandages. Eric would go up to them and ask them where they'd served and whom they'd served with, and what their situation was now. She remembered that Eric and the patients — some of whom were severely truncated; others who were severely disfigured — talked easily. But she couldn't follow the conversation, and she didn't say a word. She nodded sympathetically toward the wives and parents in the rooms, but she was stymied — there was nothing credible, and perhaps even intelligible, to be said. "Sorry" just didn't begin to cover it, and indeed, it might seem callous.

Steve Culbertson thought, as they moved from room to room, that if the rest of the parents of America could see the amputee ward, they would end the wars in Iraq and Afghanistan tomorrow. He, too, was struck by Eric's ease and composure with the men, and the respect they accorded his uniform. The troops had, Culbertson realized, all sorts of visitors — celebrities, politicians, the President himself — but Eric was one of them, had been there with them, and he spoke their language, an acronym-soaked argot Steve could barely understand. Eric asked them what they wanted to do next, and each, no matter how seriously injured, said the same thing: "I want to go back to my unit" or "my guys" or "my brothers."

The question Steve really wanted to ask at this point was: *But what if you can't go back because of your wounds? What would you do then?* That would be too bald, too cruel, though, so he began to ask them, "What do you want to do after you retire from the military?" Many of them — a surprising number, Steve thought — said that they wanted to work in the public sector: teach, coach, join the police or firefighters (again, given their wounds, these latter choices were unlikely). He began to discuss the work he did, getting young people involved in service to solve the problems that the country faced — education, poverty, climate change, housing, and so forth — and asked if they might be interested in doing something about that. Not one of them said no, although Culbertson couldn't tell if they were just being polite. Given the severity of their wounds, how could any of them think clearly at this point?

They stayed for an hour or so. There was no great *aha* moment, just the accretion of emotion and amazement at the strength of the young Sailors and Marines . . . and the realization that if their strength wasn't harnessed in some way, it might wither into hopelessness and depression. As he went from bed to bed, talking to the men about their futures, Eric found himself saying, "Great. We still need you."

It was a sledgehammer sentence. He could see it in their eyes. And he knew — he was absolutely convinced — that it was true: the country did need them. Despite their wounds — and because of their wounds — these veterans could come home and be examples in the same way the Police Corps graduates in Baltimore were.

Eric was on fire as he left the hospital. He called Ken Harbaugh, who was up at Yale Law, and Kaj Larsen on his cell phone before he reached the parking lot. "I know what we're going to do with the Center for Citizen Leadership," he told Ken. They would help wounded veterans to make the transition into civilian life by doing public service in their communities.

"Do you think anyone is doing that? Is there some program we can support?" he asked. Both Ken and Rachel spent the next few days scouring the internet. They couldn't find any.

Kaj showed up the next day to visit his sister, who was a medical student at Georgetown University. He and Eric went for one of their traditional soul-search runs — and, Kaj remembered, it was the sort of scene that would be shot from a helicopter in the movies. They ran down the mall from the Capitol to the Lincoln Memorial and back again. Eric told him about Bethesda. "Kaj, you gotta go," Eric said. "You gotta see them." He told Kaj about his public service idea. "Do you think I should do it?"

"Bro, you were *born* to do this," Kaj replied, which was not a difficult call. Eric was a creature of enthusiasms, a constant whim-machine — becoming an astronaut, climbing Mount Everest, whatever — but this was different. It had ballast as well as inspiration. It fit Eric's military and humanitarian impulses perfectly.

Over the next few months, Eric and Ken came up with a plan to offer *fellowships* — which sounded less academic and slightly more prestigious than *scholarships* — to wounded veterans who were willing to go out among the civilians and do some of the same sort of public service work they had done in the villages of Iraq and Afghanistan. To receive the stipend, they would have to find a local public service organization to sponsor them and supervise their work. The core idea was there from the start: if they were helping other people, they might not spend so much time fretting about themselves. They might make new friends, make the transition to civilian life more easily, and maybe even re-create the same sense of purpose they'd had in the military.

Helping veterans would become the work of the Center for Citizen Leadership —

which still didn't seem a very compelling or comprehensible name for this particular program. A month or so after the visit to Bethesda, the lightning bolt struck Eric as he was driving his truck. He called Ken Harbaugh and said, "Let's call it The Mission Continues."

CHAPTER 2
A CHALLENGE,
NOT A CHARITY

MICHELE NORRIS: Commentator Kenneth Harbaugh grew up listening to World War II stories from his grandfather. As a child, Harbaugh says those stories seemed fun and full of dark humor. But as his grandfather got older, his tales became more realistic.

KENNETH HARBAUGH: When I was little, I used to love a good war story. My grandfather flew bombers during World War II. And whenever he talked of his exploits, his tales always seemed to end with a punch line. War, for all I knew, was fun . . . Of course, there were stories my grandfather didn't tell until I was much older. How he came home, body full of shrapnel and a hole clean through his thigh. How his plane flying solo was ambushed by an entire squadron of enemy fighters and every officer on

218

board was wounded and bleeding with a thousand miles between them and home.

Army Captain Chris Marvin was driving home from physical therapy at the Tripler Army Medical Center on Oahu, Hawaii, listening to *All Things Considered* in early November 2007.

KENNETH HARBAUGH: When I listen to my buddies talk now about Iraq and Afghanistan, I'm struck by how similar their tone is to my grandfather's. His war was different. We all know that. But there's a strange sameness in the telling of it, the way humor is wrung from the most awful things.

Marvin had been in physical therapy for three years since his Black Hawk helicopter had crashed near Khost, in southeastern Afghanistan. His recovery had been a weird, dispiriting, otherworldly experience. He had had nine major surgeries, and he wasn't done yet. He was desperate to do something useful. The Army's idea of useful was having him work two days a week as the assistant to the assistant to the Assistant Supply Officer at the 25th Infantry Division. He didn't have a desk or computer; his duties were to show up — his presence meant that a box could be checked by the Division's Warrior Transition Unit: he had a "job." He mostly sat around doing crossword puzzles. He also learned how to speak Hawaiian, a near-useless skill — but there he was, in paradise, and the act of learning and, better still, *mastering* something esoteric was satisfying. He spent the other three days a week in physical and occupational therapy. He had lost count of the hours he'd spent doing physical therapy, but it had to be in the thousands. It was his real job.

KENNETH HARBAUGH: Bullets today aren't any friendlier than they were back then. I've seen what they do. And now there are IEDs and suicide truck bombs and all manner of horrors my grandfather never faced. War stories will never sound the same to me as they did when I was little. I see past the punch lines now. Yeah, I still laugh along with the double amputee who jokes about losing three hundred dollars' worth of tattoos. But I know how real the pain is when he tells me his only regret is that he didn't stop enough shrapnel with his own body to save his squad mate from getting hit.

Chris stopped the car in his driveway and

just sat there, listening.

KENNETH HARBAUGH: They call my grandfather's generation the greatest. But I've seen what the best of my generation has endured in Iraq and Afghanistan, and there is greatness among them. And, you know, they tell a damn good war story, too. Even if they do, sometimes, break my heart.

And now Chris was weeping. Damn, this guy had nailed it, hadn't he?

MICHELE NORRIS: Commentator Ken Harbaugh is a former Navy pilot who currently attends Yale Law School. He's also the executive director of The Mission Continues, a nonprofit that helps wounded and disabled veterans volunteer in their communities.

Now that seemed an excellent idea: "volunteering" in his community. It certainly would be more rewarding than hanging around the supply office, eye-begging the Assistant Supply Officer for some useful chore. He went on his computer, googled "The Mission Continues," found nothing. He called National Public Radio, got Ken Harbaugh's email, and sent him a note.

Harbaugh called back the next day.

"Hey, I heard your commentary on the radio," Chris said. "I want to work for The Mission Continues. I want to volunteer in my community."

"Wow," Harbaugh said, nonplussed. "That's great." The Mission Continues was maybe a month old — in fact, it could be argued that it didn't really exist yet. There had been phone calls and emails bouncing through the ether. There had been an organizational meeting in Eric's apartment. The conversations meandered, sometimes to the point of hilarity. At one point, Ken had proposed that TMC's logo be an eagle with a bandaged wing.

Eric collapsed, laughing. "That's a *terrible* idea."

They did have a general idea of what they wanted to do. But suddenly, here was an actual veteran, Chris Marvin, forcing their hand.

"Tell me about yourself," Ken asked.

"Well, the reason why your commentary struck me is that both my grandfathers were in World War Two, and my dad was a helicopter pilot in Vietnam," Marvin began. "He's career military, a Colonel in the Army National Guard. It's what people do in my family."

Chris had grown up in Bloomington, Illinois. He was straight-ahead, no frills all-American: a fine student, a four-sport varsity athlete, an Eagle Scout. He attended Notre Dame University on an ROTC scholarship and entered the Army when he graduated in 2003. He deployed to Afghanistan in April 2004 and worked out of a base near Khost, in the mountainous Paktia province on the Pakistani border. This was an ugly nexus in the war against one of the main Taliban factions, the Haqqani Network, which was supported by the Pakistani Inter-Services Intelligence (ISI). It was the most noxious entanglement of a frustrating war: The U.S. troops were fighting guerrillas armed, indirectly, by the United States, via Pakistan. The CIA had a major facility in the area, and Chris was doing some very dangerous flying, close air support for special operators on secret missions in the Af/Pak borderlands. He loved the work. He was, he would later say, 25 years old, in charge of a 25-man platoon, flying a $25 million aircraft. Where else but the U.S. military could a person his age have so much responsibility?

On August 12, 2004, he and his copilot were flying a mission near Khost when the controls jammed. Chris got down low, beneath the instrument displays, to see if he could fix the problem as the Black Hawk seriously began to lose altitude — which was a good thing, because if he had been sitting upright, he probably would have died when the helicopter crashed, very hard, on a flat stretch of hardpan desert and flipped over. He was crushed inside, stuck there for more than an hour. Fourteen were wounded in the crash; one killed.

"Is this aircraft on fire?" Chris shouted out to his men.

"No, sir," someone answered.

"Am I the worst?"

"Yes, sir." And Chris was relieved, because if he was the most severely injured, then his men were okay, then everything would be okay.

But Chris was far from good: he had broken his right foot, both of his legs, his right arm, and he had shattered all the bones on the right side of his face and broken both his knees, both of his hips, and both of his shoulders. He had broken so many things that he couldn't be put together all at once. He spent much of the next two years in a wheelchair, with an arm and a leg still needing to be fixed — there was debate among the doctors as to whether the leg should be operated on or amputated.

He was the very first casualty of the wars in Iraq and Afghanistan to arrive back at Tripler Army Medical Center on Oahu. His parents were there to greet him, which was another good thing, because his mother was a nurse, and she noticed that the doctors had him on far too many medications. "My son isn't there!" she told the doctor and ordered him to take Chris off three of the five different narcotics they had him on.

His girlfriend, Amy Miller, was there, too, appalled by his physical condition. Chris had been too broken to be properly cleaned in the field or even as he was rushed through Landstuhl Hospital in Germany, where the first surgeries were done. He was convinced that the steady diet of morphine added to the stench. But Amy — a dolphin trainer with degrees in psychology and biology from Harvard — was in for the duration. She would come home from work to make him a sandwich for lunch every day for the next three years, until he was able to use his arms again. Eventually, they would get married and have two children.

And it was Amy who pushed the wheelchair as he emerged from Tripler a few days later. Chris was swaddled by the soft tropical air, the magnificent views of Diamond Head and Waikiki Beach below. "Okay, wow," he said. "This is the perfect place to do rehab!"

A few months later, just before Christmas 2004, Chris wheeled himself out to the mailbox and found a $500 check from some charitable organization he'd never heard of — the letter talked about supporting America's heroes. And he began to get angry: this charity didn't know him. All they had was an address. So what was this $500 for? He was still on full pay, and he would retire with 100 percent disability. He owned his house and car, and he was receiving hundreds of thousands of dollars of free medical care from the military. The Army had paid for college, so he had no student loans. He had no debt at all! And here were these mushy-minded do-gooders sending him money, treating him like a charity case. They *pitied* him. They assumed he couldn't take care of himself, that his productive life was over. And yes, he was still in a wheelchair; and yes, his girlfriend still had to make him a sandwich for lunch. But he refused to be seen as an object of pity — he was a wounded soldier, looking to restart his life, and convinced that he had a lot more to offer. And yes, he had a very serious job: rehab.

He sent the $500 to a local food bank, to

people who really needed it.

Listening to all this, Ken Harbaugh was blown away. The guy was so strong, so composed: Chris Marvin seemed the fantasy version of the sort of veteran they wanted to help. He and Chris had several more phone conversations, in which Ken admitted that The Mission Continues didn't quite exist yet and asked Chris what he thought the program should be. "It should be a challenge, not a charity," Chris said. "We're warriors, not victims." And that was pretty much that.

Chris Marvin became the first official Mission Continues fellow, a status that was extremely temporary, because he was soon hired as TMC's second employee, after Rachel Wald, who was still Eric's assistant. He was named National Director of TMC's Fellowship Program in December 2007. He would do this work from Hawaii, while continuing with his operations and physical therapy. Chris accepted the stipend during his first weeks as a fellow — this wasn't like getting $500 for nothing; he was working for it — but then he found out that Eric, Ken, and Kaj were paying it out of their own pockets and refused to take any more money from them.

■ ■ ■ ■

Eric decided he would base The Mission Continues back home in St. Louis. Washington was overstuffed with organizations with names like the Center for Citizen Leadership (of which The Mission Continues was still thought to be the first of several programs). There was the Center for Public Leadership and the Center for Civic Education — countless claustrophobic centers and projects stewing in the same federal juice and trying to raise money from the same pool of donors.

It would be *distinctive* to run it from St. Louis. And he had other moneymaking opportunities back home: a teaching fellowship at the Truman School of Public Affairs at the University of Missouri, and a contract to offer Walinsky-style training to the Missouri firefighters. Washington University in St. Louis had agreed to have him teach a course on citizenship in its political science department. He was even given free office space in a downtown library building by the Gateway Center for Giving, which was an incubator for nonprofit projects.

Going home wasn't easy at first. Eric slept on an air mattress in a rented room adorned by only a clock radio and his books, organized on shelves he'd gotten from craigslist. He didn't mind the austerity so much; his Washington apartment had been thingless, too, but it had been filled with people and intellectual excitement and nonstop activity. Now, not so much. He didn't know many people beyond his family in St. Louis yet — certainly not many people with whom he could brainstorm new ideas or from whom he could learn. His old mentor Bruce Carl had died — incredibly — of AIDS. His wife told Eric that Bruce had been leading a secret life; neither she nor their children knew about it until Bruce got sick. There had never been a hint of this at B'Nai El; Bruce clearly understood that if he slipped once and even hinted at his truth, he'd be gone — and teaching the kids was too important for that. Bruce's quiet suffering seemed incomprehensible and unnecessary; the tragedy added to Eric's emptiness.

Eric's professional life in St. Louis wasn't off to a flying start either. His citizenship class at Washington University fell through when no students signed up for it. He worked out, and ran, and then worked out some more. He started learning tae kwon do; his goal was to compete nationally, and the act of learning something new, something physical, was its own reward. But the truth was, he was crawling up the walls of his apartment, frustrated and a bit worried about what came next.

He had doubts about The Mission Continues, too. It wasn't building fast enough. Ken Harbaugh also provided the first real fellow a few days after Chris Marvin signed on, the first who really *needed* a Mission Continues stipend. Harbaugh's parents ran an equine therapy center — Horses Helping the Handicapped (Triple H Equitherapy) — just outside San Antonio, Texas. They'd found a wounded Navy veteran, Mathew Trotter, who had some experience around horses and wanted to help both children and his fellow veterans heal themselves by learning how to control a horse. "Can you guys help out?" they asked Ken.

Ken and Kaj Larsen kicked in $1,000 apiece, and Eric donated $3,500 from his combat pay — and Mathew Trotter, who had endured eight surgeries on his ankles after a shipboard accident, proved to be a wise and patient teacher. A few months later, Ken's parents asked if Mathew could get a second fellowship from The Mission Continues — and he received the first Travis Manion fellowship award, funded by the Travis Manion Foundation.

The next two fellows were worthy, but not exactly what Eric had had in mind. One, Mike Paul, wasn't even an Iraq or Afghanistan veteran. And his injuries had occurred *after* he had served in the Gulf War, in a skydiving accident. He was in a wheelchair now, but he wanted to become an adaptive skiing instructor — and The Mission Continues did help him succeed in that, enabling him to go back to school to get his master's degree in teaching people with special needs. Helping Mike become a productive member of society seemed a good thing, but it was a long way from the mission Eric had imagined for himself at Bethesda. He had envisioned *thousands* of Mission Continues fellows, storming out to change the world.

Chris Marvin found another fellow in Hawaii. His name was Readen Clavier, an Army veteran from Palau who had suffered a severe traumatic brain injury when his Humvee had been blown up by an IED. Chris landed Clavier an internship at a tech company, where he could work on his fine-motor skills. This was another good thing to do, but it was vocational rehab, not public service.

And then there were others who simply did not work out at all. Two of the first six just took the money and ran. One was going to start a Student Veterans of America chapter at his Ivy League college — and simply disappeared. Another was going to do peer counseling at a VA hospital in Maryland. He showed up for a while, but his appearances became intermittent and then stopped.

Eric was frustrated by these failures. He knew that veterans were being pelted with gifts — The Mission Continues was being pelted with gifts: tickets to the ballpark, golf balls, blankets, cash like the $500 Chris Marvin had sent to the food bank. He figured that a lot of veterans saw The Mission Continues stipend as just another gift. "Oh sure, I'll do some service work," they'd say — and they might even intend to do it, or try it for a while, but they were not conditioned to see it as a rigorous, military-style commitment. Chris Marvin's line, "It's a challenge, not a charity," resonated with Eric. The *challenge* had to be TMC's in-your-face opening offer to any veterans who were looking for help. This wasn't a freebie. This was purposeful work.

But there had to be more to it than a slogan. Eric needed to learn for himself how a fellowship actually might work. How could you monitor the thing and make sure that valuable service was being performed? What else could TMC provide the fellows in addition to a stipend? And what about the local agencies hosting the fellows — obviously, someone had to stay in touch with them and find out if they thought this was working. Ken Harbaugh and Chris Marvin had found the first five TMC fellows. Eric hadn't been responsible for any of them. "We need a St. Louis fellow," he told Rachel Wald.

There was a sociologist named Amanda Moore-McBride over at Washington University's Brown School of Social Work. She had studied the effects of civic engagement on AmeriCorps members. Eric visited and told her about The Mission Continues. "Hey Monica, c'mon over here," she called out to her colleague across the hall. "You've got to meet this guy."

Monica Matthieu was a speed-talking, no-nonsense Cajun, who had actually worked with veterans and had her heart broken by the opacity and intransigence of their psychological wounds; her default position was a defenseless, loving skepticism. She had met more than a few vets who had come home and wanted to help others who had returned from Iraq and Afghanistan — half of them were stuck and scarred and scattered, trying to figure out how to help themselves as much as others. But Eric Greitens was something different. He was an academic, for one thing — the fact that he'd written a doctoral thesis about the treatment of children in refugee camps meant that he understood research and how to determine whether something actually worked or not. He could speak her language. But more important was his idea, which actually had a working precedent. A third Brown School colleague, Dr. Nancy Morrow-Howe — the place was cluttered with hyphenated sociological brilliance — had studied the impact of civic engagement on the elderly. There was a robust and hopeful literature about the beneficial effects of community service on senior citizens: those who helped out in their communities were healthier and happier, and they lived longer.

In one Ohio State University study, two groups of elderly patients in senior day care were asked to make gift baskets. One group made the baskets for themselves; a second group was told they were making the baskets for homeless people in their community. The second group experienced a greater sense of satisfaction and psychological well-being than those who were simply making the baskets for themselves.

The similarities between elderly people and wounded veterans were eerie. They were both operating at less than their optimal capacity — physically and sometimes mentally — and both were very much aware, and depressed by, the things they could no longer do. Senior citizens tended to lose their sense of purpose and community when they retired. They felt isolated. They grieved for friends and family lost. Matthieu hadn't put the pieces together before, but it made total sense: community service might be a terrific antidote for post-traumatic stress. And this was fresh new sociological turf — there was no formal research, no literature on this subject — which was the functional equivalent of a perfectly spiced crawfish gumbo for a bayou sociologist. "What can I do for you?" she asked Eric.

"I need a St. Louis fellow," Eric said. "This is where we're going to be based, and I want to have a strong presence here. I want to monitor this thing, see how it works, see how we could make it better." This was just what Matthieu wanted to hear. She hoped Eric would agree to monitor his fellows with strict sociological metrics to see if it was actually working.

"Yes, I want to do that, but first I need

some fellows," Eric said. "You work with veterans. Do you know anyone who might be right for a fellowship?"

"Actually," she said, "I think I do."

Tim Smith was pure St. Louis. He came from the south side, from a solid family. His dad managed logistics in a warehouse; his mom worked for a Catholic charitable organization. He was a very good athlete, a basketball player for the University of Saint Mary in Leavenworth, Kansas, but not exactly a devoted student. He wandered away from school and started working in an Irish pub back home, where he met Terri Farias. They were just friends at first; then Tim enlisted in the Army — he missed being part of a team — and started sending Terri letters, and they fell in love. They were engaged before he was sent to Iraq; the assumption was they'd get married if he came back.

Tim wasn't wounded, at least not physically, in Iraq, but he came back strange. His best friend, Doc Grayson, had been killed with seven others by an IED in Sadr City in April 2004, one of the bloodiest months of the war. Their unit moved to Mahmudiyah in the Triangle of Death, just south of Baghdad. The war was very bad there, too. FOB

St. Michael — their Forward Operating Base — was pummeled by mortars and rocket-propelled grenades every day. Tim was never physically injured, but he was seriously rattled — and that began to manifest itself physically. He developed an allergy to dust. His eyes swelled and shut with severe conjunctivitis whenever he went outside. Tim figured his body was telling him something important: don't go outside.

The conjunctivitis continued when he redeployed to Germany, where Terri joined him — in fact, his eyes began to swell and shut every time he had to go out to the gun range. His unit returned to Iraq, but Tim stayed back in Germany, managing the chow hall.

Tim and Terri were married in Germany. They lived there for nearly two years and had their first child, Tim Jr. Terri didn't notice much of a change in Tim at first, aside from the conjunctivitis; he was happy in his work, had good friends in his unit, and had a precise daily routine.

But Tim began to change dramatically when they returned to St. Louis in February 2007. Loud noises jolted him; there were nightmares and anxiety attacks. He slept with a gun under the bed. He wasn't funny and outgoing the way he'd been before. Much of his personality had been deleted — and he couldn't tell her why and wouldn't tell her what had happened over there. He couldn't tell her much of anything.

He was also having trouble finding work, or even rousing himself to go look for work. They went on food stamps and were ashamed of it. On the evening of July 4, 2007, the extended family gathered for a picnic in their backyard, which was adjacent to Sublett Park, where there would be a big fireworks show. As the sun set, and just before the fireworks began, Terri noticed Tim rush back into the house — something was definitely wrong — and she decided to follow him in. He was sitting on the bed, weeping. She had never seen him cry before, and it terrified her. "What's wrong, Tim?" she asked, but he didn't answer.

She sat there until the sobbing left him, like a slow-moving storm turning to drizzle and then steam on a summer night. It was the fireworks, he told her. He couldn't even handle the damn Fourth of July fireworks show — it was right out there, and obvious, the noise predictable, but it brought back all those months of being mortared. He looked at her, bleary, lost. "We've got to do something about this," Terri said.

They went to a counselor at the Veterans Administration, which was where Tim met Monica Matthieu. She was struck by how determined Tim was to push past the PTSD and get on with his life. He had just found a veterans' preference job at the central post office, working midnight to six. He began taking classes in the morning at the University of Missouri–St. Louis. He was fifteen credits short of a BA in social work. After class each day, he would go home, study, sleep for four hours, then report back to the post office at midnight. "What should I do when I get my degree?" he asked Matthieu.

"What do you want to do?"

"I'm not sure, but I do like helping people."

She told him that he should think about getting a master's in social work at Washington University.

"Really?" Washington University was where the rich kids, the smart ones, went. Tim figured it would be a real stretch for him. He was still feeling semi-paralyzed, especially when he was alone in the middle of the night at the post office. He was still semi-terrified every time he left home.

"Why not?" Matthieu asked, and in asking, she knew. "Don't worry, I'll help you." And she did. Tim worked on his grammar and writing and read the books she told him to read. "This guy," she thought, "is the only man I ever met who does exactly what I tell him to do."

He was still suffering, though. There was a morning at UMSL when he left a building after class, and the sun was at a certain angle or something — he wasn't quite sure — but he was back in Iraq, freaked and sweating profusely. He ran back inside the building, gathered himself, took deep breaths, and went to his next class. Sticking with it, day after day, took incredible courage and determination, Matthieu thought. Tim persevered without a fuss.

So it was a no-brainer when Eric Greitens told her that he was looking for a fellow. She told Tim about the program, the idea of veterans volunteering in the community. She told him he should meet with Greitens, and of course he did.

"Tell me about yourself," Eric said, opening the first significant interview to take place on his old brown leather couch in St. Louis. Tim spoke hesitantly, in a swallowed Midwestern mumble, but he told Eric the whole story: what had happened to him in Iraq and, more significantly, what was happening to him back home. He found that talking to Eric was easy, even though he was an officer. Tim told him more than he'd ever told Terri.

"How would you like to do a Mission Continues fellowship?" Eric asked.

"What's a fellowship?" Tim replied.

Eric explained the program, and Tim said, "Wow. That sounds like a pretty good deal. I'd love to do that."

"Well then," Eric said, extending his hand, "welcome to The Mission Continues. Where do you want to serve?"

Tim wasn't sure. He mentioned several possibilities: he had volunteered at the Boys Club in the past, teaching basketball to the kids. But he was also interested in working with some of the veterans he'd met at the VA. Eric said he would help Tim figure it out, and they went together to both the Boys Club and the VA. Tim was amazed by the amount of attention that this Navy SEAL Lieutenant Commander was lavishing on an E-5 Sergeant. He was also a bit daunted by Eric's expectations for him. But it felt good. One night Eric took Tim and Terri out for dinner at a restaurant in St. Louis's famed Italian neighborhood, the Hill. It was the start of a new life, Terri thought. Tim was animated, excited after all those zombie months. He was cracking jokes again. She had almost forgotten that side of him.

Tim decided that he wanted to work with his fellow veterans at the VA, where he'd been offered a job as a volunteer peer counselor, sitting in on the group sessions, sometimes even leading them.

"Well, that sounds pretty good to me," Eric said. He told Tim the fellowship would be funded by the Travis Manion Foundation — and that there were several other duties he would have to perform in addition to the service. Eric wanted him out in the community, spreading the word about The Mission Continues, finding more potential fellows at the VA, working on service projects.

Tim was game for all that, even if he wasn't sure that he'd be very good at it. His first public appearance as a Mission Continues fellow was particularly daunting, at the St. Louis Country Club, where about fifty potential donors had been gathered to hear Eric's pitch and also — this was the hard part — listen to an actual Mission Continues fellow.

"Do we all sit at the same table?" Tim asked hopefully, as he, Eric, and Rachel Wald walked in.

"No," Eric said. "You sit there," pointing to a front table. "I'll sit at this table, and

Rachel, you go over there." Tim was wearing his only suit, which he'd bought for job interviews, and his only tie. The people at the table were very nice. He was reluctant to talk about his time in the Army, lost when they talked about investments, but better when they talked sports, and he was sweating. He went back and forth to the bathroom, mopping himself off and fussing with his tie.

Eric spoke first, and Tim thought he was very effective. Then he introduced Tim, and as they passed each other at the podium, Eric gave Tim a "go get 'em, I *know* you can handle this" nod. And Tim went, nervously, into the fire.

He wasn't terrific. He made it through, and the audience was sympathetic. But he hadn't learned how to talk civilian yet. His language was laced with military acronyms, FOBs and COPs and RPGs, E-5s, and Chinooks. "You did a good job," Eric said, "but one thing I noticed you could do better is speak in terms they understand." He continued to bring Tim along to his public relations events. And each time, they would do a postmortem. "You were a lot better on the military talk," Eric would say, "but you still seem a bit frightened. Don't be. These people want to like you. Don't be afraid to be enthusiastic."

And Eric found, just as Monica Matthieu had, that every time he asked Tim to work on something, Tim worked on it. He would never be a polished speaker, but he became a more confident one. The sweat tsunamis abated. Soon Eric was sending Tim out by himself to meet with local organizations — the Red Cross, the St. Louis zoo. "I need you to sign up ten organizations as possible hosts for future fellows or sources of volunteers when we organize service projects," Eric said, and Tim did it. By the time his fellowship ended that autumn, Tim had been offered a full-time job as a peer support counselor at the VA and had been accepted into Washington University's Master of Social Work program.

Eric was named Grand Marshall of the St. Louis Veterans Day parade in 2008. He decided to use the occasion to celebrate the first anniversary of The Mission Continues, and he invited his core group of friends and fellows to come to St. Louis and celebrate.

The wisdom of moving to St. Louis was obvious by now. He never would have been the Grand Marshall of the Veterans Day parade if he'd stayed in Washington. The Mission Continues was receiving a steady stream of local press coverage. The St. Louis business community was pitching in with donations. A World War II veteran named Jack Taylor who had started Enterprise Rent-A-Car — named after the USS *Enterprise,* on which he'd served — gave Eric a $50,000 donation. With real money coming in, Eric decided to hire a young social worker named Paul Eisenstein to run the business side of the operation. Greitens continued to work as a volunteer.

On Eisenstein's first day in May 2008, Eric handed him a very military and rather official Commander's Intent memo that began with a mission statement, followed by fifteen goals. Most were very specific, including:

"Raise $500,000."

"Create 15 successful Mission Continues fellowships."

"Involve over 100 wounded and disabled veterans in service [projects]."

"Produce over 5,000 hours of volunteer service."

"Ensure that we meet the highest standards of nonprofit governance. (Be on track to achieve the equivalent of a Gold Star or Five Star rating from at least two, hopefully three, charity review boards.)"

Eisenstein had never been exposed to the

military before. He had been an Ameri-Corps volunteer, which had impressed Eric: "You served your country." He found the unblinking specificity of the Commander's Intent document bracing. This wasn't going to be some sloppy do-gooder deal. Would he be able to accomplish all those goals in seven months? Probably not, but he liked being pushed. (And in fact, he aced fourteen of the fifteen.)

Eric seemed a big SEAL in a small city, Eisenstein thought. He watched as Eric recruited local businesses and political royalty like the Danforth family, owners of Ralston Purina, to the cause. Eric also convinced Southwest Airlines to provide round-trip tickets for The Mission Continues friends and fellows who came to the Veterans Day celebration. He seemed to go into every meeting with the absolute expectation of success, and he handled crises with Obi-Wan calm. This, too, was something Paul had never seen in the not-for-profit world.

The crowd was sparse enough on Veterans Day that the TMC core group made an impression. Steve Culbertson and Ken Harbaugh had come in from Washington; Kaj Larsen came from California; Chris Marvin, Mathew Trotter, and Tim Smith were there, as was their first woman fellow, Sonia Meneses from Tennessee, who had lost most of her hearing in an explosion downrange. And they were all, unwittingly, in a uniform — black leather jackets and jeans. They looked like a motorcycle gang. Eric was dressed like a politician: blue suit, white shirt, red tie, no overcoat. He figured that he was going to have to do something about how his people looked.

But he also felt gratified: the fact that they'd all come dressed the same way seemed a silent ratification that something important was happening. The Mission Continues not only existed — the Center for Citizen Leadership would soon die a quiet death — but it also had achieved a unique, tough-minded outlaw status in the world of veterans' service organizations.

The official Mission Continues polos and T-shirts would be a sharp royal blue. The logo would be a compass pointing a few degrees off course. Eric's idea was that if you change your course just a little bit, as Tim Smith had done during his fellowship, you would wind up in a completely different place in life. Beneath the compass was a slogan, courtesy of Chris Marvin: "A Challenge, Not a Charity."

CHAPTER 3
ONE SKY SOLDIER FALLS, WE ALL FALL

Two years after he was sure his life had ended, Mike Pereira decided to google Eric Greitens. Mike was beginning to entertain the possibility that his life wasn't over after all, that he might actually have a second act, and Greitens was the first person in authority he'd ever met — certainly not his parents or teachers or his other superior officers — who took an interest in his future and told him he had real potential.

He had met Eric in Balad, Iraq, in the autumn of 2006. It was weird, too, because Greitens was a Navy officer. In Mike's experience, Navy officers tended to be — well, there was no other way to put it — assholes. In the Army and Marines, junior officers were out downrange with their troops, eating and fighting and crapping with them; the camaraderie began to dissipate as the officers climbed the ranks, but some hint of it always remained. The Navy, however, had this profound, antique class segregation; they acted as if enlisted men were servants. They took out the dry cleaning, served tea. The Navy was hoity-toity, and Mike was a guy who had a large WORKING CLASS tattoo on his back, with the "C" portrayed as a hammer and sickle, the symbol of communism, which later proved embarrassing: he'd gotten the tattoo when he was fifteen and a jerk and had no idea what the hammer and sickle meant.

From the beginning, Greitens was different from any other officer he'd served under — and it was a difficult start, because Mike's opening move was a screaming, crying, tearing-his-hair-out fit. Eric was the headquarters intelligence liaison for SEAL Team Six at the time; Mike was a private contractor, an intelligence analyst who assessed the information coming from the interrogations of high-value Al Qaeda prisoners held at Balad. The Army had asked him to retire in order to join this special contract unit — it was a complicated business and too secret to be described — but he was still a Sergeant in his soul, still living the military life, and still eating from the Kellogg Brown & Root dining facility (D-Fac), even though he no longer had to wear a uniform.

The work was fascinating, but frustrating. Mike was there in perpetuity, but the officers on the SEAL side of the intel chain came and went on seven-month tours. Just as the SEAL guys were beginning to distinguish Abu-Azzaz from Abu-Ayyud, they were sent home. Mike, meanwhile, had created a four-foot-high, fourteen-foot-wide Wonder Wall — it looked like a circuit board — that mapped out the connections between almost every conceivable Abu of value. There were a thousand names linked on the wall. Greitens was blown away when he saw it.

The problem was, the new military intelligence guys — the ones perpetually rotating in — always felt the need to establish their own bona fides. They had a stream of info, too, coming in from the SEALs downrange, and very often it was excellent information. Sometimes, though, it was not so good. In this particular case, the SEALs were going with a new source who turned out to be a drug addict with a gripe against a particular family. Mike had tried to stop it. "No, not *that* family, *this* family. *These* are the guys you want to hit." But the SEALs had been adamant and hit the wrong family. They had blown open the door and there had been people — innocent women and children — sleeping near the door, and now they were dead, and Mike was unloading on this spiffy Lieutenant Commander Greitens, yelling and pounding the plywood table and pulling his hair. Unnecessary deaths could set Mike off this way. Eric just sat there, calmly eating a bowl of rice — and Mike was getting pissed at him, too, because why didn't he tell Mike to put a cork in it?

Finally, after Mike had drained his fuel tank, Eric asked, "What can we do to make it better?"

Whoa. Now *that* was novel. But Greitens actually was interested; he wanted to know what Mike knew. He sensed Mike knew a lot. They began to work closely together on a new target set that would integrate ground intelligence, signals intelligence, previous missions, and intel gleaned from detainees. The leader of Al Qaeda in Iraq, Abu Musab al-Zarqawi, had recently been killed. He'd been succeeded by Abu Ayyub al-Masri, who was now the number-one target. Mike put together the intelligence, Eric edited it, and they brought it to the Colonel of a Unit-That-Cannot-Be-Named, who simply loved it. Eric didn't take the credit the way most officers would; he told the Colonel they had a gold mine in Mike Pereira. Mike received a commander's coin — a currency of respect in the military — and felt that he had reached his pinnacle of effectiveness.

He and Eric became friends. They ate together. They talked about the future. Eric talked about how he wanted to combine the wisdom of older people with the ambition of younger people back at home. "What are you going to do?" he asked Mike. "What about college? What are your goals?"

Goals? College? He had always wanted to go to college. But no one in his life had ever expected him to do it or told him he *should* go to college. "You should go to college," Eric said. "Let's figure out how to get you to the right place."

They scheduled a career-counseling meeting. It took place in the Charlie Beckwith Conference Room — Mike would never forget that because it was one of the most important meetings of his life — and Eric became his academic adviser. Eric had taken the time to write out notes about how to find the right school, how to get through the admissions process, and how to establish himself as a force to be reckoned with in the world. "When you get out of the military," Greitens told him, "you have as strong a possibility of becoming a leader as you do here."

But you couldn't just say remarkable things like that to Mike Pereira. You had to understand where Mike was coming from, why all of this seemed so implausible; Mike insisted on it. And so he told Eric about his life, and Eric patiently listened.

Mike had come up very hard; indeed, he'd come from several generations of hard. He was Portuguese, from the Azores, on his father's side, and Mexican on his mother's. His father, Ron Pereira, better known as "Doc" because of his otherworldly ability to fix engines of all sorts, had emerged from the human equivalent of primordial slime: Doc's father had walked out on his mother, who became a prostitute and a drug addict, and then the mistress of a mob guy who dumped her, and then a prostitute once more. At times, she was strung out for days on end. One time Doc had found her covered in blood on the floor: she had tried to cut her hair and cut her ears instead. Another time she was carrying a bottle of drugs in her vagina and it broke; Doc had to clean that up, too.

Doc Pereira started stealing cars when he was ten, just to get by. He was in juvenile prison by the age of twelve and out by the age of fourteen. His mother was murdered when he was fifteen; Doc figured it was his fault for not protecting her. He ran away from the funeral, unwilling to submit himself to foster care. He overdosed on heroin at the age of sixteen and went into rehab. He came out of rehab and began driving long-haul trucks from Canada to Phoenix and selling drugs on the side. He spent four years in jail, when Mike was a boy, after he was caught hauling a shipment of marijuana.

Mike's mother, Cynthia Lopez, was a Mexican Cinderella. Her parents had crossed the river to get to America. She found solace in religion, deep in religion — and so Mike got deep into religion, too. The family moved around in the San Francisco area, from Watsonville to the East Bay — a house several miles from the epicenter of the 1989 earthquake. Doc had been working on an engine in the basement when the shaking started; Mike and his sister, Amanda, were upstairs, terrified, as the house was falling apart all around them — and then Doc rushed in, swooped them up like Superman, and deposited them in the storm cellar. They moved to Bellingham, Washington, after that. Mike was eight years old. The house was just outside the city line in a rural area; it had a barn out back that Doc used to store and fix cars; in effect,

Doc had transformed the property into an auto wreck-yard. The upside was that he had stopped drinking and drugging, and he finally settled into work on a regular basis.

Doc was a big guy, six foot three, 250 pounds, and unpredictable, Superman one minute and the Hulk the next. He was a terrific musician who played guitar with some of the better groups in the San Francisco Bay area and built his own guitars. There was often music and laughter in the house — but he also had a temper. One of Mike's earliest memories was a pushing match with Amanda, who went to their dad and said that Mike had hit her. Doc grabbed Mike and whipped him with an extension cord. Cynthia took him into the shower to clean him up afterward, and — this was one of his first, indelible memories — he saw his blood running down the drain as she washed him off.

As Mike grew older, the situation with his dad grew worse. He was a rebellious, mouthy teenager. Doc insisted on respect. A lot of the fighting was about standard teenage stuff. Mike had to do chores, lots of them. He'd refuse, he'd taunt Doc, Doc would flash — Cynthia's first instinct was to protect her boy, which would make Doc even angrier. Even when they weren't yelling at one another, life pretty much sucked — even the potentially good moments. Cynthia decided Mike needed new carpet for his room, and his dad told him to come along: they were going to the carpet store. But they didn't go to the carpet store. They went to the Dumpster around the back of the store, and his dad pulled out a hideous piece of orange carpet. "That's a really nice carpet," Doc said, and then he threatened, "You better not eat or drink on it. You better keep it clean."

Mike's brains were spotted quickly by the powers that be: he was placed in the Gifted and Talented Education (GATE) track in elementary school. His father did acknowledge it from time to time: "For a smart kid," he said, "you're pretty fucking stupid."

He could do extremely well in school when he was interested in something, but he wasn't interested in much, and if the teacher was even remotely reminiscent of his dad, he just wouldn't go to class. His high school algebra teacher was, for example, a primo jerk, and Mike decided to boycott. He skipped everything but the tests, which he aced, just to show the guy how little his actual teaching mattered. He was in constant trouble with the principal, suspended, reinstated; he dropped out, came back, got suspended and reinstated again. When he was fourteen, his mother walked out. She took Amanda with her, but not Mike. He remained in the wreck-yard with his father, who took out his frustrations by beating up cars. One time Doc was trying to get the brakes off a car, and he was sweating and cussing, and he slipped and cut his hand open and began slamming his fist into the car, blood flying everywhere. "She's going to kick, she's going to buck, she's going to fight, she's going to make you sweat, she's going to make you bleed, but you can't let that motherfucker win," he told Mike, who found it hilarious and terrifying — and ultimately, years later, inspirational: his dad had taught him to do a tough job, how not to quit, how to fight for what he wanted. But he'd only realize that later.

After six impossible months with Doc, Mike left. He moved around from friend to friend — the hospitality usually wore out after a couple days — until one friend's parents invited him to stay forever. They said they wanted to care for him as a foster child. What they really wanted, he soon realized, was the money that came from the state for doing that. They were in debt, and Mike could liberate them. When the foster care deal fell through, they kicked him out.

He took to living in his car, spending nights in the First Baptist Church parking lot. The minister knew him and took pity on him and allowed him to shower inside every so often. His diet consisted of hot dogs and soda, a combo he could buy at Home Depot for $1.60 — he found the money by stealing small change from unlocked cars. His one actual meal each week came on Sunday, when his mother took him to Denny's.

Mike's parking-lot life ended when he turned sixteen and got a part-time job in a Les Schwab tire store. He saw an ad for a room with extremely cheap rent; it turned out to be a house populated by seven ex-cons who had just come out of halfway houses. It was old and ramshackle, and the ex-cons ranged from sad to creepy, but it was better than living in his car, so he took it. He was needed at the shop, and at times he had to skip class to work there. "Look, I'm on my own. I've got to work to live," he told the principal, who decided to cut him some slack. But some slack wasn't nearly enough. His boss at the tire shop wanted him full-time, so he dropped out of school — which put him a rung above most of his friends, who had dropped out of high school and were either in juvie hall or dead into drugs. A few weeks later, he came back to the house one night and looked at his hands. They were filthy. They looked like his father's hands. "I guess everyone in my family is fated to live with grease under their fingernails," he said to himself. He thought about the tire shop. He was the youngest person working there; there were men in their sixties who had worked there all their lives. He couldn't imagine living that way, raising a family and having kids that way. "I've got to throw myself out into the world," he thought, "and see what happens."

He went to an Army recruiter. They took him on a tour of Fort Lewis, which was nearby. They showed him the firing range. They were all hoo-ah about shooting guns and blowing stuff up. But that didn't impress Mike very much; he'd experienced far too many explosions at home. Then they took him to the D-Fac. He had never seen so much food. It was like a dream. There were hamburgers cooking on a grill, hot dishes, a pasta bar, a long row of fruit and desserts, vegetables, a pile of grilled cheese sandwiches, and ice cream. "Sign me up," he said. He felt as if he had been recruited into heaven.

He needed a high school diploma in order

to sign on the dotted line, and he threw himself on the mercy of a guidance counselor named Sue Jamtsa, who approached his various teachers and promised that Mike would be in attendance and socialized for his last semester of school. He graduated from Squalicum High School that spring.

Mike loved the Army from day one. He loved boot camp. He loved having a secure place to sleep every night. He was amazed that he had access to the D-Fac any time he wanted to go there. And his aptitude test results were off the charts. The Army decided to train him as an intelligence analyst and sent him to Germany.

Germany was like a theme park. American soldiers were rock stars — even if they'd been wreck-yard scum back home. Maybe not all the girls, but a lot of them, wanted to be with G.I. Joe. And for those who couldn't find a girl, there was a brigade of prostitutes, some of whom were not bad at all. But for Mike, the real thrill was the knowledge that he was no longer alone in the world. The other intelligence trainees were very much like him — high school fuckups with big IQs from tough families. Everyone had a story. One guy had been abused by an uncle. Another guy had a sister who was into drugs and prostitution.

Camaraderie — real brotherhood — for most troops was forged downrange; camaraderie for the intel trainees was forged in the back alleys of Sachsenhausen, helping a fallen comrade who had just been punched in the nose by a prostitute and was bleeding profusely. Camaraderie was learning that, rare as they were and antisocial as they had been, they could talk about the most terrible stuff freely, without being betrayed.

Mike did well in training. He was sent to Italy to be part of an intel analysis operation focused on the Middle East, which was located on the same base as the 173rd Airborne Brigade, the "Sky Soldiers." He did well enough there, too, and was sent to PLDC — Primary Leadership Development Course, a training program for Sergeants. "It's like a ritual," he would later say. "You go to the woods for a few days, they beat the hell out of you, and you come back a Sergeant." The first time he was singled out and told to drop and do push-ups, he realized that someone next to him had also dropped, unbidden, and was doing push-ups — and the trainer was yelling at the guy, "What are you doing down? I didn't tell you to drop."

"One Sky Soldier falls, we all fall," Dante Cannelli responded. After that, every time one of the seven guys from the 173rd was told to drop, they all dropped. Cannelli was a medic, a gentle soul, and he quickly became the best friend Mike Pereira had ever had. They had barbecues together, got drunk together, started dating two Italian girls who happened to be friends.

Mike met Georgia Rostirolla at a bar called the Crazy Bull, which was — it was clear from the name — a place for Italian women to meet G.I. Joes. His friend Curry, a charismatic counterintelligence expert, had dragged him there. "Pereira, we gotta get you out on the town," Curry said. "And here's how we're going to do it. You're going to walk up to the ten most beautiful women in the bar, and the odds are that one of them is going to want to talk to you." Georgia was number four. She was small, but an absolute stunner. She spoke impeccable English. Mike was not the most confident Casanova; he was good-looking in a nerdy, ectomorphic way, with an intense, academic air about him. He was right there, Georgia thought. There was nothing duplicitous about him. Nothing dangerous either. He was a good guy. They started dating in September 2003 and were living together by February 2004. Soon after that, both Mike and Dante were sent to Afghanistan.

Mike went to the detainee interrogation unit at Bagram Air Base, just north of Kabul; Dante went downrange to Paktia province with the 173rd Airborne.

Mike was able to do some serious work at Bagram. He interrogated prisoners — but quickly realized that no one was cross-referencing the intel coming from the interviews, and he set out to do that. Before long, he was interrogating both the regular detainees and the high-value prisoners held by the special operators in a separate shed. In July 2005, four high-value Al Qaeda prisoners broke out of Bagram, probably with the help of Afghan guards. Mike did a quick analysis of all the information that had been gathered on them and found that all four came from the same small town in Pakistan. He requested SIGINT (signals intelligence — drones, phone monitoring, that sort of thing), and the four were found in their hometown and apprehended. Mike became something of an intel celebrity after that; he received accolades all the way up the chain of command to Vice President Dick Cheney.

Mike would receive the daily U.S. casualty reports — two killed in action in Kandahar, three wounded in action in Helmand — but they were abstractions, and he didn't think about them. He was far more obsessed with the bad guys. He had pictures of them, in most cases; he had compiled thick dossiers on them, their movements, their families, their residences. He felt he knew the Al Qaeda networks cold; he was so caught up in Mondo Mike and special ops that he lost track of which conventional U.S. units were where, with one exception. He knew that the 173rd Airborne was operating in Paktika, and one day there was a report of two killed in action, members of the 173rd Airborne . . . and he wondered. Mike had interrogated prisoners who were members of an IED cell operating in Paktika; they turned out to be part of the group that had laid the IED that killed the soldiers from the 173rd. Mike had known that the rest of the group was still out there. He had felt *almost* confident enough to put together a contingency operation for special ops troops to hit the members of the cell who were still at large. He had their homes, their schematics . . . but not quite enough.

Then Georgia called. "You heard, right?" she asked.

"Heard what?"

"About Dante."

Fuck. No.

"He was killed in an explosion" — an IED

explosion, *the* IED explosion in Paktika. Mike had *killed* Dante. It was the only way he could think about it. He had absolutely been responsible for his best friend's death.

After that, every KIA had Dante's face. Mike felt responsible for all of them. Each time someone was killed or wounded, Mike would go through the "if only I had" stations of the cross. He rarely left his work area, rarely ate, rarely slept — finding the bad guys was now a 24/7 operation. Later, he would realize that he had gone off the deep end and probably should have checked himself into sick bay and sought counseling. Instead, the excellent, if insane, quality of his work put him in line for the offer to go to Iraq with the private contractor who dare-not-be-named. He would have access to a lot more assets, and he could be a lot more effective than he'd been in Afghanistan and prevent a lot more American deaths, and he leaped for it.

The fact that Mike met Eric Greitens in Balad helped a lot. Eric was an anchor; his sanity and friendship kept Mike from flying off too far. But Mike figured that he wasn't going to have access to the LT for very long. Eric was like a lion in a shoebox, Mike thought, desperate to get downrange, see

265

real action, test himself. Eric pushed himself physically far beyond anything Mike had seen before; he pushed so hard running a treadmill one day that he broke it. (Eric would win the Fallujah marathon that year — an event that took place within FOB Fallujah, in which the runners were given maps that included bomb shelters in case there was a rocket attack.)

And so Mike wasn't surprised when Eric went downrange to lead an Al Qaeda targeting cell in Fallujah. He was pretty much alone then. He had become a necessary piece of the machine, and he was respected, sort of. But he hadn't trained with any of the guys in his secret intel unit — Mike believed you couldn't really know a guy unless you'd trained with him — and they were pleasant and smart enough, but they weren't *brothers*.

He did have one friend, a prisoner. We'll call him Hamid. He knew Mike as "Stanley," which was Pereira's *nom d'intel.* He was a lot like Mike, same age, a nerdy, introverted ectomorph. He was a jacked-up Al Qaeda communications expert. He'd built the laptop for Abu Musab al-Zarqawi that was traced by American intel and led to Zarqawi's death. Hamid was from Kuwait, the younger brother of a major Al Qaeda leader. He was working in an electronics store in Syria while doing his secret work, and his parents were on his case: Why couldn't he be a fighter, a martyr for God, like his brother? The family had connections to Zarqawi, and Hamid eventually agreed to go to Iraq to be part of Zarqawi's team. He was caught up almost immediately in the battle of Fallujah — which terrified him. "All I could do was cry," he told Mike. "They wanted me to drive a suicide car. I drove it a little ways and then jumped out and ran to another village, where I knew some of my brother's friends were."

Having demonstrated a distinct inability to be a martyr for God, Hamid was put in charge of the Al Qaeda websites and chat rooms, which were sometimes used to send instructions for terrorist missions. He was captured on the "Night of a Thousand Daggers," when forty-eight different high-value targets were taken by American special forces, one of the most effective operations of the Iraq War. Mike was not the first person to interrogate Hamid, and he didn't want to be the last: when a prisoner was deemed no longer useful, he was turned over to the Iraqi judicial system, which was usually a death sentence.

Hamid had two wives and a kid. He spoke

excellent English and had a sense of humor. Mike loved the guy but didn't trust him entirely. He was, after all, Al Qaeda.

Mike's world began to crater in late March 2007, when he heard that Eric had been blown up in the chlorine bomb in Fallujah. It was a huge bomb, and Mike assumed the worst. He was shattered — everyone he'd really cared about seemed to die. When the casualty reports came in, Mike exhaled — Eric wasn't seriously wounded — but the anxiety lingered, even after he actually saw Greitens one last time, on the flight line at Balad. Eric was on his way home, and he was humble about the bomb; he just said that it had been tough and that a close friend had been badly hurt, but he was fine. "Don't worry about me," he said. "And keep in touch. Let me know when you get back home."

When you get back home . . .

Okay, it was time to think about that. Georgia certainly thought it was well past time. But . . . *home* — nothing good had ever happened for him back home. And yet: He was a private contractor. He had about $100,000 in savings. All he had to do was walk into the office, sign a few papers, and he'd be out of there.

Three days after he said good-bye to Eric,

the special operators asked him to come on a field operation with Hamid. They were going to Ramadi, where Hamid was supposed to identify a target. When they got there, Hamid couldn't, or wouldn't, identify the guy — and the special ops guys took him away and beat the crap out of him, breaking his nose and jaw. They put him in the back of a flatbed truck with a bag over his head. He was sobbing quietly. "Stanley," he whispered. "Stanley, are you here?"

"Yes, right here."

"Will you hold my hand?" Fuck it, Mike thought. He held Hamid's hand.

They were piled onto a dual-rotor Chinook, the primary troop- and load-carrying military helicopter. They were dragging a sling-load of supplies to the town of al-Assad. But the load was too heavy for the chopper, which strained to get off the ground and then began to falter and groan when it was aloft. Mike could hear the Chinook's crazy wheezing, and then he could see the engine on the other side of the bird was on fire. And they were going down.

People were screaming. He could smell them pissing and shitting their pants. He was pushed up against the bulkhead. He was going to be crushed to death. "Please,

God," he prayed. "Please, God, let me live to see another morning."

Somehow, everyone lived. The pilots crash-landed the Chinook, and people were wounded, but everybody lived. Mike rolled out onto flat land and just stared at the stars. He had prayed to God, and he'd been allowed to see another morning — but how weird was *that*? How weird was praying? Was it really God who had spared him or the brilliant helicopter pilots? He had lived with God for a long time and never questioned Him. But now — and Mike realized that this was so *him,* so perverse — a prayer had been answered, and Mike had lost faith.

And then there was Hamid. He'd been fooling himself about that, too. Sooner or later, Hamid was going to have to be remanded into the Iraqi judicial system. He would undoubtedly be hanged. There was no way around that. And there was no way around the fact that Hamid's fate was Mike's responsibility. He was the interrogator who knew him best — but, when it came right down to it, how well did he really know Hamid? And could he put his affection for the computer geek ahead of the safety of American troops like Dante Cannelli?

He signed Hamid over to the Iraqis, and

then he went to the contractors' office and signed himself out. "I'm done," he told them.

He was very much done. Everything had died in the chopper. God was dead. His friends kept dying. He had signed Hamid's death warrant. His life was over.

He tried school at Whatcom Community College in Bellingham. It was said to be a good school, a feeder for the University of Washington, but Mike lasted only a few weeks. He took a political science class, and they were discussing Iraq. A girl said, "I don't know what we're doing there, aside from raping women and killing babies." Mike held his fire, but then they showed a film about the war that had a scene of burning bodies and . . . Mike was back in the Intensive Care Unit at Bagram, interrogating severely burned detainees. The greasy smell of cooked flesh was in his nose, and he simply got up and walked out of the class.

He had rented — this was really weird, when he thought about it — his old house from his parents, who had gotten back together and moved to a newer place. It was a small three-bedroom set on three acres, with a red barn that his dad had used as a mechanic's shed and a yard that was still filled with wrecked cars. He settled in very deeply with his memories. He played *Rainbow Six* nonstop on Xbox with a couple of Albanians in New York. He pushed Georgia away. She didn't want to leave, but he told her that she had to — and she went back to Italy. That was August 2007.

Trash and pizza boxes and empty bottles piled up around the house. He felt a near physical craving for the order of military life, for his guys, for the way things had been in Germany. He would haunt the local Army recruiting station, not to re-up, just to talk; the soldiers there began to think he was nuts. He put an ad on craigslist, seeking other veterans to talk to. No one responded.

One night, alone in his mess, Mike pulled out his 9mm Smith & Wesson pistol. He put a bullet in the chamber and put the barrel in his mouth. He figured his life had more value as a statistic. The pain of living every day like this was excruciating. He put his finger on the trigger — and . . . he began to think: Dad had a really fucked-up life, but he made it through somehow — was he really that much more fucked up than Doc Pereira? And if he took the gun out of his mouth right now, he might be of service to others — you didn't have to commit suicide, no matter how fierce the pain. And then he thought about Eric Greitens: *he* had believed in Mike. And what if Eric was right, that Mike could be not just a person of value, but a leader? Leadership seemed implausible — he couldn't even lead himself at that point — but becoming a person of value was within range, even if he wasn't quite sure how to get there. He took the gun out of his mouth. He kept the bullet.

Before she left for Italy, Georgia had sent out an all-points bulletin that Mike was really in a lot of trouble. She went to the authorities at Whatcom Community College and told them; she went to the Student Veterans Club. And about a month after Mike took the gun out of his mouth, there was a knock on the door — Tim Nelson, the president of the Veterans Club at Whatcom. Tim was a Marine, a force of nature, the perfect opposite of lugubrious, and lugubrious was where Mike still was. They started to talk. Tim had done three tours in Iraq. They talked about the military; they were both proud to have served, but their pride didn't match with the mortal suck of the situation in Iraq and Afghanistan, the friends they'd lost — and for what? Tim didn't mention the utter squalor of Mike's place until near the end. "So, Mike, you're so proud of being an NCO [a noncommissioned officer, a Sergeant]," he said. "How come you're living like a Private?"

Mike cleaned up the house. Then he went back to school, and it was sort of like being in the military again. He didn't go back to school just for himself; he did it for Tim. And for the first time, he took it seriously: he aced every class. Every day, he could feel it — moving away from the squalor and depression, moving toward peace. He went to counseling at the VA. He moved out of his parents' house into an apartment. Georgia came back in the spring of 2008. She wanted to go to school at Whatcom and become an accountant. "I'll let you stay here for ten days, and then you've got to leave," he told her. Ten days later, he desperately didn't want her to leave, and they were back together.

Mike became active in the Veterans Club with Tim Nelson, and over time, it turned out that Tim needed Mike as much as Mike had needed Tim. He would show up at Mike and Georgia's house in the middle of the night, crying, unable to sleep. Mike would take him to Denny's for an early breakfast and let him talk it out. There were a thousand signs that Tim was in deep trouble, but Mike couldn't process that: Tim was his superior officer, his Eric. Tim had been trained in suicide prevention; he had taught Mike how to keep the gun out of his mouth.

Tim took a shotgun and blew his face off in July 2008. Mike had to hold up Tim's father at the funeral; the old man kept collapsing. Mike was collapsing inside, too — another Sky Soldier down — but this time, Mike was holding it together, in part because the other Whatcom veterans were looking to *him* for leadership. Tim's wife had taken their daughter to her home in Spokane, and so it fell to Mike and his fellow veterans to clean up the mess, wash the walls, and pack up all of Tim's things. Mike wasn't sure he was ready for leadership; he wasn't sure he was going to hold it together; he was back to dark as the reality of Tim's death settled in.

That was when Mike googled Eric Greitens, looking for advice. He was impressed by The Mission Continues website. There were video links to speeches Eric had given. Mike had never thought about the notion of community service as a means to reenter civilian life before. He really wanted to talk to Eric about it — he really wanted to become a Mission Continues fellow — but he couldn't just cold-call him. He had to do something that would impress Eric first.

Mike looked for a local program that encouraged veterans to serve in their community, but he couldn't find any. There was one program that was targeted for convicts. "If they take convicts," he told the guys in the Veterans Club, "maybe they'll take veterans."

He met with Allie Hoover, the woman who ran the program for convicts. "We'd love to have you guys," she said. "What do you want to do?"

"Anything," Mike said. "Give us the things no one else wants to do."

"You've GOT it," Allie said.

And they were in business, scrubbing mold in basements, cleaning roofs, helping the elderly and the disabled and those who were dying of cancer. Mike's group grew from three veterans to thirty during the course of the year. They focused on helping the disabled and those who were ill. By the spring of 2009, they were helping six hundred people — doing chores, cleaning and shopping for them, taking them to doctor's appointments, keeping them company.

Finally, he was ready to send a letter — a nine-page, single-spaced letter — to Eric Greitens, asking to become a Mission Continues fellow. "Sir, you may not remember me," he began. Eric laughed when he read that: How could you not remember Mike Pereira? "You've really got something here," Mike wrote. "I've seen how service changes lives. It saved my life."

Eric invited Mike and Georgia to come to St. Louis for dinner. He was impressed, once again, by Mike's acuity, but even more by his story: he had created his own Mission Continues fellowship and lived it without the stipend. Eric continued to think about Mike after he and Georgia returned to Bellingham. The Mission Continues was now almost two years old, and it was beginning to grow exponentially. There were now thirty-two Mission Continues fellows, past and present. But there was no one to keep up with the fellows, really keep up with them, to help them through the rough spots and challenge them if they weren't meeting their service obligations. He was interviewing people to become Fellowship Director, and he realized the best interview he'd had was dinner with Mike.

He called Mike and said, "Hey, Mike, I've been thinking about something. You've already done the equivalent of a Mission Continues fellowship. In fact, you've done more than that. You've organized veterans, and led them, and helped them through the tough times. I need someone to do that here. Would you be willing to come to St. Louis with Georgia and become my Fellowship Director?"

"Are you kidding?" Mike asked. Eric said he wasn't, and the job would pay $30,000 a year.

"Of course I'll come," Mike said.

"One other condition," Eric added. "You've got to promise me that you're going to go back to school and graduate from a four-year college. I don't think the job I'm offering you scratches the surface of your potential."

For the second time in his life, Mike Pereira felt he'd been recruited into heaven.

CHAPTER 4
LIVING THE HERBALIFE

Clay Hunt smiled, and that was it for Robin Becker. They were in a bar in Huntington Beach. Clay was there with friends; Robin was there with friends. They were in a group, sitting around a table. The club was well beyond noisy, full house in full plumage. The guys were ripped; the women, paragons of breezy tan. Later, they'd go out and play beach volleyball. You've seen this in beer ads.

And it all seemed the primal usual: joking, teasing, pheromones, grenade bursts of too-loud laughter. Everyone entirely aware of everyone else's performance art. But Clay's smile seemed to exist on a different level of reality — or rather, *in* reality, rather than preen and display. He was actually looking at her, saying a hundred knowing things about where they were, without saying a word.

The next day, they walked the beach and

talked about war and friends and family. He was sensitive without seeming gooey, a safe kind of sensitive. He wouldn't hurt her. They talked about doing stuff together — surfing, hiking, biking, just hanging out. They both enjoyed outdoor stuff. He was stationed out at 29 Palms, and soon he would be deploying to Iraq for the first time. He put his hand on the small of her back, guiding her up through the dunes.

This was sometime in late summer of 2006. He came back the next weekend, and the next. There was an immediate mesh, Robin thought, a million shared synapses — their own little world. They were entirely there for each other, full attention every weekend. There were others along for their ride, of course. There was Jake Wood — really good guy, she thought, the center of the show, much more out-there than Clay. The two of them were total charmers, each in his own way — preternatural best friends; you could spot the bond a mile away.

Clay deployed in January 2007, and in the blink of an eye — by early March — he was home again with his wounded wrist. Robin visited him in the hospital and met his parents. Eventually, their weekend life resumed, and Robin didn't notice much of a difference in Clay. But he did begin to spend a lot of time with the mother of one of his friends who had died.

Audrey Nitschka — Blake Howey's mom — had operated the Hotel Howey in her home for Blake's Marine friends before they deployed to Iraq. She lived in Glendora, just east of Pasadena, and was thrilled to have Blake's friends sleeping all over the living room floor and playing flag football in the backyard whenever they had liberty from 29 Palms. Audrey was recently divorced, kind . . . and cool; she knew how to handle Marines, and these Marines were still kids. They called her "Mom," and they needed a mom; they adopted her seven-year-old daughter, Taylor. They left boxes of their belongings in her garage before they deployed.

How outrageous that Blake was the first to die. His best friend, Nathan Windsor, called and said, "I know I can never replace Blake, but I'll be your substitute son, Mom, and I'll be Taylor's big brother." Windsor was killed two weeks later. And Clay was shot in the wrist a few days after that.

Clay had never been part of the Hotel Howey scene; he spent his weekends at the beach with Robin. But he called Audrey soon after he returned from Iraq, while he was still in the hospital, and asked if he could visit her.

"Of course," she said.

He seemed to hesitate. "There's a guy here in the hospital who knew Blake. Can he come with me?"

"Of course," she said.

Sergeant Rosenberger was terrified to meet Howey's mom. He and Blake had been in the same Humvee the night Blake died on Route Reds. They should have stopped to check the bridge for IEDs, but they were running late. The squad they were supposed to be rescuing was still out in the boonies, stuck in the mud in the dark. He had ordered Blake not to stop, to drive on, straight into the IED. He was responsible for her son's death. He had to apologize to Audrey.

Audrey had heard others, Blake's friends, blame Rosenberger as well, and she didn't know how she'd react to him. But now, with the culprit — a shattered twenty-three-year-old boy — in her living room, she couldn't summon the slightest twinge of anger. "It was my fault," Rosenberger said. "I don't expect you to ever forgive me."

"There's nothing to forgive," Audrey said. "It's war. It's crazy."

Clay was amazed and touched by that. Howey had been his bunkmate, a close friend — and Rosenberger may well have screwed up — but people screwed up all the time, and Clay's reaction had been the same as Audrey's: Rosenberger was a good guy; he had *insisted* on confessing his guilt to Howey's mom. There was no way Clay could be angry with him. His job now was to help Rosenberger through this; that's just what you did.

And he had a responsibility to Howey's mom as well. She had handled herself with such grace. When the rest of their unit came home from Iraq in the summer of 2007, Clay brought Blake's squadmates to see her — and, as in the past, they stayed; Hotel Howey reopened for business. These kids were as close as she would ever get to Blake again. She watched them asleep on the floor in the family room at night, twitching and groaning, sometimes shouting, refighting their wars. She had to be careful when they were asleep; if she came through the door loudly on her way in or out, they'd be up with a start — Clay would be up punching. He'd nearly decked her once when she'd had to wake him. He slept with his combat knife; the others slept with guns. They seemed obsessed with their guns. She didn't understand that at all; guns scared her. She asked Clay why, after all the scary, terrible violence, he and the others still talked so much about guns and went off to the range to shoot them.

"It's a release," he said. "You want to go to the range with me? I'll show you how to shoot."

The thing was, Clay was right. It *was* a release. Pulling the trigger, the noise, the violence of it, trying to kill the damn target — it did make her feel better on some deep level that she couldn't understand. She bought herself a pistol and a gun locker and made her Marines check their weapons at the door. Eventually she would own five pistols.

Audrey didn't see Clay very often during 2008. He was in sniper school and then in Afghanistan, and he was spending most of his weekends with Robin. He kept in touch, told her all about Robin, about how athletic she was, good to go for long bike rides and hiking and surfing. But Audrey sensed something was missing.

For her part, Robin couldn't see much difference in Clay after he came home from Iraq. Their weekend world didn't change at all. Or maybe, just a little, when Jake and Jeff Muir came home from Iraq in August — it became more about the Band of Brothers, less about Clay and Robin, which was understandable but annoying. But Clay was still there with her most weekends — and then he was getting ready to deploy again. She had no idea that he had been diagnosed with PTSD. She didn't ask him about Iraq. Her impression was that you weren't supposed to talk about it — unless Clay wanted to, and he never mentioned it. He seemed strong. He was proud of graduating from sniper school. And now he was pestering her, "What's your ring size? What's your ring size?"

She tried to back him off. What did they really know about each other? They said, "I love you," which was absolutely true — on weekends. He seemed the *sort* of guy she'd want to spend her life with — but did you just get engaged, get married, without spending a week using the same bathroom? They never talked about the future; he never talked about what he would do when he left the Marines. She was a hard worker, but she didn't talk to Clay about what she did for a living (telemarketing, not much income yet, but she had ambitions). He didn't know that side of her at all. And yet, he was all over her, saying they needed to be together, that if they got married and something happened to him in Afghanistan, she'd receive his benefits.

He *was* sweet. And she did think she loved him. "Yes," she finally told him, "but let's keep it a secret until you get home. Then we can have a real wedding." They were married at a courthouse in Orange County. Then he was gone for what seemed a very long time.

While Clay was in Afghanistan, Robin found her trade: selling Herbalife products and convincing other women to sell them for her. The term of art for this sort of business is "multilevel marketing"; detractors say it resembles a Ponzi scheme — and while Herbalife had pyramidal elements, Robin believed that there were, at bottom, a range of nutritional and skin care products that people, especially women interested in losing weight, found helpful. For Robin, it wasn't the door-to-door selling as much as it was the promise of building a sales force. She dived into it; with Clay gone, there wasn't much to distract her.

When Clay came home in late October 2008, he moved in with Robin in Brentwood and very quickly noticed that she had changed. She was distracted, busy, colder somehow. She gave him orders, chores, and nagged him to get his act together, get a life. "The woman I came home to," he told his mother, "is not the woman I left."

True enough, Robin thought. But someone had to take out the trash and clean the dishes. Clay seemed to think that she could have long, leisurely lunches with him every day, as they'd had on weekends past; he seemed offended that he wasn't getting her full attention. Robin was on her computer, on her phone, out driving around to her sales reps all the time. Years later, she would be unable to remember many details of their time together.

She did notice that he didn't sleep very much. He would try. He would lie down in bed with her for ten minutes, and then he would be up and out, saying, "This ain't gonna happen," and he'd go to the living room, where he would stare out the window or read a book. If he had nightmares, she never heard them. She knew he was taking some sort of calm-down medicine prescribed by the VA, but a lot of people she knew were taking calm-down medicine. He wanted more from her than she could give — or maybe, he just didn't know what he wanted; or maybe, she wasn't prepared to give very much; or maybe, all of the above. They began to fight. He would accuse her of not caring about him; she would tell him to get his act together, go to school, start working, do something. The fights ended, as often as not, with him storming out of the house and going for a long bike ride or drinking with his old crew in Huntington Beach, most of whom were jerks, she thought. She didn't have the luxury of storming out; she had a business to build.

They went to Texas for Christmas in 2008 and spent some time with Clay's dad and then with his mom. Both Stacy and Susan, separately, came to the same conclusion about Robin: she wasn't a bad person, but she wasn't very warm either, and Clay had always gravitated toward warm. She seemed far more interested in her computer and her work than she did in socializing with them or being with Clay. All the gifts she gave them that Christmas were Herbalife products.

A few days after they returned to California, Clay and Robin had a pretty bad fight. "Why don't we go live in Texas?" he said. "I can go to school there and you can do your work."

"Texas?" They had barely tried living in California, Robin thought. They didn't know how to live together yet. "Why?"

"It's home," Clay said. "I feel safer there."

Safer? What did that mean? "You can go back and live in Texas, but I'm building a network here, and I'm going to stay here."

It descended from there to free-range shouting and Clay storming out with his bike and without any money or identification or a helmet. He sped along Wilshire Boulevard toward the beach, pushing hard in the sunshine, trying to let out the frustration. A Jeep was crowding him, and he began to shout at the driver: "I have a right to be here, too." The driver shouted right back: "You're slowing everybody down." Fuck you. No, fuck you. Asshole . . . and the driver swerved into Clay's bike, or maybe Clay swerved into the car, but the jolt was violent and Clay was knocked down, out cold, and the Jeep didn't bother to stop.

He awoke in the emergency room at UCLA with a severe concussion and a chipped tooth. He was extremely foggy, but he remembered Robin's phone number, and she came with his wallet. The doctors wanted to do some tests, an MRI of his brain — and the tests came back strange. They said that he had suffered a traumatic brain injury. Totally weird: two tours in Iraq and Afghanistan, and he rings up a TBI on Wilshire Boulevard. "They say there are three damaged spots on my brain," he told his mother.

"How do you *feel*?" Susan asked.

"Scattered," he said. "I'm having trouble remembering words."

He apologized to Robin. He still loved and needed her. He wanted to stay married. He proposed that he and Robin spend the next two years in California — he'd finish college there — and then they'd talk about going home to Texas. He applied to Loyola Marymount University, a tough Jesuit school, and got in — he wanted to be a physician's assistant, a paramedic of some sort. Robin was heartened by these efforts, and yes, she was willing to go ahead with the wedding, which Clay's dad agreed to pay for.

They were married that spring in a lovely glass chapel in the mountains overlooking the ocean. Jake was best man. Clay asked his surrogate mom Audrey Nitschka to give a speech. She tried to talk about how Clay had been so kind, how he'd brought Blake's friends home to her, and then she started to cry. "I'm sorry," she told Clay later. "I was pretty drunk."

It was a sunny day, a perfect setting; the Marines were blinding and beautiful in their brass buttons and dress blues. Robin was hopeful that a corner had been turned.

Clay seemed okay. He had found comfort

that spring riding his bike with other veterans, part of an organization called Ride 2 Recovery, led by a former professional cyclist named John Wordin whom Clay had found through the VA. They'd had a good conversation and then a good ride down to the Santa Monica pier. "I'm really a mountain biker," Clay said.

"Okay, we'll do one of those up in Topanga, too," Wordin said. "But if you really want to have some fun, you should come on one of our challenge rides."

The challenges were week-long, 350-mile structured rides — from San Francisco to Los Angeles, for example. They were limited to two hundred wounded veterans and were almost always fully subscribed. The veterans would ride for six hours a day and take frequent breaks, sometimes visiting schools, newspapers, or community centers along the way, telling their story. Wordin was a calm and devoted presence; each evening during the challenge, he would run a conversation — about what they'd experienced that day, about their troubles, about what they wanted to forget and get past. He told Clay about the shop he'd set up in his garage, where he built bikes for amputees and even for some paraplegics. "It's a lot of guys like you and some who are much worse off," Wordin said. "They're all folks who enjoy the outdoors and haven't found their way back to civilian life. You said you had trouble sleeping? *Nobody* has trouble sleeping during a challenge ride."

Clay was a strong rider and a natural leader, and he became a regular on the rides. He was great in the evening group meetings as well, doing his eloquent Clay thing, talking about the friends he'd lost, how he should have been the one who died, how he had suicidal thoughts but programs like Ride 2 Recovery were helping him through.

Clay entered Loyola Marymount in the fall of 2009. He was ten years older than most of the other students, which was weird and a little uncomfortable — to feel old at such a young age — but the kids looked up to him, and that meant something. He was asked to speak at the school's Veterans Day celebration. He talked about the war — simply, without the oo-rah — and about how he had come to believe that Iraq and Afghanistan were mistakes. Lives were being lost. People were coming home with PTSD, people like him — he talked about having suicidal thoughts at times. But he was working his way through that. He was in counseling, and he had Robin. "She's my rock," he said. "I'd never make it through without her."

Robin was there and moved by his eloquence. He *had* that audience, she thought, and if he could do that, why couldn't he do everything else?

That fall, Clay burrowed deeper into the veterans' movement; he joined Iraq and Afghanistan Veterans of America (IAVA), which was the best-known of his generation's advocacy groups. It had begun as a protest organization in 2004, led by an Army Captain named Paul Rieckhoff. "We love the Army but hate the war," Rieckhoff had said, which summed up the military experience for more than a few troopers who had volunteered after 9/11 and found themselves fighting a war that made no strategic or military sense. There was a difference between IAVA and the Vietnam generation of veterans' protest groups: IAVA quickly developed a pragmatic agenda that could be cheered by the war's supporters and opponents alike. Rieckhoff had been infuriated by the fact that his company had inadequate body armor in Baghdad and that their Humvees were soft-skinned, with no steel protection. His unit actually had to raid the Baghdad junkyards to find pieces of metal that they'd strap to the sides of their vehicles. So IAVA mounted a lobbying campaign that shamed the Department of Defense and the Congress into providing more effective body armor and up-armored Humvees. As time went on, Rieckhoff would lead teams of veterans to Washington each year for Storm the Hill missions to lobby for an expanded G.I. Bill of Rights, more money and attention to the problems of traumatic brain injury and PTSD, and reform of the Veterans Administration, which was an impossible bureaucratic muckswamp that swallowed applications for disability benefits and couldn't seem to spit them out. Rieckhoff was controversial because of his nonstop advocacy and his willingness to call out malfeasance at the VA, especially under the cloudy rule of former four-star General Eric Shinseki, who was appointed by Barack Obama and disappeared into a deep public relations hole, overwhelmed by the bureaucracy, unwilling (or perhaps unable) to advocate for Iraq and Afghanistan veterans who were flooding the system with fresh wounds and unprecedented problems. Rieckhoff — huge, bald, energetic, and smart — pierced the vacuum Shinseki created and emerged as the most effective spokesman for his generation of veterans.

Hearing that Clay Hunt was a talented speaker, Rieckhoff invited him to attend Storm the Hill 2010 — and Clay convinced IAVA to let Jake come along. Before that, though, IAVA asked Clay to do some speaking in California. He became something of a poster boy for PTSD; he was in two televised public service announcements. "I've seen and done things that people should not have to see or do," he said in one. But it was his presence more than his words: Robin watched the TV spot and saw flickers of that same smile, the clear-eyed decency. She still loved that Clay. But he wasn't there, with her, very often.

School was hard. He was having real problems holding his attention in class, writing essays, taking tests, remembering anything. He told Audrey Nitschka that he wasn't sure if it was the traumatic brain injury, his old ADHD, or the combination of drugs the VA was giving him, but something was making him screwy. He was having erectile problems, too, he admitted. But he was trying, really trying, to keep it together.

And then, on January 12, 2010, the earthquake struck Haiti. Clay was Jake's first call. "You in?"

"Shit. I've got to go to Houston for my stepbrother's wedding. But I'll get down there. I'll find a way."

Haiti was a bright-line for Robin. She knew Clay was desperate to go with Jake — it was the sort of saddle-up, let's-go thing that Clay laid on her all the time. When they returned home to California from the wedding, Clay devoured Jake's blog reports and photos from the scene of the earthquake. There weren't many posts — Team Rubicon had been there for only two days — but Clay kept reading them over and over. "You coming to bed?" Robin asked.

"Yeah, in a minute."

The next thing she knew, it was the middle of the night, and Clay was waking her up brusquely and saying, "You need to take me to the airport."

"Ohhh-kayyy," she said, trying to convey her frustration. But she could tell that Clay wasn't in the mood for a discussion. This was Band of Brothers business. They rode to the airport in silence. Robin couldn't trust herself to open her mouth; she didn't want to send him off to a dangerous place angry. So she hugged him at the airport and said, "I love you," and let him go.

But her anger festered, and when he came home, jubilant, stoked by all the good things they'd done in Haiti — he told her about the incredible Doc Griswell and the medic Mark Hayward and said he wanted to be a medic, just like Doc Army; he was full of new plans — she let him have it. "Clay, you just walked out of this house — you woke me up in the middle of the night and *told* me to drive you to the airport. That's not right," she said. "We're married. That's not what married people do. You didn't even discuss it with me. We could have done it together, we could have planned it . . ."

"There was no time for that," he said. "I had to go right then."

"But you could have talked to me about it, shared it with me . . ."

And then she stopped. She could see Clay was crushed. He had been glowing, more excited than she'd ever seen him — and she had been a total buzzkill. She sensed that she had crossed an invisible line, betrayed him somehow. It was going to be hard to recover from this. A few days later, he was gone again — off to Washington, D.C., with Jake for IAVA's Storm the Hill campaign to lobby for better veterans' benefits.

A blizzard had just dumped nearly two feet of snow on Washington; another would arrive in a few days with ten inches more —

the D.C. locals called it Snowpocalypse. The twenty-eight Storm the Hill veterans who had gathered to lobby Congress were pretty much confined to quarters at night — which forced them to commandeer the hotel bar, probably what they would have done anyway. They were hungry for one another's company.

They arrived on Super Bowl Sunday and had a day of orientation, dividing into four-person teams — Clay was in Delta Team; Jake was in Fox. They learned how to make presentations to the congressional staffers they'd be visiting, the details of the issues they'd be raising, and how to deal with the media. They were given talking points; they divided each presentation into four sections, so each of the vets would have a role. They were asked to act and dress respectfully. The men would wear jackets and ties; the women, nothing flashy. Clay chose a champagne tie to go with his white shirt and dark suit. His role in Delta Team was to tell a story about a friend he had met through Ride 2 Recovery, a Vietnam veteran who'd had to fill out a twenty-six-page disability claims form when he came home from the war forty years ago. "I came home from Afghanistan last year, suffering from PTSD," Clay said. "And guess what? I had to fill out a twenty-six-page paper form to apply for my disability. And there was no way to keep track of it. It just disappeared somewhere in the VA. If my parents can send me a FedEx package from Houston to Santa Monica, and I can track it all the way on my phone, shouldn't we be able to keep track of our disability claims?"

Clay was articulate and persuasive without being angry, thought his assigned roommate, Anthony Pike. Jake was also effective, but fiercer than Clay. He'd gotten into a confrontation with the conservative Oklahoma Senator Tom Coburn, who — to tell the truth — had been asking for it. "You know what's wrong with your generation of veterans? You just want stuff," Coburn said. "You guys come in here with all these plans for policy change. But you know what you didn't come here with: a plan to pay for it."

Jake wanted to assault the guy, but he kept his temper, sort of. "Senator, with all due respect, it's not our job to figure out how to pay for it. That's your job. That's why you were elected to the Senate."

The other veterans were blown away by the energy and style of the two Team Rubicon guys. Jake was always at the heart of the action when everyone gathered at the hotel bar at night. Clay would hang back, except when Haiti came up — and then he was transformed, jazzed about the joys of being out there with fellow veterans, part of a team again, actually helping people. Storm the Hill was sort of like that, too, but without the physical challenge. Pike was envious of Clay's Haiti experience, and he wasn't alone. Rieckhoff began to tout Team Rubicon when he did media interviews. TR was the answer to Senator Coburn's complaint: it was veterans doing good for themselves and their communities.

And Clay became the model. He was candid about the problems he'd suffered through, the suicidal thoughts he'd had — but he hadn't sequestered himself in a dark room. He was out in the world, doing something about it. He was enthusiastic — and flat-out, unalloyed enthusiasm was not a common symptom of PTSD; he was attending college to develop medical skills that he could use on TR missions. Jake was the face of Team Rubicon, but it was Clay — vulnerable, kind, with that killer smile — who captured the hearts of the IAVA staff.

After a week in Washington, buoyed by the support, convinced that he'd really turned a corner this time, Clay went home, where Robin was waiting, still frustrated, still hoping to have a real conversation about their life together. He wanted to tell her how good he felt, how the other vets not only had his back but also seemed to respect him for what he was doing. He *knew* what he was going to do now: he would work for and with other veterans. They would do great things. He would go out and proselytize for IAVA and help get Team Rubicon off the ground. He would go back to Haiti; there would be other Team Rubicon missions, other Ride 2 Recovery challenge rides. He and John Wordin were planning a challenge to honor Blake Howey.

"What about school?" Robin asked. "You're already behind."

"I can't handle this," he exploded, suddenly knowing his own mind. "You have no fucking *idea* . . . I want a divorce."

"A *divorce*?" Robin was infuriated. "Three months ago, you told the whole world that I was *your rock*. You remember? Veterans Day? And now you want a divorce?"

"You're just not fucking there for me. You even saw me with the gun out and you didn't do anything about it."

"You *always* have the gun out," she said. It was reflexive, onanistic: he was always cleaning it, oiling it, going off to the shooting range — how was she to know that he was actually thinking about using it on himself? He never told her what he was thinking.

And yet other people knew what Clay was thinking and feeling without asking. Audrey Nitschka knew; Jake and his girlfriend, Indra Petersons, certainly knew. All his friends knew that he could dive very deep, very quickly, into an extremely dark place; the exhilaration of Haiti and Storm the Hill was simply the other side of the coin.

As for Clay, there wasn't time or space or, if the truth be told, very much desire for him and Robin to hash out their situation. He was adamant about the divorce; Robin, indignant.

Within a matter of days, there was a massive earthquake in Chile, and he was gone again.

CHAPTER 5
THE HERO'S JOURNEY

"Mike," Eric Greitens said. "They're honoring Gold Star families at the Soldiers Memorial downtown. I want you to represent us."

"Really?" Mike Pereira asked warily, sensing a setup.

"Yes," Eric said. And yes, it was a setup. Challenging Mike's post-traumatic stress was part of Eric's training program in the months after Pereira arrived in St. Louis in August 2009. He knew Mike was uncomfortable in public with people he didn't know; he would be especially frazzled in public with people he didn't know who had lost their children in Iraq and Afghanistan.

"I don't know," Mike said. "I don't know if I can do that."

"Why not?" Eric could see the gears spinning, the tension rising.

"Because I don't know that I can keep it together. I don't know what I can do for them. I'm going to be thinking about . . ."

"Yeah, but this isn't about you," Eric said gently. "This is about those families. They need our support; they need to know we're here. We have to get the word out. Look, Mike, if you're going to work here, you're going to have to handle a lot of uncomfortable situations — and if you're going to work with people who have PTSD, you've got to understand that we don't accept any excuses, not even from you. You know that. You're serving others here. You're going to that ceremony."

Mike knew that Eric was right, of course. He knew this was a test he was going to have to pass, part of the relentless tutorial that he was getting from Eric. There had been reading assignments, starting with the Robert Fagles translation of *The Odyssey.* "It's the first book ever written about a soldier coming home from a war," Eric said. "It's a journey."

Mike latched on to that — the idea that he was on a journey upward toward enlightenment. Eric asked him to read other books about the mythic quest: *The Hero with a Thousand Faces* by Joseph Campbell, *Shop Class as Soulcraft* by Matthew B. Crawford, *Iron John* by Robert Bly. They all pointed in one direction: the hero went on an adventure; along the way he faced challenges, suffered, and died a spiritual death, and only then, on the way home, he began to rebuild strength and character while suffering through even more perilous adventures. Eric introduced Mike to his favorite poem by Aeschylus, famously recited by Robert Kennedy in the Indianapolis ghetto after the death of Martin Luther King, Jr.:

He who learns must suffer,
And even in our sleep pain that cannot
   forget,
Falls drop by drop upon the heart,
And in our own despite, against our will,
Comes wisdom to us by the awful grace of
   God.

So Mike went to the Soldiers Memorial, and soon he was spending hours with the Gold Star families who showed up at the office, which became a gathering place for veterans and their spouses and families as word of The Mission Continues spread through St. Louis. Eric would invite them — and students, and people he'd met in the business community — to clean playgrounds and refurbish schools and community centers. The projects would draw media attention, and media attention drew more candidates for fellowships — and others, veterans and civilians, who just wanted to be part of something good.

Mike had bureaucratic responsibilities, which he performed with no relish; his main concern was helping veterans who were having problems, especially those he sensed were heading down the suicide slide. He would stalk them, working the hardest with those who were least prepared for a Mission Continues fellowship; he would work with them for months, trying to get them to write an acceptable application essay.

One of Mike's first projects was Ian Smith, who had been a close intel analysis buddy of his in Germany. Ian was now in Nashville, working three jobs — mowing lawns, delivering pizzas, serving as the janitor at a local church, while carrying a 4.0 average at Volunteer State Community College. But he wasn't sleeping very well; he needed booze to get himself down. And he wasn't treating his girlfriend, Christy, very well; he was never violent, but his temper was horrific. He was sleeping with a gun every night. He had gained sixty pounds. He was disconsolate.

"Sounds to me like you've got what I have," Mike said.

"No way," Ian said. "Nothing bad happened to me over there. I wasn't hurt . . ."

"I wasn't either," Mike replied. "But just sitting there, helpless, watching my friends get blown up . . ."

Ian had certainly experienced *that*. His first deployment with the 101st Airborne to Mahmudiyah, in Iraq's Triangle of Death, had been infamous: one of the soldiers in the unit had raped an Iraqi girl in front of her family, then killed the family and set them on fire. A book, *Black Hearts,* had been written about it. Every day, Ian sat in the TOC in Mahmudiyah, surrounded by big screens showing sky views from drones and helicopters, watching IED explosions. He lost friends on patrol almost every week. Four soldiers he knew were kidnapped by the Iraqis and later found dead. The FOB was mortared or hit by rocket-propelled grenades most days.

But still, he hadn't been in combat. He hadn't been hurt.

His second tour, as part of a MiTT team in Baghdad in 2007 and 2008, had been a triumph. The war had turned around by then. His team worked with an Iraqi Army unit trying to rid a mostly Sunni neighborhood of Jaish al-Mahdi (JAM) forces — the Shiite militia run by Muqtada al-Sadr — and they ultimately succeeded. "I *won* my war," Ian told Mike. "Why should I have PTSD?"

"I don't know," Mike replied. "Why do you need that gun? Why can't you sleep without booze? Why did Christy leave you?"

Ian wasn't budging, but Mike wasn't giving up. He told Ian to go out and buy an Xbox and headset, so they could play *Call of Duty* together and talk. They spent hours on the headsets, wasting hajjis and, occasionally, talking about Ian's situation. Mike could hear the numb in Ian's voice. He sounded too much like Tim Nelson, who had blown his head off in Bellingham. That simply could not happen again. He tried to get Ian off the couch, over to St. Louis for a weekend. He told him about The Mission Continues — Ian thought Mike made it sound like a cult, with Eric Greitens as Jesus — but Mike kept talking about it and asking Ian about what he was doing and whether he had friends nearby, service buddies, anybody to keep him in the world.

The truth was, except for Mike, Ian was alone, the pizza boxes — the signature nutritional artifact of post-traumatic stress — piling up in his dark room. He was playing with his gun, cleaning it, loading it, putting it to his temple. He was going through the motions of his life, mowing lawns, cleaning the church. He started doing some emergency ambulance work, which he thought would add some purpose — but almost all of his runs involved moving dialysis patients to a clinic and back. He was pissed off at everyone, all those civilians who had no idea about anything.

Mike sent Ian a copy of *Black Hearts,* and Ian devoured it and was freaked by it. The book brought everything back in Technicolor and surround sound. His unit had been driven nuts by war. He hadn't been outside the wire very often, but he'd been playing in the same crazy sandbox. And he simply could not understand why he was acting the way he was. Life in Nashville was cratering. Without Christy, there wasn't enough income to keep the house; he was going to have to move into a trailer. He was pulling out the gun almost every night, playing with it. "One of these nights, I just may put a bullet in my head," he told Mike.

"Hey, why don'tcha come *this* weekend?" Mike offered again, trying to sound calm. "We're doing a service project at a children's center, cleaning it up. It's good. It's like saddling up again. You get to hang with people like us, shoot the shit. No pressure. You can stay with Georgia and me. Ian, listen man, you need a road trip."

Much to Mike's amazement, Ian came. The service project was at the Edgewood Children's Center in St. Louis. Ian found himself in a room with a paintbrush and a handful of other vets. They were immediately familiar to him — they looked like he did, tough and tatted on the outside, confused and angry on the inside. It was like looking in a mirror. They began to talk as they worked, basic stuff, like where they'd deployed and with which unit and "Hey, did you know so-and-so?" They told war stories and stories about coming home and stories about how retarded civilians were. They were laughing. And suddenly the room was done — it looked great! — and they started painting another. You couldn't argue with this, Ian thought. There was no downside to painting a school for disabled kids. There was no bad in this. He understood, suddenly, the silly cliché: it's all good.

That night he slept the sleep of the just on Mike's couch, ten hours without nightmares. It had been how long — months? years? — since he'd slept like that. He woke up happy, pretty near euphoric. Man, he thought, if I can capture just a little bit of what we did yesterday and hold it close to my heart, I think I could do all right.

Ian moved to St. Louis, got counseling at

the VA, made a living driving EMT ambulances. He started working out, lost the sixty pounds; eventually he began to run, swim, and bike in triathlons. He became a Mission Continues fellow and then a TMC staff member. He specialized in organizing service projects all over the country. Eventually, Eric sent him to Washington to serve as a White House intern in Michelle Obama's Joining Forces initiative for veterans.

The success Mike had with Ian was narcotic; repeating that success was pretty much all he cared about. The fellowship program needed to be tightened. There were still too many failures. There were fellows who didn't show up for work at their local sponsoring organizations or used their stipends to buy drugs or couldn't control their anger. Eric wanted a foolproof system. He wanted every fellow to succeed. At the same time — and this was the hard part — he didn't want to reject anyone. It was okay if recruits said, "No, this isn't for me." But Eric couldn't bear the thought of turning away anyone who really wanted to serve, no matter how debilitated. He wanted Mike to stick with them, prepare them for the moment when they'd really be ready and purposeful enough for a fellowship. But what did "ready" mean? What were the parameters for selecting a Mission Continues fellow?

"Why don't you make a list of the qualities we need to see when a fellow applies?" Eric asked Mike.

Mike huffed and sweated and came up with a list of ten. He handed the list to Eric, who said, "Can you recite all ten from memory?"

Mike couldn't. "Why don't you work on this?" Eric said. "Pare it down. Come back to me with a list of two or three absolutely essential qualities."

That was how it was in 2009: systems and processes and metrics. It seemed to Mike that The Mission Continues staff was plodding down a slow, sludgy river on a raft, while Eric was zooming about in a Jet Ski, stopping in occasionally to fire off a set of instructions or bring news of another $10,000 or $50,000 raised — and pushing them always, always, to develop ways to measure the efficacy of the program. They were having individual successes like Ian Smith and Tim Smith, but those two had served in St. Louis, under close supervision. What about the fellows in the rest of the country? It was time for Monica Matthieu to step in and do a proper study; she recruited both Mike and Ian — former intel analysts were natural sociologists — to help with an exit questionnaire for the fellows. The problem was, there still weren't very many of them, maybe twenty or so, past and present. They were choosing their fellows carefully, adding them one at a time.

In the spring of 2009, Eric was invited to speak on a panel about the post-9/11 generation of veterans at Harvard's Kennedy School. He gave his usual Mission Continues pitch, looking prohibitively spiffy in a dark suit, white shirt, and canary yellow tie. Out in the audience, a young doctoral student named Sheena Chestnut took the message to heart. Her father, a doctor, had recently crushed his leg while working on a home construction project. The leg had been amputated below the knee — and she realized that a service program like The Mission Continues might have done her father some good as he rejoined the world, physically diminished after surgery.

Sheena had come to the event with a friend who knew Eric through her own national service work. Afterward, they went to Grendel's Den, a famed campus bar down the street from the Kennedy School. The conversation was easy, fun; no one, not

313

even Eric, dominated. Sheena was an East Asia expert, about to spend the summer in China. Eric regaled her with stories of his own China trip; he talked about singing "Row, Row, Row Your Boat" after his first Chinese banquet and had everyone laughing. Sheena told Eric about her dad, about her reaction to the panel. She was petite, very attractive, with bright hazel eyes, a small voice, and dark hair. She was a Highland dancer who'd competed in national and international tournaments, so she knew all about the pain and discipline that boxing and SEAL training had required. She was right there with him, on the same wavelength, from the moment they started talking. And when he stood up from the table, Eric heard a voice say, "This is the girl you're going to marry."

This was well beyond weird. Eric was not one to hear voices. He had been burned badly once. He had fallen in love with a fabulous, willful young woman from Wales when he'd been at Oxford; it was all youth and passion, two qualities Eric had rarely indulged. They went to refugee camps together. They were married at a castle in Wales. She came to California for his SEAL training but couldn't seem to settle herself there. Eric tried, too hard, to help her figure out her future, but he had trouble reading her. He was away sixteen hours a day in training and exhausted when he came home — and then she left abruptly, just after he'd completed SEAL training. Eric was crushed. He blamed himself for the divorce: it was the first time that he had failed at anything so totally, with only pain as a lesson. He'd had a series of girlfriends after that. They were of a type: smart, attractive, unchallenging. He was, in fact, boggled by women — was it possible to find someone who was thrilling but also a source of stability? He doubted it. "You don't settle for anything less than the best in any other aspect of your life," Adam Walinsky said to him. "Why should you do that with women?"

He and Sheena exchanged business cards as they left Grendel's. He promised to keep in touch but, daunted, he didn't. Six months passed.

He was back in Boston that October for a Mission Continues fund-raiser downtown. He called and asked if Sheena would like to go out for a drink after it was over. He figured that it would end about nine p.m., but several of the potential funders seemed real possibilities and wanted to get to know him better. He had to stay on. Finally, at about ten thirty, Sheena texted him, "Are we still going to do this?"

He called her. "Do you still want to? It's pretty late."

"Do *you*?"

"Yes. Absolutely."

She took a cab from Cambridge to downtown Boston, where he was staying. He realized that he was starving. He hadn't eaten dinner. "Do you mind if I get something to eat?" he asked. She didn't mind at all — but it was late, and nothing was open except a pizza shop that sold slices. Then he realized he had credit cards but no cash — and they took only cash. "Can you help me?" he asked her. "Can I owe you?"

"Of course," she said. There was something endearing about such a handsome, dynamic guy being so clumsy. He was embarrassed but didn't try to bluff his way through it. There was no pretense to him, she thought: charisma without pretense was something new under the sun.

They sat on a cold stone wall at the edge of the Boston Common. It was a chilly autumn night, but all the periphera — the pizza, the temperature — soon fell away, and they talked as easily as they had the first time. She told him about her summer in China; he told her that a publisher had asked him to write an autobiography. He

316

was talking it to an assistant, Tim Ly, who would transcribe the sessions; then Eric would write off the notes, but he wasn't sure it was any good. They talked about their families. Hers was pretty conservative; both her parents were doctors.

Eric put her in a cab back to Cambridge, and she said, "Are you going to let another six months go by?"

No. No way. They began a nomadic courtship. Their first six dates were in five different cities. Eric soon sent her the manuscript of his autobiography, *The Heart and the Fist,* and asked for her opinions. It seemed a perverse act of intimacy, incredibly forward in its way. There was a fair amount of ego involved but also an open sort of earnestness: he was saying that he really respected her, that he really valued her judgment — even though he barely knew her. She decided to return the intimacy; her comments would introduce him, in the most precise way, to the way her mind worked. She wasn't going to be easy on him. She would give the book a stern but appreciative read, marking up the pages with questions — "Can you find a better way to say this?" — and corrections: "Yugoslavia was *not* a Soviet satellite state."

Eric fell in love with her corrections. He

could not have hoped for a better reaction from her. She came to St. Louis — he gave her an extensive tour, quietly trying to make the case that this was as good a place as any for a China scholar to live — and she passed the Rob and Becky test easily. He went for runs with Kaj Larsen in California and St. Louis, wondering whether this was the real thing, whether he should take the plunge. Kaj — who was having too good a time to take any sort of plunge himself — told Eric he wouldn't know unless he tried.

"I don't want to be a two-time loser," Eric said, but he knew that was not an answer.

On Veterans Day, 2009, a major study of returning veterans called "All Volunteer Force: From Military to Civilian Service" was published with much aplomb, including the support of Michelle Obama.

The results were stunning:

— Only 13 percent of post-9/11 veterans strongly agreed that their transition home was going well.
— 92 percent agreed that service to their community was important to them, and 90 percent agreed that service was a basic responsibility of every American.
— 95 percent wanted to serve wounded

veterans; 90 percent wanted to serve military families; 88 percent wanted to do disaster relief; 86 percent wanted to serve at-risk youth; 82 percent wanted to help older Americans; 69 percent wanted to help clean up the environment.

The survey was the work of a young woman named Mary Yonkman, a blonde, somewhere-way-beyond-intense Hoosier who was married to a Navy helicopter pilot. Yonkman worked for a small Washington think tank called Civic Enterprises, which had been founded by John Bridgeland, a former director of George W. Bush's Office of Faith-Based and Community Initiatives. She had studied the various organizations serving returning veterans — there were more than 200,000, but few seemed to reflect the spirit of this new generation, and more than a few were outright scams, raising money, allegedly, for veterans but distributing only a tiny fraction of what they raised. One exception that Yonkman found was The Mission Continues, and it was tiny.

She latched on to Greitens and picked his brain about ways to make service a more accessible option to help returning veterans make the transition to private life. She and

Bridgeland spent the next five months planning an all-star Veterans Day release for the study, a conference that would feature speeches by the First Lady and Dr. Jill Biden announcing their joint effort to help veterans, Joining Forces. Eric, and a handful of veterans who had actually volunteered in their communities, would also speak.

"Mike! I need you in my office," Eric said a few weeks before the event.

Uh-oh. Every time the summons came, Mike knew, the probability was pain. And now Eric told him about the ceremony in Washington, featuring the First Lady, and said, "I want you to speak for us."

Mike was terrified but also excited. He really wanted to tell the world about The Mission Continues. He had given speeches about veterans back home in Washington, but this was a very different Washington. Michelle Obama would be there. It would be televised. He worked late into the night at the office and presented Eric with a draft a few days before the ceremony.

"Well, you've made a start," Eric said. "You're here," he added, raising his left hand, palm down, just over his desk. "I need you to be here." Eric raised his right hand, palm down, several feet over his head. "I need you to inspire them."

The speech, about two and a half minutes long, is recorded for posterity on YouTube. Mike seems somber, disciplined. He talks briefly, in a restrained way, about how he quit school, lost his wife, and had his best friend commit suicide when he came home from the war. He talks about how service gave him a sense of purpose, saved his life. The presentation is crisp, fairly confident — not a barn burner, not Mike at his passionate best (which was probably a necessary precaution, given Mike's Vesuvian tendencies) — but good enough to win an ovation from the audience and a thumbs-up from Greitens.

After the Joining Forces ceremony, Eric had a sense that the world was about to rush his way. It seemed inevitable that The Mission Continues would be drawing more attention and funding now, and it just wasn't ready to handle all that. He called Mary Yonkman a few weeks after the Veterans Day ceremony and said, "Mary, you did an excellent job. The report is fantastic. But what are you going to do now? You can continue to work in Washington, D.C., and think great thoughts, or you can come and work for me in St. Louis and make this happen."

Then Eric lowered his voice, from pitch to plea, and said, "I just want you to keep in mind that this is *your husband's* generation of veterans, and you'll live with this for the rest of your life."

The next day, Yonkman walked into Bridgeland's office and said she was going to work for The Mission Continues.

On April 1, 2010, Eric dispatched Mike Pereira to Los Angeles to make the TMC pitch in a contest to win an $8,000 grant, organized by mobilize.org. Ten different veterans' groups would try to sell their ideas, and one hundred veterans, gathered by the sponsor, would vote on which was best. The event was held in one of those dreary airport hotels near LAX, but the feeling in the place — again, the camaraderie — was warm and easy. Mike met Kaj Larsen for the first time, who was there to cheer on the cause — and Eric was there, too, to give the keynote address in the morning; he left immediately thereafter. The ten-minute grant presentations began in the afternoon.

Mike was looser this time, and more personal. He talked about the program for the elderly that he and his fellow veterans had started in Bellingham, how that experience had turned him around, and how The

Mission Continues was unique in its quest to make veterans whole and purposeful through community service. The reaction to his pitch was very good, he thought.

But after he spoke, three Marine noncoms got up and talked about how they had provided disaster relief after the Haiti earthquake two months earlier. Jake Wood led the presentation with slides of the devastation and slides of Team Rubicon members saving lives, saving *babies'* lives — uh-oh, Pereira thought, these guys have their shit together — and then Will McNulty talked about how the trip had been organized with help from the Jesuits. Finally, Clay Hunt told his story, about how he had been flailing around since he'd come home from the war, how he'd even contemplated suicide, but in Haiti, for the first time, his problems just didn't seem so serious anymore.

That night, Mike sought out the Team Rubicon guys at dinner. "Hey, why don't you guys think about becoming Mission Continues fellows?"

"Why would we want to do that?" Jake asked.

"Because we'll pay you a stipend to do what you're already doing for free."

"What's the catch?"

Well, when you came right down to it, there was no catch, other than making an application and writing an essay.

Clay reminded Jake that *this* was the program he'd mentioned on the plane home from Santo Domingo. Eric Greitens was the Navy SEAL dude. "They also have Kaj Larsen," McNulty said. Kaj had gotten a job as a television journalist, doing real investigative reporting from all over the world for *Vanguard* on Al Gore's Current cable channel. McNulty was a fan. He had spotted Kaj during a break that afternoon and said, brilliantly, "You're Kaj Larsen."

"And you're the guy from Team Rubicon," Kaj replied. "I'd like to come along with you on one of your missions, do a story about it."

Wow. Was it going to be that easy?

Kaj made the TMC fellowship pitch to McNulty that afternoon, but William was ineligible because he hadn't been wounded downrange. Clay had been shot in the wrist, though, and had a PTSD rating; and Jake had his foot, which had required yet another surgery after the Afghanistan deployment.

Team Rubicon won the $8,000 grant the next day. The Mission Continues finished a very close second in the voting. But Mike Pereira left LA stoked: Jake and Clay had said they would apply for fellowships. They were exactly the sort of fellows Eric had had in mind. Mike had lost the competition, but he believed he'd come home with a bigger prize.

In December 2010, Eric went to Spokane for the holidays. On the day before Christmas, he asked Sheena to go with him on an errand — he'd always liked the English tradition of Christmas crackers with crepe-paper crowns and tiny gifts in them. He took her to a dollar store and got a bunch of joke gifts — Groucho glasses, a fake hand grenade, candy — and went home to wrap them. After dessert on Christmas night, the family opened their gifts. And then Sheena opened hers, a small box with an engagement ring inside.

"Will . . . will you . . ." Eric was suddenly very nervous. The room was silent, in mid-gasp. "Will you marry me?"

Sheena said yes and began to cry, then her mother and sister and everyone was crying and hugging. Later, Eric fell asleep on the couch, watching a British Premier League soccer match. Sheena was touched by this public display of sheer comfort. "Well," her mother said. "That's good to know. He has an off switch."

CHAPTER 6
MY LIFE IS A TRAIN WRECK

Chile wasn't as compelling a mission for Team Rubicon as Haiti had been. It was a developed country; there was a disaster relief infrastructure. The Chilean Army took charge of post-quake operations, which left TR with not that much to do aside from occasional first aid work. But it was good to be back together again — Jake, William, Clay, the super-medic Mark Hayward, and Zack Smith, a firefighter from Sacramento. They landed in Argentina and crossed the Andes in taxis, a rousing ride along switch-back roads. The Chilean Army asked them to do reconnaissance in the seaside towns north and south of ground zero, and they did — it was nice to be doing *something* — but they were seeing only a handful of patients a day. Helicopters were dropping tons of food and medical supplies. The hospitals were fully staffed. They went home after a week.

Jake and McNulty figured there would still be a need for Team Rubicon in the more desperate places on earth, but after Chile, they realized there were limits to its potential — and Jake was more convinced than ever that this was going to be a part-time thing in his life. He had been accepted to UCLA business school on a full ride; he and Indra were set in her apartment near Pasadena.

Clay was alone in Santa Monica now; Robin had left and taken all the furniture. Clay's mom flew in and tried to make the empty place a home. She bought him sheets and pillows and towels, stuff for the kitchen. He seemed okay to her, but drifting. Spring semester at Loyola Marymount was lost — he received incompletes in all his classes — but he was determined to return in the fall. The VA hadn't come through with his disability benefits yet. He had the $1,000 a month from The Mission Continues, but no other sources of income. He certainly wouldn't be able to keep the Santa Monica apartment if he didn't find work of some sort, especially if the VA didn't come through. Indra gave him a key to their place; he would come over, unbidden, when he was feeling down and lay it all on Jake. Taking care of Clay was a heavy burden, and

Indra began to wonder if the Band of Brothers thing might not be the untrammeled fabulousness that they made it out to be.

McNulty saw Clay frequently during the summer of 2010 as well. He had decided to move to Los Angeles — it would be a much more convenient locale for his Title X film company — and he bunked with Clay when he came to town, looking for a place to rent. They hung out with Kaj Larsen, running on the beach, working out, chasing girls. Clay was itching for another TR deployment, thinking about going back to Haiti on his own.

Kaj became an easy liaison between The Mission Continues and Team Rubicon, able to bridge the cultural gap between Eric's rectitude and Jake's casual charisma. Eventually Kaj would serve on the boards of both organizations. His real-life career was going well: he had moved on from Current TV to CNN's investigative unit, and he figured that Team Rubicon's next mission would make for a great story.

It came that August, when the torrential waters from an epic monsoon season in Pakistan cascaded down from the Hindu Kush and flooded the Indus River Valley. Millions of people were displaced; thousands were dying of waterborne diseases like cholera. As Jake and Will began to plan the mission — Will would lead it; Jake and Clay would stay home and go to school for real — McNulty received a phone call from Dr. Eduardo Dolhun, one of the original eight in Haiti, who was desperate to get to Pakistan.

Dolhun had a family practice in San Francisco and an idealistic streak — like Jake, he'd simply bought a plane ticket and decided to see if he could help in Haiti. He knew his way around disaster areas and was especially obsessed with cholera, a disease that was essentially a vicious form of diarrhea. It was the second greatest killer of children in the world; an estimated 1.9 million died each year (pneumonia was first and malaria third). The worst part was that there was a simple treatment for cholera, used and distributed by the UN's World Health Organization (WHO) — a magic mix of glucose and salts that immediately rehydrated the body — but the WHO formula had a severe limitation: it tasted horrible. It worked wonders when transmitted intravenously, but no one seemed to want to swallow it. There were commercial versions of the product — the most popular was Gatorade — but those messed with the essential WHO formula, adding in more sugar and reducing the salt. That was fine for sweaty athletes in the heat of a game, but too much sugar dehydrated the body and would only speed the death of a cholera patient.

Dolhun decided to experiment with the WHO formula, reducing the salt slightly, adding flavoring to the mixture. He worked on it for years, through research fellowships at the University of California Medical School and Johns Hopkins University. He had talked nonstop about Oral Rehydration Solutions (ORS) in Haiti, about the lives they were losing that could be saved. He was still experimenting with his formula. By August 2010, though, he had something he thought would work. He had a batch produced and packaged in eighty-eight-pound bags, which he would ship to Pakistan. He called his product Drip-Drop.

And Drip-Drop was the star of the show when Team Rubicon deployed to western Punjab. The conditions were worse than Haiti because such a vast area was affected, the government response was feeble, and the problem was compounded every day as more and more people drank the filthy floodwaters to survive and then fell ill. The TR team flew into Islamabad, and then traveled in vans down into Punjab, where a doctor, Yasmina Rashid, sent them with translators to one of the more remote areas, the town of Muzaffargarh. They had to walk the last miles in flooded muck, toting the Drip-Drop sacks.

Kaj Larsen recorded all of this for CNN, eventually editing it down to two five-minute reports. The highlight was an infant named Ali, who was near death, comatose, limbs floppy. Kaj's camera crew shot Will McNulty picking up the baby and taking him to Dolhun, who fed him Drip-Drop orally through a syringe. Within minutes the baby was alive, crying, hungry, thirsty, revived. The stuff actually worked.

Word of the magic potion spread through Muzaffargarh, and crowds began to gather. At night, the Team Rubicon crew would sit at a table — like drug dealers harvesting a haul — separating the Drip-Drop into plastic baggies, which they'd distribute with clean water in the mornings. This was Dolhun's ultimate test: whether the parents themselves could administer it to their children. They could. For two weeks, Team Rubicon moved from village to village distributing and administering Drip-Drop until their supply ran out.

There was excitement back in California. Team Rubicon now had two strategic advantages when it came to disaster relief — their military skills and Drip-Drop. First Lady Michelle Obama had seen Kaj's reports on CNN, and in late September she mentioned TR as a group that was doing really important things in a speech to a packed crowd of potential funders at the Clinton Global Initiative. She even mentioned Jake by name — but he had mixed feelings about that. The publicity was nice but sort of phony. He hadn't been able to go to Pakistan; McNulty had led the mission. Jake was just another MBA student at UCLA . . . and, he had to admit, school just wasn't very interesting compared to saving lives in West Punjab.

And then Dolhun made Jake an offer: come work for Drip-Drop, be our COO. "We can build this business together," Dolhun said. "We can build it through TR missions and start marketing it throughout the world. We can take it to the WHO and have a comparison test with their product." The doctor loved the idea of Jake as a front man — handsome, articulate, an obsessed military humanitarian. Jake was tempted, but careful. He had promised Indra that he would get his MBA and settle down. He was excited, though; there were all sorts of possibilities now.

■ ■ ■ ■

After skipping the spring semester of 2010 at Loyola Marymount, Clay tried again in the fall. He was really motivated this time. He wanted to be like Mark Hayward, the super-medic who had been so brilliant in Haiti and Chile. But his brain was fried, he couldn't retain anything, he had trouble retrieving words, and he had trouble sitting still in class. He tried different combinations of drugs at the VA, but nothing seemed to work — he would be woozy or antsy or nauseated or scattered. He was worried about money, too. He hadn't received his G.I. Bill education benefits because of the wasted spring semester, so he had paid for the fall semester with his credit card. He was still waiting to hear from the VA about an enhanced disability rating because he was now suffering from both post-traumatic stress and a traumatic brain injury. He couldn't afford the apartment anymore and moved out. He spent some nights at Audrey Nitschka's house and others with John Wordin at his home in the San Fernando Valley.

On September 15, Susan Selke received a call from her son. "Mom, you may have to come get me," he said. "I can't function very well."

"I can't get there tonight, Clay," she replied. He sounded terrible, scared and shaky. She was terrified. "I can get there tomorrow. Can you get to the VA? Can you drive yourself there?"

"Yeah, I can do that."

"You do that, and then call me when you get there."

But Susan wasn't convinced that Clay could or would do that, so she called Wordin. "John, I don't know what to do. I'm in Texas. I'm coming tomorrow . . . but he cannot be by himself tonight."

"I'll call him right now," Wordin replied. "I'll get him to come here." Even if Clay managed to deliver himself into the impersonal bureaucratic maw of the VA, Wordin feared that he might be left sitting alone in a bleak, fluorescent waiting room for hours, which would be the very worst thing for him. "I'm calling him on the other phone right now," he told Susan. Wordin reached Clay, who actually was on the way to the VA, and told him to turn around and drive to his house.

A day later, it was as if nothing had happened. "I'm not sure what was going on," Clay said to his mother.

"You were a mess," Susan said.

"I know."

"I can still come out there and get you."

"No, I'm okay here with John. I'm going to live here with him for a while. He's got an extra room. I'm going to help him build some bikes for the next challenge ride." He sounded strong, firm, almost normal.

As the weeks passed, Wordin began to get a better picture of Clay's illness. If John let him, Clay could go on, obsessively, about how he'd let down his fellow Marines in Iraq. The exact same words, the same stories every time, the same guilt. That was one of his fixations. The other was Afghanistan: how useless and stupid a war it was, how backward the people were. "It was surreal, John," he'd say. "They had no idea that we were trying to help them. And they were probably right. I don't know that we were helping at all. I think we probably weren't. We watched Echo, Fox, and Golf do company-sized sweeps through Taliban lands — they were always 'successful' and then the Taliban would come back. We didn't accomplish a fucking thing."

Sometimes Wordin found Clay up by himself at two or three in the morning and suggested, "Don't you think you should try to sleep?" But the only way for Clay to sleep was Ambien, and John wasn't convinced that, or the fusillade of other pills that Clay had been prescribed, was doing much good.

What worked was work. If Wordin could keep him busy in the bicycle shop, Clay was fine — in fact, he was excellent in the shop, helping to build hand-crank bikes for paraplegics and customized models for double, triple, and, in one case, a quadruple amputee. They built a pull-along bike for a quadriplegic named Chuck, which they called the Chuck Wagon. Clay worked quietly, with a purpose — and then, after they cleaned up for the day, he would play catch or shoot hoops, or he'd play Xbox with Wordin's son, Josh. He was terrific with Josh; they were like two kids playing together.

Clay's parents would call each day, sometimes both Stacy and Susan, asking for a report. When Clay spent the night at Audrey Nitschka's house, his mom would find him there, too. Susan didn't mind that Clay called Audrey his "second mom." Sometimes a kid just needed someone like that in his life, and she wanted all the eyes-on supervision she could get for Clay. Audrey had all the time of the day and night for him. They would watch television, and then they would stay up and talk.

"I think Jake and William are getting sick of me calling," Clay said one night. "I bum them out. All I can talk about is this shit."

"Yeah, well," Audrey said, "that makes two of us. All I can talk about is this shit, too." She'd never really recovered from her son's death; it was as if she had PTSD, too. She went to a shrink who said she was suffering from agoraphobia, anxiety, and depression. Her marriage had fallen apart, but she had found a boyfriend who was *extremely* understanding — even when Clay, who seemed to have no boundaries, would come into their bedroom in the middle of the night and want to talk. There were times, too, when Clay would call in from some bar, bruised and shit-faced, and her boyfriend would go retrieve him.

Audrey and Clay compared medications. He was on Lexapro, Ambien, Valium, and several other drugs. She was on Xanax.

"I just feel like I'm so fucking damaged," he said.

"Clay, we're all damaged," she said, but she worried about him. There were times when Clay was just crazy amped — she wondered if he was bipolar — and he'd talk about going to live in Haiti or becoming a ski bum in Colorado or reenlisting in the Marines.

337

"Clay, you don't want to do that," she said. "Please don't go back in."

"I was good at it."

But look where it landed you, she thought. She didn't say it, because she didn't want to compound his agony. His best times, in a way, were with her daughter, Taylor, Blake's half sister. He would shoot hoops with her, attend her basketball games, go to her dance recitals. Taylor called Clay her "pretend" brother. Audrey had mixed feelings about that, too.

Jake lasted a semester at UCLA business school. He could handle the MBA material, but it lacked the rush and import of a Team Rubicon deployment. In late autumn of 2010, Dr. Dolhun finally convinced him to become COO of Drip-Drop. "It's entrepreneurial and humanitarian," Jake told Indra. "It just makes sense for me."

"Just be sure you sign a contract," she told him, assuming that he wouldn't. And he didn't: there was too much else to do; the legal stuff was a diversion. There was a marketing plan to concoct, and there were obvious potential customers to contact — the U.S. military, the UN relief agencies, the Red Cross — there was the overwhelming question of how to bring the product to scale. Jake was commuting up to San Francisco for organizational meetings with Dolhun.

There were still plenty of Team Rubicon things that needed to be done in preparation for the next mission — fund-raising, publicity, stocking equipment on both coasts. McNulty tried to get Clay to do some of the bureaucratic chores, like getting permits from the city of Los Angeles to store the array of medicines they used on disaster operations, but Clay whiffed on them. He was too scattered and scared, and sometimes he couldn't leave the house, whichever house he happened to be living in at that moment. Worse, he was calling Will all the time now — and it was always the same Ancient Mariner routine: everything was awful, he was depressed, he was having problems with the VA. By late fall, William dreaded seeing Clay's number come up on his phone. Sometimes, to his own horror, he wouldn't pick up.

Jake was burdened by Clay's calls as well. He just didn't have time for all the bitching and moaning, even from a brother, and he felt heartsick about that . . . because it was so easy to be an asshole. You would say to yourself: I'll call him back later. And then you'd get involved in something else, and later would slip by and never happen.

In early December, Jake got a phone call from Audrey Nitschka. "Have you seen Clay?" she asked. "He spent last night with us and he was supposed to go to Taylor's recital, but he told me this morning he wasn't coming because he just couldn't handle it. And now I can't find him anywhere. Jake, I'm really worried."

Clay answered Jake's call on the first ring. "Hey, dude, you're freaking out Audrey," Jake said.

"I know," Clay said. "I wasn't answering because I felt guilty about not going to Taylor's thing."

"So why didn't you go?"

"Because I keep thinking about Blake," Clay said. "I'm in a bad place right now."

Jake told Clay to meet him at the Pasadena apartment. He bought a case of beer and asked Indra to go upstairs. "Clay's not good," he said. "I've got to deal with this."

Clay was shaking visibly when he arrived. Jake could tell that he'd been crying. "Hey . . . hey, dude, what's going on?" Jake asked.

"I feel guilty about Blake," he said.

"Why should *you* feel guilty?" After all, Jake figured *he* was the one who should have died on the bridge that night, if Rosenberger had only let him lead the convoy. "You weren't even there."

"I suck at everything. My life's a fucking train wreck." And he began to recite his personal stations of the cross.

"Hey, let's hit the reset button," Jake said, "and get your mind off this."

They went out to hear some live music at a local dive, but Clay remained catatonic, shaky. When they returned to the apartment, he collapsed, crying. It was shocking; Jake had never seen him this bad. And again, Clay sobbed and talked about how he'd failed at everything — he had dropped out of Loyola Marymount; he hadn't made it through recon school; he was a failure at marriage. "I know I'm dragging you down, Jake," he said. "I've been thinking about using the gun. Really thinking about it."

"C'mon, dude, you don't want to do that." Jake tried to comfort him. He didn't know what to say.

"I don't have any fucking idea *what to do*," Clay said. "Maybe I should drop all this shit, go to Colorado and be a ski bum. That's the only place I've ever been happy."

The only place he'd ever been happy? Jake had seen Clay happy plenty of times in California, happy for long periods of time. He'd been happy in Haiti. He'd been happy in D.C. Jake knew that Clay expected him to be responsible, to tell him, "You're an idiot. Stop acting like a baby. Get your shit together. Get back into school." But Jake was in the midst of his own process of dropping out — and he knew that Loyola Marymount had been torture for Clay. School would only make him worse.

"Look, I think you've got two choices," Jake said. "You can go to Colorado, have some fun, chill out or . . ." Jake hesitated here. "Or you can go back to Haiti. We're trying to arrange a trip with the International Medical Corps to go down and work on the cholera epidemic there. They need teams to go to the remote towns, up in the hills, and set up clinics there. We may go right after the first of the year, if we have the money for it. But I'll fucking bankrupt Team Rubicon to send you there, if you think it will help you get your shit together."

Clay brightened immediately. This sounded like a plan. He would go to Colorado and do some snowboarding. Maybe he'd go to Houston and see his parents for the holidays. And then, he'd go back to Haiti. It would be exactly a year since the earthquake.

He lasted two weeks in Colorado. He moved into a basement apartment with some friends, but felt claustrophobic. A big storm was coming, he told his mother, and he could be trapped there for weeks.

"Then leave right now," Susan said. "Come home."

Home was, in a way, more stable than it had ever been before. Both Stacy and Susan had remarried — and, as they struggled through the Clay situation together, they had actually become friends again. Susan and her husband were just moving into a new house, so Clay stayed with his father and stepmother. Stacy had plenty of friends in the construction business, and he found Clay a job as a site superintendent-in-training. Clay liked the idea — it was outside work; he'd be using his hands — and he began to make plans to settle down in Houston. He went to the VA and asked to have his files transferred from Santa Monica.

But before he could really settle in, the Haiti trip materialized. He left in mid-January and stayed for several weeks. He joined Matt Pelak, an Army National Guard Sergeant and Poughkeepsie, New York, firefighter, as the two Team Rubicon representatives. Matt was a classic hyper-efficient TR type: big and quiet, smart in a humble, no-nonsense way. His first mission had been to Pakistan, where he'd impressed McNulty with his utter reliability. "He's solid," McNulty told Jake when they got home.

"Let's make him our East Coast Co-ordinator," Jake said. "He lives in New York. It would be smart to store medicine and equipment on both coasts, right?"

In Haiti, Clay introduced Matt to Brother Jim Boynton before going up into the mountains. Jim was burned out and preparing to leave the country. He said the Haitians had learned nothing from the earthquake. The country was a horror show. Clay was bummed by the visit, but once they arrived in the hill town, he was all business. He was, in fact, exemplary, Matt thought: Clay just dived right in, setting up a tent roof over the clinic, washing down the place, doing some rudimentary first aid work, playing with the kids. When he finished whatever tasks Matt gave him to do, he'd come back for more — with a smile. No wonder Jake and William love the dude so much, Matt thought. Clay was a total pro, a happy camper — he even bolstered the spirits of the rest of the team, some of whom were rookies when it came to disaster relief and were having a tough time handling the devastation, which was stomach-turning. The Haitians didn't understand that if they washed the victims' bedsheets in the filthy river and brought them to the clinic, they would get rid of the stains, but not the germs.

One night Matt and Clay stayed up and talked — they were the only two military veterans on the team; the rest were medical personnel — and Clay told Matt all the old stories about Iraq and Afghanistan and guilt. The tremor in his voice, the repetition of the stories, told Matt a lot more than anything Clay said.

They were staying in a rudimentary guest house, and Matt had been given a very large room with an entirely unexpected king-size bed. In the middle of the night, Clay came in without a word, lay down on the far side of the bed, and fell asleep. He didn't mention it the next morning, so Matt didn't either. It was all, "What do we need to do today?" And he was back at it, radiating happiness and optimism. The Haitians gravitated toward him; he was a rock star in the field.

Matt left that night. Clay stayed on for two weeks, then went home to Houston and found that the VA hadn't been able to move his records from California. They were lost somewhere. They had disappeared in Muskogee, Oklahoma — at least, that was what one of the desultory geeks in the VA office told him. He came back a week later and found that there might be another possibility: the computer in Houston was having trouble communicating with the computer in Santa Monica. Or something. But still no medical records.

He started the construction job, which was okay some of the time. It kept him busy, but it didn't have the satisfactions of Haiti. He thought about taking the exam to become a firefighter. Matt Pelak loved the job and had talked to Clay about it in Haiti. It was sort of like the military, Matt said. It was organized and an opportunity to help people. "It's not as good as TR because we don't run it," Matt told him the night of their long conversation. "You've got a bureaucracy, you have to get approvals for some things or wait while the higher-ups decide which way to go. But it's good work."

Clay kept at the construction job. The physical part was good, and the pay was great; the crew was mostly Mexican, hard workers, fine people. He would go out with them after work; he began dating.

"Dad, I've got to find a place of my own," he said to Stacy in early February.

"Why?"

"Well, if I meet a lady," Clay said, smiling,

"it's kind of hard to say, 'Hey, wanna go to my dad's house for a drink?' "

Stacy laughed. "Well, we've got plenty of apartments." He gave Clay a list of some of the vacant units in complexes that his company managed. Clay chose one in Sugarland, on the southwest side of town, an area chockablock with recent immigrants, especially Arabs. Some of the women in the complex wore hijab. There was a halal grocery store on the corner. Clay wasn't aware of the demographics until he moved in and then he told his mother that the place freaked him a bit; it reminded him of Iraq — but he was working, had started dating a very nice young woman; he seemed better than he'd been in California.

Except for the VA, which was driving him nuts. His papers still hadn't arrived from California, and now he had to replace them. They asked him to fill out a long, maddening form, listing his entire medical history, which Clay found impossible. He tried to remember his various maladies and hospital visits in chronological order: When had he first gone to the VA for PTSD? Which drugs had he taken? The very process of filling out the form sent him into a slide. He needed to get his Lexapro prescription filled. An appointment was set for early February, but it was with a psychologist, who couldn't prescribe medications. He had to go to a *psychiatrist.* The soonest possible appointment with a VA psychiatrist was early March.

The psychiatrist prescribed the Lexapro and sent Clay to the VA pharmacy, where he waited for more than two hours before a clerk told him they were out of the drug. "We can mail you some as soon as we get it in," the clerk said.

"How long will *that* take?" Clay asked.

"Ten days to two weeks."

Clay stormed out. He had missed an entire day's work — for nothing. He called his mother and said, "I won't go back to that damn place. I don't know what to do. I don't think I can wait two weeks, Mom."

Susan asked a friend for some Lexapro, and she was able to get enough pills to tide Clay over until the prescription arrived in the mail.

Jake called Clay in March. He said that he was going to India on vacation with Indra and his sister for a couple of weeks. Things were going well with Drip-Drop. There was the possibility of another TR mission, this time to a real war zone — Libya — in partnership, once again, with the International Medical Corps. Clay was ready to roll.

"So how's work?" Jake asked.

"It's work." It wasn't Team Rubicon; he wasn't helping anybody. He wasn't helping himself. "I need the team," he said. "I'm thinking about reenlisting with the Marines."

Jake had heard it all before. But he'd do what he could to keep feeding Clay new missions.

"Hey, Mom, you doing anything on Friday?" Clay asked Susan near the end of March.

"No. Why?"

"I'm getting myself a new truck." He was moving up to a Toyota Tacoma. "It's bigger. I need it to haul my tools and stuff around for work. Plus it's a really cool truck. I'd like you to take a look before I buy it."

This was good news, Susan thought. Buying the truck seemed a statement: Clay was settling in. He had the cash to buy himself something expensive. It was spring in Houston; flowers were blooming before the heat and humidity got crazy. Susan allowed herself a moment of hope.

Clay showed the truck to Stacy on Saturday and they went out to lunch to celebrate.

Clay wasn't talking much about his plans, but he wasn't talking about his problems either. In fact, Stacy was the one who raised PTSD that day. He and some real estate friends had agreed to help a local group of recent veterans build a retreat called Camp Hope, where they could do a lot of the outdoorsy things that Clay liked to do. "They're having a meeting on Wednesday. Maybe you could go, tell them your story, tell them about Team Rubicon. These are all guys with PTSD and maybe you could help them."

"Sure," Clay said, but Stacy sensed he wasn't very interested, which was odd: Clay usually got all het up over veterans' programs.

Clay went to dinner and a movie with his mom and stepdad that night. He wanted to see *The Lincoln Lawyer,* but Susan and Richard had already seen it. Instead, they went to see *Limitless,* a tense, mind-bending movie in which Bradley Cooper plays a blocked writer who becomes omnipotent after he takes a secret drug.

Clay seemed okay going in, although he did insist on sitting down in the handicapped row — his lone seat was the closest to the door. Susan and Richard sat farther along the row, past the spaces for wheelchairs, but Susan had a clear view of her son, who seemed completely immersed in the movie. And as she watched, she began to worry that this was probably not the best thing for Clay to see — there were harrowing scenes in which the main character became addicted to the drug. But he learned how to control the addiction. Eventually, he was stronger and smarter than ever. She watched her son, transfixed by the movie, alone at the end of the row.

Stacy called Susan the next day. He told her about Camp Hope, and how he thought it might be a good thing for Clay to go to the meeting on Wednesday. Maybe she could nudge him. "Maybe you could go with him," Stacy said. "I'm going to be in Austin. He could tell them about Team Rubicon and that might help them."

"*Clay's* the one who needs help," Susan replied, but she thought the meeting might be good for him and told Stacy she would call Clay on Monday. She usually called Clay every day. There was no answer on Monday, so she left a message. He didn't call back. She called again on Tuesday with the same result. She was beginning to get worried. Clay was usually pretty good about returning her calls. And nothing again, on

351

Wednesday. She called Stacy to see if he knew anything.

On Thursday morning, March 31, Stacy called her from Austin. "Susan, apparently Clay hasn't shown up for work the past few days. Have you been in contact with him?"

"No, and I'm worried," she said. "I'm going right over to the apartment."

She raced over and saw both Clay's old and new trucks in the parking lot. So he was there. Maybe he'd just gone on a bender. She banged on the door as hard as she could; no answer. The apartment was on the ground floor, and she tried looking through the windows, banging on them and screaming crazily, "Clay, it's Mom! Mom's here!" But nothing.

She called her husband, Richard, who said he'd come right over. She called Stacy, who said he'd get the building manager over there right away. The building manager, a woman, came with the keys, but the door to Clay's apartment was dead-bolted, and she said she'd send some maintenance people with a crowbar. Susan handed the woman her phone and said, "Dial 911. He's a veteran and he's had some suicidal thoughts in the past." She slumped down then and pushed her back hard against the brick wall of Clay's apartment, trying to be as close to her son as she possibly could.

The Fort Bend County Sheriff's Offi[ce] arrived about the same time as the mainte nance people with the crowbar. The cop[s] came in force, as did the maintenance people — five of them with a crowbar. Sud denly there were police lights spinning; sud denly there was a crowd. It was like a scene from a movie. Just a moment ago, Susan had been alone.

One of the maintenance men started working the crowbar. The police drew their guns. "No!" Susan screamed. "You don't have to do that. He's fine," she added hope fully. "He's just asleep."

"Is he armed?" the police asked.

"He does have weapons," she admitted — but that seemed irrelevant, ridiculous. Everything was so far past that now. "He's a veteran and he does have firearms."

"Well," the lead police officer said, "then we have to do this."

The maintenance man was the first through the door, and he came out wide- eyed. He couldn't speak English, but he gestured hopelessly with his hands. Nothing else needed to be said.

Susan made a move for the door, but the lead detective stopped her. "You don't want to see this," he said. "He's been dead about

ay and you don't want to see this . . .
is is not the memory you want."

A few weeks later, Susan Selke received a
letter from the Department of Veterans Affairs addressed to Clay. She could barely
handle it; it seemed radioactive. She struggled to open it and then read: Clay's claim
had finally been processed, after two years
of trying. He had received a 100 percent
disability rating for post-traumatic stress
disorder.

■ ■ ■ ■

PART IV
THEIR MISSION
CONTINUED

■ ■ ■ ■

CHAPTER 1
LEGACY

Jake was in a Mexican restaurant in Huntington Beach with William and several other core Team Rubicon members. His phone rang, a 713 area code number he didn't know, so he let it go to voice mail. It rang again, then again. What was 713? Houston, he realized. He picked up the phone on the third ring.

"Is this Jake Wood?" a woman said.

"Yes."

"Could you hold for Stacy Hunt?"

Jake went out to the street, his mind racing — immediately fixing on *his* responsibility, *his* letting Clay down those past few months. Clay was hurt, was dead. He was probably dead. "Please don't let it be suicide," he said aloud. If it wasn't suicide, if it was just a car crash, he could live with that.

Stacy came on the phone, shattered. "Well, Jake, we lost him."

"What do you *mean*?" Jake responded fiercely.

"Clay. He's dead. He shot himself."

They continued talking, mouths flapping, arrangements . . . Jake would call Robin, Audrey, the other Marines . . . the funeral would be . . . Stacy and Susan would . . .

And Jake felt his knees go out from under him. After fifteen minutes, McNulty went outside to see what was going on, and Jake was on the ground, in fetal position, sobbing.

When Jake looked back on it, everything that had happened in March 2011 was of one piece, a calibrated series of events intended to punish him for his complicity in Clay's death. His car had been broken into, and his wallet was gone — credit cards, license, and everything. He had to have two root canals; his face was pounding. And then his Drip-Drop job was snatched away from him suddenly, and rather violently. He had sensed that something squirrelly was afoot for weeks. Eduardo Dolhun was involved in negotiations with a military contractor who wanted to buy a piece of the company. Jake thought this was a good idea at first. It was the quickest, easiest way to move to scale: the contractor knew how to sell to the U.S. military — Drip-Drop would be a natural product for them to stock — and he had other potential clients throughout the Gulf region. The contractor also promised that he would make a major grant to Team Rubicon.

But the tone of Dolhun's emails was sliding south, ever more evasive, in the days before Jake was supposed to leave with Indra and his sister for a vacation to India. For some reason, the military contractor didn't like the idea of Team Rubicon going to Libya with International Medical Corps. Jake tried to find out why. No answer. He made a last-minute check of his email in the LAX departure lounge, and there was one from Dolhun: the contractor didn't want Jake to be COO of Drip-Drop any longer.

Jake sent an email to Dolhun: "Does that mean I'm fired?"

He received the answer in Mumbai: "Yes."

Wow. Now he had . . . nothing. Indra, as usual, had been right: she could have gone double I-Told-You-So. She had told him to finish the MBA; she had told him to get a signed contract from Dolhun. He had a contract, sort of — but it was a flimsy document, worthless. Dolhun was one of the original eight in Haiti; he was a stepbrother, sort of. Drip-Drop had become an integral part of recent Team Rubicon missions. It saved lives. It had never occurred to Jake *not* to trust Dolhun.

And then, Clay's death. Jake had absolutely no doubt that he was responsible. He was clear on that. He thought about all the things he should have done, all the phone calls he should have answered. He knew that he had abandoned his post; he had pushed his brother away. He thought about Clay at his best, in Haiti, surrounded by children. The thoughts swirled and ramified: What kind of an asshole am I to let him die like that?

Jake made it through Clay's funeral, fueled by beer and his sense of responsibility — he had to hold it together for Clay's family. Stacy Hunt felt culpable for Clay's death, too. There was a lifetime of things he could have done; there were all of his impatient reactions to Clay's ADHD. Jake comforted him, told Stacy there was nothing he could have done, and he did so with real conviction. Because Jake knew the truth: *he* was the one responsible for Clay's death.

Mike Pereira went down to Houston for Clay's funeral as the official representative of The Mission Continues, carrying Eric

Greitens's condolences. Clay was the first TMC fellow to kill himself, but he was not well-known in St. Louis. Jake and Clay had been left to their own devices, starting Team Rubicon; they'd had less contact with the TMC staff than most fellows did. Eric barely knew him. But Mike did: he had spent a lot of time on the phone with Clay, especially toward the end.

Mike had known what was happening. He'd heard the near-death voice twice before, with his mentor Tim Nelson in Bellingham, whom he had failed, and with Ian Smith, whom he had helped to save. Actually, three times: he remembered his own death voice and the cruelly impersonal taste of cold steel in his mouth. He tried everything with Clay. He would talk about what Clay had accomplished in Haiti and how to bottle it. That worked, sometimes. Mike would try to widen the focus, talk about Clay's life as a hero's journey, talk about Homeric values. At times, Clay could be lured out of his despair; toward the end, though, he was less responsive. "The world is dead to me," he told Mike.

But that was part of the process, Mike argued. The hero *comes back* from the near-death experience . . .

Jake Wood, shattered, gave a beautiful

eulogy at the funeral. Afterward, Mike, Jake, Will McNulty, Matt Pelak, and Paul Rieckhoff of IAVA pulled away from the crowd and talked briefly: What were they going to do about this? Clay had been a nexus — integral to IAVA, to The Mission Continues, to Team Rubicon — and they still couldn't stop him from killing himself. Suicide was becoming an epidemic among their brothers and sisters. The Veterans Administration was estimating that twenty-two veterans killed themselves *each day.* (Many were older — Vietnam era — but weren't they brothers, too?)

"He kept saying, 'I'm all alone,' " Mike said. "Isn't that always the way it is?" But how could you — how could *they* — break through that? Jake had no answer. He wavered between catatonia and fury. The night before the funeral, he'd almost gotten into a bar fight with some of the other Marines because he'd kept shouting, "Fuck you, Clay . . . Fuck you . . . You asshole. *Fuck* you."

And now what? Actually, Jake didn't have the wherewithal to think about what came next, but McNulty was lobbying him to drop everything and do Team Rubicon full-time to honor Clay.

"And who pays our salaries?" Jake argued back. "How do we live?" The situation was complicated by the fact that the military contractor who was trying to buy Drip-Drop hadn't delivered on the $100,000 grant to Team Rubicon. In the interim, Jake and McNulty had hired a woman named Joanne, whom Clay had known and recommended from Loyola Marymount, to do the administrative work that no one else had the patience to do. The plan was to pay her out of the $100,000. "How the fuck are we going to pay Joanne?" Jake asked.

"We'll figure it out," William said. "Look, Jake, you know that this idea is a game changer. It can change the world." Having uttered the words, McNulty knew that was precisely the sort of grandiose argument that would not work with Jake, and then he thought of a better one: "It could have saved Clay."

Jake scoffed, but he knew McNulty, as usual, had grabbed onto a piece of the truth: Clay was closest to whole when he was on deployments. But there just weren't that many deployments. International missions were expensive; it cost an average of $3,000 to insert a TR volunteer into an overseas disaster relief role. It was hard to raise enough money to make a significant impact.

At the funeral, Matt Pelak — who had just been with Clay in Haiti — suggested that maybe they could respond to domestic disasters, too. There were lots of those. But what would be their role? Unlike in Haiti, there was plenty of infrastructure in the States. The local authorities were well trained to run things; even the Federal Emergency Management Agency (FEMA) had gotten its act together after Hurricane Katrina had wrecked New Orleans.

Jake and William went to Miami almost immediately after Clay's funeral. They were going to tell their story at one of the social entrepreneurship conferences that seemed to be happening every third week; it was a good way to make contacts and troll for funders. They were in their hotel room the first night, when Jake received a call from Dolhun. He put it on speaker, so McNulty could hear.

"Jake, I'm really sorry. I'm really embarrassed. I did a bad thing," Dolhun began. The deal with the military contractor hadn't worked out. "I couldn't sign the papers," he went on. "I couldn't just sign away Drip-Drop to someone I wasn't sure about."

He wanted Jake back. "We'll really make it work this time," he said.

"I don't know," Jake said, as McNulty

shook his head no-no-no. "You really fucked me, Eduardo. How can I trust you now?"

Jake agreed to think about it. McNulty wanted none of it. "Dude, how can you even think about trusting that asshole?"

"Yeah, but how am I going to make a living?"

Jake looked at William and knew what his answer would be. "I don't know, Will," he said.

"Let's do it for Clay," William replied.

A few days after they returned home to Los Angeles, Joanne retrieved the mail from their post office box. There were bags of it, thousands of letters filled with money — in memory of Clay Hunt. There was $60,000 in small contributions.

"We can pay Joanne," William said. "Jake, let's give this thing a shot. These mailbags are telling us something."

Jake wasn't sure. Team Rubicon would live on because of Clay's death? It seemed ghoulish. On the other hand, there were all these people — thousands of people — who wanted the work to continue.

Eric Greitens reassured the stunned Mission Continues staff on the morning after Clay's death, but he saved his most important words for his core executives privately, after the meeting. "Our attitude toward suicide has to be this: warriors do not commit suicide," he said. "A true warrior helps people. Suicide does the exact opposite. It devastates the people who are closest to the warrior. We should be thoughtful and sympathetic in these cases, but we can't glorify them. We have to send the message that suicide is simply unacceptable."

It was a hard message; some on the staff, especially those who dealt with prospective fellows, found it a little too hard. Mike Pereira believed that Eric was right about the bottom line and — in theory — about the strategy, too. In practice, though, dealing with suicide was more desperate and wrenching than that; it was the toughest thing in the world. Mike loved Eric and thought he was leading The Mission Continues in the right direction, with rigor, but he was growing further away from the lives he hoped to save.

Indeed, Eric was getting ready to move on, and most people at TMC sensed it. His autobiography, *The Heart and the Fist,* had made the *New York Times* best seller list. He was appearing on national television. He had also been wildly successful raising money in 2010; the first segment of a five-year $6.7 million grant from Goldman

Sachs had just arrived. Home Depot was about to kick in $1 million to supply Mission Continues service projects; Target, Southwest Airlines, and several private foundations were on board as well. TMC needed a professional executive who could actually manage the transition from tiny to . . . relatively small.

Eric was scheduled to meet with his first choice for the job, a former Army Black Hawk pilot named Spencer Kympton, the morning after he received the news of Clay Hunt's death. He asked Mary Yonkman to call Kympton and postpone the meeting. "Spence, I've got bad news. We've had our first suicide," Mary told him. "The scene in the office might be tense and emotional tomorrow. It certainly won't be the usual Mission Continues experience. You might want to come another day."

"No," he said softly. "I'd still like to come, if that's all right. Tomorrow is exactly the sort of day I'd like to see The Mission Continues."

Kympton was a West Point graduate from an Army family. He had left the service just after 9/11 and taken a familiar career path for the military's brightest officers: a Harvard MBA (with honors, of course) and then a stint at McKinsey, the Green Berets of corporate consulting. He didn't find the corporate work very satisfying, though. He drifted to the not-for-profit side of McKinsey, fascinated by the burgeoning public school reform movement, and then to full-time work as a Director of Recruiting for Teach For America — a program that Eric considered the gold standard for public service in the civilian sector.

Spencer loved working at Teach For America, but he was an outsider. The rest of the staff had spent two years teaching under duress in desperate schools; they had their own jokes and rituals. He wasn't part of the tribe. By 2011, the travails of Iraq and Afghanistan veterans — including some of Spencer's friends from West Point — had become a big, gruesome story, and he thought: *There's* a culture where I'm an insider. Maybe I can do something to help there.

Spencer was tall, fit, sandy-haired, and soft-spoken. He felt an immediate bond with Eric. They didn't tell war stories. They talked process. Spencer understood that The Mission Continues, up till then, had been inspired chaos. Mary Yonkman had been working on bringing it under control, but Mary was pregnant and going back to live with her husband in Virginia. Eric told him about the big grants from Goldman and Home Depot coming in. He also talked about the fellows and how it felt, as a former military officer, to be leading them again in community work. "How do you feel about getting dirty?" he asked Kympton.

Spencer was thrilled by the prospect.

Mike Pereira knew that his time at The Mission Continues was coming to a close. He had been in a constant roil with the bureaucratizing forces at TMC. There had been some bad scenes. Changes obviously were afoot. Spencer was soon hired and so was a former Army officer named Meredith Knopp, who would be Mike's immediate superior and organize the fellowship program. The Mission Continues was becoming more like the Army: officers and grunts and civilian POGs (Persons Other than Grunts). As always, the grunts felt that the officers were too far from the front lines.

Mike knew that there had to be an officer class if TMC was going to grow. But after Clay's death, he also thought — and Mike was vehement about this — that the fellows had to become a team. They had to get to know and care about one another, even though they were spread across the nation. No TMC fellow should ever again feel as alone as Clay had. He pestered Eric about this, and his pestering meshed perfectly with the thoughts of the officer class: Spencer and Meredith had the same gut feelings, but they talked about them in business school terms, about the program's "identity" and "branding." The Mission Continues didn't have a strong enough "profile" in the nonprofit world; it didn't even have a particularly strong profile among its own fellows — most had a deeper connection with the local charities that sponsored them than they did with St. Louis. "We've done a lousy job organizing our alumni," Spencer told Eric, top down. "And we haven't done much of anything to bond the fellows to the organization."

"These people need to feel more of what we had in the military," Mike Pereira told Eric, bottom up. "People like Clay Hunt need TMC battle buddies they can depend on when things get tough."

A decision was made to bring all the fellows — past, present, and future — together in St. Louis for Veterans Day 2011. They would have a "lessons learned" conference, and then they would have a big public event that would, in effect, announce The Mission Continues 2.0, with three hundred new fellows planned for 2012. They would do it up, have a gala, invite potential funders, make it black tie, host a banquet at the famed Chase Park Plaza, with dinner and dancing. They could add star power by giving an award to some famous supporter of The Mission Continues — Tom Brokaw was soon recruited — and have several of their fellows tell their stories to the TMC funders and local media.

The event was an explosion of unexpected emotion from the start. The fellows, nearly one hundred strong, grabbed hold of one another at the "lessons learned" conference and couldn't seem to let go. There were sessions during which three and four at a time told their stories, sometimes hilariously, sometimes in tears. All sorts of suggestions were made to improve the program; Spencer, Meredith, and the rest of the officer class took furious notes. The similarity of their experiences was ratified by the academic study of fifty-two early fellows Monica Matthieu had done with her Washington University colleagues — and also with Mike Pereira and Ian Smith of The Mission Continues, whose names appeared on the final paper. The results were extremely promising: 86 percent of the fellows reported a positive life-changing experience, 71 percent had gone on to further their education, and 86 percent said the program helped them transfer their military skills to civilian employment. This was especially impressive, given that 52 percent of those studied had suffered traumatic brain injuries, and 64 percent had been diagnosed with post-traumatic stress. Matthieu urged caution. The sample size was tiny. There weren't many of the usual academic regulators, like a control group that hadn't experienced TMC. But there was the smidgen of an inkling of a possibility: it seemed, as she had expected, that community service might be a viable treatment for post-traumatic stress. (A 2013 update of the survey confirmed the 2011 findings.)

That afternoon, Spencer was working out in the hotel gym when he overheard two fellows who'd just finished their PT. "I've got to go upstairs and iron my Mission Continues shirt for the dinner tonight," one said. He said it with great pride and responsibility, and Spencer was moved: Eric really had created a new branch of the service, a new unit, for these young men and women. And this meeting was the missing piece: they had restored camaraderie and unit pride to the tribe.

The next morning, the day of the gala, Ian Smith organized a service project for all the returning fellows and some high-profile members of the St. Louis Rams football team: they would put together eight hundred "reverse" care packages for kids in the community. There were TV cameras; everyone seemed thrilled and happy to be part of the event. Eric walked into the room and saw his father, among others, hard at work. Rob Greitens looked up, beaming. "The energy in this room is amazing," Eric told Ian Smith, grabbing him by the shoulders. "Thank you."

Afterward, Rob approached his son. He was a man who worked to keep his feelings under control. But he was having trouble with that now. "Eric," he said, "this is really good."

"Thanks, Dad," Eric said, unable to say more.

That night, Tom Brokaw was followed to the stage by Army Major Anthony Smith, a huge black man wearing a blazing ivory suit and scarf, with a black collarless shirt that featured an embroidered zircon crucifix in a shield. He began to tell his story: he'd been blown up by a rocket-propelled grenade and left for dead in a body bag. He'd survived only because one of the medics unzipped the bag to get Smith's dog tags and found that he was still breathing. Smith lost an arm and a leg and suffered traumatic brain injury. He spent sixty-four days in a coma and had endless surgeries. And then he started to recover, and then he began to work out. He competed in triathlons, running on a prosthetic leg; he became a karate champion using his hand and his stump, and then he mastered tae kwon do. "But I felt a void," he continued. "I'd spent all my life helping others."

He did his Mission Continues fellowship at the Boys and Girls Club in his hometown of Blytheville, Arkansas, "down by the river, where we black folks live." He started his own martial arts dojo, teaching boys and girls how to defend themselves — and more: "We have six maxims. Be polite. Be patient. Be alert. Be brave. Do your best. And respect yourself and those around you . . . And so that's my story.

"Today, I am known in the military as Major Anthony Smith. I am known in the martial arts community as 'A-Train' . . . but that 'A' doesn't stand for 'Anthony'; it stands for" — and here he leaped into a brilliant falsetto — *"aww-some!"*

The place went wild, and Smith — who seemed perfectly conscious of where everyone was: the fellows on the left-hand side of the audience, the funders and supporters on the right-hand side — turned to the funders and said, "I am a living testament to Never Give Up. I am a *Mission Continues* fellow. Are you ready to help out? Are you ready? Because if you didn't know before, *now you know.*"

There was a mob scene afterward. Everyone wanted pictures taken with Smith and Tom Brokaw. But that wasn't the most memorable thing for The Mission Continues staff: a stream of fellows surrounded them and thanked them and asked, "Why didn't we ever do this before? Can we do this more often?"

Spencer Kympton and Meredith Knopp looked at each other with the same thought: *Can* we do this more often? Within days, they approached Eric with a plan: they would divide the 2012 fellows into four classes — Alpha, Bravo, Charlie, and Delta — and they would begin each class with an orientation and a big community service project. There would be a real induction ceremony. They would take an oath together. They would identify themselves as Mission Continues fellows from day one, as Spencer and Meredith wanted; they would bond as brothers and sisters, as Mike Pereira had hoped.

CHAPTER 2
TRANSFORMATION

A monster tornado touched down in Tuscaloosa, Alabama, less than a month after Clay's death. Hundreds of people were dead; the wreckage was biblical. Team Rubicon put a siren alert on its website, calling for volunteers. McNulty stayed home to run the logistics; Jake went out to run the deployment. He was joined there by old friends like Shawn Beidler, his sniper-team leader, and Matt Pelak, who drove down from Poughkeepsie in his truck, with several chain saws. There were others, several dozen in all, who came and became part of Team Rubicon's national core. A local doctor contributed his hunting camp as an operating base — it was out in the piney woods, down a mile-long dirt road. The living room's rude wood walls were festooned with deer heads; there was a bedroom crammed with bunk beds and a no-frills kitchen.

Team Rubicon was on the ground the day

after the tornado, doing general cleanup work. Matt Pelak's previous TR missions in Pakistan and Haiti had been staffed mostly by medical personnel, but now he was surrounded by fellow veterans. They were doing mucky, heavy, muscular chores. They'd drive up to a house with a tree crashed on the roof and start to work the chain saws and wheelbarrow rubble from the yard. They worked steadily all day, and it was as perfect a mission as you could get. The residents were extremely grateful — and astonished: recent military veterans volunteering to do cleanup work? It was satisfying on the most personal level for Matt; it was making him *feel* good; his endorphins were running. He was very conscious of the people working around him; there were a lot of smiles and backslaps. That night, Jake introduced the team to another Haiti tradition: the nightly debrief, with a couple cases of beer. They set a fire in a pit amidst the loblolly pines, cooked dinner, and sat around the campfire. It was the first time Pelak had experienced anything like it; people were talking emotionally about how much it meant to be together, deployed in this way.

The next day's work was more of the same. But that night, Matt received a text message from his girlfriend: Osama bin Laden was dead. The volunteers raced to their pickup trucks to see if the news was on the radio — but they were so deep in the woods that regular reception was impossible. Eventually a straggler drove up, and he had satellite radio in his truck. They gathered around, and there it was: bin Laden had been killed, shot dead by Navy SEALs. They were screaming and hugging. Eventually, they sat around the campfire and talked about it. The son of a bitch who had started the whole thing, who'd blown up the Twin Towers, whose minions had killed and maimed their brothers and sisters — that sick bastard was finally wasted. Around the campfire, some were weeping as they remembered their losses. "I don't know about you," Jake said, "but right now, I wouldn't want to be anyplace else on earth than with you guys."

Two weeks after Tuscaloosa, there was an even bigger tornado in Joplin, Missouri. Jake was out in Oklahoma, storm-chasing with Indra and some of her meteorologist friends, and he quickly moved to take charge of the Joplin deployment. It was another success.

And then things began to calm down; the spring storms abated. Jake found himself alone — Team Rubicon still didn't have an office — with too much time to think. He was having nightmares. He grew distant, testy, near-mute. Indra wondered: Where did he go?

She also began to wonder about Team Rubicon. The deployments were fabulous. Great work was being done. But they were sort of *narcotic,* too, weren't they? The Band of Brothers would gather together, wear their uniform — gray Team Rubicon T-shirts and red baseball caps — organize themselves into teams, tease one another, knock things down, build things up, impress the civilians with their discipline and efficiency, sit around the campfire drinking beer . . . and then they would come home, alone again, and crash.

Indra believed that Jake had been suffering few of the effects of post-traumatic stress before Clay died. He'd never been a great talker in private; when he wasn't *on* in public, he was the guy in the corner glued to his laptop. But he hadn't been suffering either. The *war* hadn't put him where he was now. There had been some bad memories, but Jake seemed able to handle those. This was different, though; this had been precipitated by Clay's death. Jake's war-related post-traumatic stress hadn't happened in Iraq or Afghanistan. It had happened in Los Angeles. And it wasn't just the shock of Clay's death: it was the corrosive emotional bends, the too-fast decompression that came from leaving the Marines, a tight-knit organization with a sense of higher purpose, and being dumped, alone, in a society with no organized purpose at all except for making money and having fun. Jake had moved, reflexively, toward restoring his military family almost immediately after he left the Marines in October 2009. Within three months, he had organized the Haiti mission, and he'd been on a dead sprint until Clay died. It was subconsciously brilliant: he had lost a community and then he and McNulty had created a community to replace it.

Now he was in full retreat. Indra sensed he was pushing her away, and she was right. Jake was locked in his own prison, under arrest for the death of his friend. He didn't deserve Indra. He had let Clay down; he would let Indra down, too. How could he take responsibility for Indra after what he'd allowed to happen to Clay? Maybe it was better to be dumped; he worked at it almost every day. But Indra was not going to play that game. She was Nordic tough in that way: she had made her commitment to him, even if he seemed to be trying to sneak away. She loved the guy he had been before he checked out — and she was going to force him to check back in again. She was right there, in his face, all the time; she wanted to know what the hell was going on. But he didn't know what was going on. He hoped, on some level, that she would kick him out of the apartment; he didn't have the courage or the strength just to move out. He dreaded that she might kick him out. Where would he go?

Will McNulty had no idea this was happening — in fact, he thought the exact opposite was happening: Jake was becoming a public big shot, and sometimes he was taking too much of the credit for Team Rubicon. There were times Jake didn't even mention his partner, McNulty, when he gave his oo-rah Team Rubicon talks.

Jake was invited to the Clinton Global Initiative, where Bill Clinton himself announced that the CGI would be funding Team Rubicon to train five hundred combat medics. The Big Ten cable sports channel was buzzing around, filming Jake for a big feature on its newsmagazine — the Badger football player who had become a humanitarian all-star. *GQ* magazine was scouting Jake as a possible humanitarian of the year;

he was a finalist, competing against Eric Greitens. The winner would be announced at a celebrity-clotted New York gala in October. (Jake won.)

In September, Jake was invited to preside over the ultimate temple of American masculinity: Monday Night Football. He would introduce, on film, the game between his beloved Green Bay Packers and the Minnesota Vikings. The 57-second spot was filled with all the usual testosterone tricks: trumpets, drums, football players crashing into one another intercut with a Marine drill team doing its thing. And Jake, the coolest guy on the planet, introduced as a *Decorated Marine and Veteran Advocate,* walking through the players' tunnel into a stadium . . .

I was part of a team . . .

Then a full-on shot of Jake, raising his head.

The Marines . . .

Enter the Drill Team.

So I know what it takes to succeed . . . to work for a common goal.

Enter football players crashing and celebrating.

It takes precision, discipline, leadership, and pride . . .

Drill team chanting and tossing their rifles around.

My Packers have all that . . . with just one goal in mind:

Jets scorching across the sky, fireworks exploding over a football stadium, orgasmic mayhem.

To win.

Marines folding a giant flag, Packers celebrating.

At legendary Lambeau Field, on our turf . . .

Jake, full-on:

In our country, for the undefeated Packers . . .

Shots of Packers triumphant.

And the Armed Forces . . .

Marine rifle squad firing. American flag, with Packers flag beneath it, being raised at dawn.

I'm proud to welcome you . . .

Clarion trumpets and martial drums, scenes of ecstatic touchdown celebrations.

To Monday Night Football.

A dramatic profile shot of Jake, saying softly:

Oo-rah.

A few weeks later, Jake and Indra were in Madison for the Wisconsin homecoming game. He was to give a speech on the Thursday before the game. There was a dinner. He was testy throughout; he and Indra rattled through the evening on a low bicker. Later, he wouldn't remember what the bickering was all about — it was just the way things were between them, typical.

Back in the hotel room, Indra asked him what was going on — what was *really* going on? And Jake exploded in sobs. It was shocking, like watching a building collapse in slow motion. He let it all out — his guilt about Clay, his pain, his loneliness, his attempts to push her away.

"Oh, baby," she said, comforting him. "We need to get you some help."

Mike Pereira left The Mission Continues a few weeks before the St. Louis gala and matriculated at Washington University. He left behind a legacy of mad compassion for the fellows that would continue to inspire the noncoms at TMC; indeed, his legacy had a name — Tiffany Garcia.

Anthony Smith, the star of the gala, would never have become a fellow if Tiffany Garcia hadn't stalked him. She was famous for that. If Tiffany thought you had the makings of a TMC fellow, you couldn't get rid of her. She was a former Marine mechanic, ridiculously candid. "I've been fired twice and I'm a lousy mother," she told Eric when she first visited the St. Louis office. But she proved a brilliant recruiter. Mary Yonkman would listen to her on the phone with some poor soul in a dark room and think: This girl is a genius. She knows how to play every chord in the hymnal.

In the months before and weeks after Mike Pereira left, Tiffany faced her greatest recruiting challenge: a Marine named Natasha Young.

Young had skin cancer, Lyme disease, and a child out of wedlock. She had seen a lot of awful in Iraq. She had been the Gunnery Sergeant for an Explosive Ordnance Disposal (EOD) company. She had lost five close friends — one especially close — in bomb disposal detonations, and when they died, her job was to gather their effects (and scrub their laptops for embarrassing personal stuff as well as official documents) and accompany the caskets to the airfield. She prayed alone over each casket.

Young — everyone called her "Tash" — had been born in Lawrence, Massachusetts, the daughter of two troubled teenagers. Her father was a crack addict who moved furniture; he was murdered when she was eighteen. Her mother loved Tash desperately, but she had drug-related health problems as well. Tash was molested regularly for years by her mother's second husband. She hid that somewhere deep inside, under a devastating facade of mouth and energy. She was an indifferent student with a foghorn Boston accent and a wild streak of blarney; she took shit from nobody and ran with a crowd so rough that the FBI was watching them for drug dealing. In her junior year, two federal agents stopped her as she was driving her boyfriend's car and said, "It's just a matter of time."

Natasha was no dummy: she figured the feds were right. She was going to wind up dead or in jail; all her friends were. She needed an out. The summer before senior year, her cousin Tommie took refuge with her mom — her family was screwed up out to three or four degrees of separation; Tommie needed protection from an even worse mess than Natasha's. "I'm getting out of here," Tommie said. "I'm joining the military."

"You are out of your mind," Natasha replied.

Tommie had applied to all the different services, but when the recruiters began to call, she got cold feet. One day the Marine Corps guy called, and Natasha answered the phone. "Tommie's not here," she said. "I don't know where she is."

"How about you?"

"What about me? I'm too young. I'm still in high school."

"How old are you?"

"Seventeen."

"You're old enough. You can sign up now — pick your specialty — and then join up after you graduate."

"I don't know about that."

"Give me five minutes and I'll change your life," he said. "I'll be there at two thirty."

The guy just wouldn't take a no. "I'll give you three minutes," she said, knowing that she wasn't even going to give him that. She slipped out of the house fifteen minutes before the recruiter was supposed to arrive the next day . . . but he was already there, waiting outside. That was her first taste of the Marines. And he looked seriously spiffy in his Charlies: a short-sleeved khaki uniform shirt with his Staff Sergeant stripes and dress-blue pants. She thought about the contrast between this guy and her friends: this guy was put together. She gave him more than five minutes. She lost track of time.

He tried to sell her on the benefits — education, health care, the chance to pick a specialty and learn a skill — but that wasn't what got her. It was the *you can be part of something really special.* You can be part of something important. You're going to have to work hard to win it; the Marines were a world-class, kick-ass physical and mental challenge. She was going to have to be tough. But, he said, he sensed something in her. "I believe in you and I know that you can do it."

And that was it. As with Mike Pereira and countless others, this was the first time anyone had said the magic words. Why would anyone believe in her? She had never really been part of anything, unless you counted her family (and yes, she did love her poor mother and her stepsisters and stepbrothers, even though her mother was so out of it in those days that her youngest stepbrother got on the school bus in his pajamas every morning until the social workers came; Natasha wound up taking custody of him, but that was another exhausting story).

In boot camp, she learned something else. She was a very good Marine, but she was more than that: every night the recruits in her squad got together, sat in a circle, said prayers — *I can do all things through Christ* — and gave thanks. On occasion, and much to her surprise, her fellow Marines gave thanks, out loud, in public, to Recruit Young for helping get them through the day. She was a natural leader; she'd never known that either. Her peers voted her "Molly Marine," the most admired recruit in the unit.

So Natasha absolutely *loved* being a Marine, even when her engineering specialty turned out to be bulk fuel: "Pumping gas and kicking ass." That was a bummer. Worse, it put her in the bull's-eye of a maniac in her unit who blasted into her room at the Cherry Point Marine Air Station in North Carolina, wearing a ski mask and orange shorts with white piping, and attacked her sexually with such a testosterone rush that she could not fight him off — she screamed for help and finally bit him in the chest. A week later, they found the guy — but a local girl claimed that she had bitten him, and he got off. Natasha filed that away with her stepfather. She wasn't going to let one asshole ruin everything.

She rose through the ranks quickly, serving two tours in Iraq — the second one with the EOD unit and the caskets. Then she came home and spent her last three years as a Marine recruiter in Massachusetts and New Hampshire — and she had to admit, she was every bit as good as the guy who had recruited her. She was selling a product that she loved. But she was also careless one night with one of her fellow recruiters; that's when she became pregnant.

After she gave birth, she was sick and overweight, and she was ragged by her superiors about it. She was subjected to humiliating public weigh-ins at the recruiting office. She worked out constantly, but it was no use. The weight just wasn't coming off. She later learned that she had trouble processing glucose. She was paralyzed, and sometimes she was worse than that. She had weapons in the small new house she had bought in Lawrence, the one perpetually flying the Marine Corps flag. She knew how to use a gun; she'd think about it, but there was her son, Julian. She was determined to be a good mom. Still, her retirement from the Marines felt like exile; she was at home, but far, far from her real home. There was a constant ache; her energy was gone.

Tiffany Garcia heard about Natasha Young from a Mission Continues fellow named Julian Jaramillo, who said that she was his sister — not *really*, not genetically, but . . . really, they were emotional twins. They had become close in the Marines, stateside at Camp Lejeune; each needed a safe friend, Natasha especially, after she was raped. And if they really were alike, Tiffany thought, well then, that was something very good: Julian — everyone called him "J" — was a compelling mess at first, living alone in a tiny tent in a Florida campground, but he was strong in all the important ways. His fellowship with Habitat for Humanity had worked; he was a Harley mechanic now. "Tiffany, you gotta get my sister," he said in the summer of 2011. "She's not out yet, but she's all fucked up."

Tiffany called Tash and said that J had told her to check Tash out. "Not interested," Tash said.

Tash called Julian, "What is this shit?"

"It saved my life," he said. "You know where I was . . . Where are *you* now?"

"You drank the Kool-Aid," she said. "Service? What do I need that shit for? I just served. I'm done with service."

Tiffany called again. Natasha shut her down. Tiffany kept calling. She didn't know *why* she was doing this; she just sensed something about Natasha — as a recruiter, she knew a potential recruit when she heard one on the other end of the phone . . . and this potential recruit was a recruiter herself; Tash knew all the tricks. It became a contest.

Natasha was on retirement leave, getting paid to do nothing — which she did with aplomb. She told friends that she had deployed to "Camp Couch, where I'm the commanding officer and my MOS is to stay on Camp Couch." She did her best to take care of her son. During her postpartum illness, she'd gotten a service dog — Josh — who protected her in crowds, could actually turn on the bedroom light when she had nightmares, and reminded her when she had to take her medications; all together, that was more than enough family. She was okay.

She was released from the military on October 24, 2011 — the same day her father had been murdered in 2000. She was back to her same old factory town, but she was — she knew this — different now. She had skills. She landed a job as a counselor at the local technical center, but she hated the kids. They weren't well-off, but they were . . . entitled. How had *that* happened? Even after she taught them how to write résumés, they'd ask her to do it for them. They'd whine about not being able to get jobs. When she asked them where they'd looked, she got blank stares. She wanted to drill sergeant the lot of them, kick them in the butt, PT them until they puked.

Tiffany called again. "Did you get your DD214?" — her discharge papers.

"No," Natasha lied.

Tiffany called Jaramillo, who said that Natasha had indeed gotten her 214. "She's ducking you," J said.

Tiffany called Natasha back and played her last card. "You're fucking lying to me. If you don't realize that you *need* my program, you don't *deserve* my program. You're not *good enough* for my program." And then she hung up.

"Oh, shit," Natasha thought. "That bitch just did it." Tiffany had challenged her — she wasn't good enough? "Okay," she thought. "I'm gonna show you who can do what — and then I'm gonna kick your ass."

She called Tiffany back. "Okay, I'm ready."

"If you want to be in Alpha Class, you're going to have to get moving," Tiffany said, quietly satisfied. There were essays; there was an interview. Tiffany helped her through the essays. And Alpha Class? That implied that there were going to be others in the same boat with her. When Natasha thought about it, that didn't seem bad at all.

A few weeks before Alpha Class convened, Tash learned that she had uterine cancer. She was told that it was curable, but it was cancer, the civilian equivalent of a million-dollar wound: she had a gold-plated excuse to remain on Camp Couch for the duration. But The Mission Continues paid cash money — a $6,000 stipend over six months

— and she needed that. She decided to tough it out; she was going to have to do The Mission Continues and uterine cancer simultaneously.

Alpha Class — thirty-four strong — convened in a St. Louis hotel in late January 2012. Each was given TMC swag: a blue T-shirt with FELLOW written across the back, a blue polo shirt with TMC's compass insignia and slogan "A Challenge, Not a Charity" embroidered over the heart, a Mission Continues plastic water bottle, power bars, other stuff. They met in one of those anonymous hotel meeting rooms, part of a larger ballroom; it could have been anywhere. But Natasha looked around and saw people who were very much like her: more women than in the standard-issue military, mostly from the enlisted ranks, and guys — Marines, some of them — with tattoos nearly as elaborate as her own. There was a fancy buffet chow line. There were cold drinks and snacks.

Spencer Kympton had been thinking about what he would say to Alpha Class ever since he'd heard the fellow at the St. Louis gala proudly talking about how he had to iron his Mission Continues polo shirt. To start, he showed Alpha a series of PowerPoint slides: who they were demographically, what branches of the military they'd served in, how many were officers and enlisted, how many were men and women. "Every one of you voluntarily signed up for the military," he said. "That's one bond you share." Another bond was that each of them had volunteered for The Mission Continues. That meant they were ready to continue their service, "And *we still need you*. We believe you still have a lot to give. Look to the left of you, and to the right of you. *This* is your new unit. *This* is your new branch of service. So stand up and shake hands with all your new brothers and sisters in Alpha Class of The Mission Continues."

There was a whoosh in the room, a massive exhale, an almost palpable sense of relief.

There was a guy at Natasha's table who really stood out — older, scarily emaciated, an officer — Lieutenant Colonel Mark Weber. He wasn't a fellow; he was there as an inspirational speaker. A year earlier, as he prepared for a staff job with General David Petraeus in Afghanistan, LTC Weber had gone for a physical and was told that a rapacious cancer was rifling through his innards. He was told he had six months to live.

Natasha's cancer wasn't so serious, allegedly; she would get a hysterectomy, and that would be it. She absolutely believed that, or tried to, most of the time. But here was this guy, an officer no less, who was on the clock — he didn't know how many *days* he had left — and there he was, with them.

There was no pretense, no woe-is-me, no fake machismo, absolutely no bullshit when Mark Weber got up to speak. "They keep telling me to have positive thoughts," he said, and laughed. "That's nice, but there are days that are just knee-buckling. I have four children; it's not hard to have positive thoughts about them. Positive thoughts are good, but they're not as important as *this:* seeking perspective. I love it when people say, 'Today was the worst day of my life. My boss yelled at me.' " He waited for the laughter to fill the room, then continued, "But the truth is, somebody always has it worse than you. The way to stop feeling sorry for yourself is to focus on your achievements, the things you accomplish every day. For me, sometimes it's as simple as 'Hey, I got out of bed today.' " In fact, Weber was still working for the Minnesota National Guard; indeed, he was thinking about becoming a Mission Continues fellow himself — he wanted to serve with

Outward Bound.

Everything the guy said was real, Natasha thought. There was not a false note:

"It's okay to take a knee every once in a while. There's nothing wrong with being mad, frustrated, crying . . . Have your pity party, then get up and move on.

"Denial gets a bad rap . . . But it's essential for me. I'm dying. According to the doctors, I should be dead. But I'm not going to stop living. People ask me all the time, 'Why are you still doing this? Why are you going to St. Louis to talk to a bunch of veterans? Why don't you spend more time with your family?' And I say, 'Because I can.'

"Every one of you has an excuse. I use mine all the time. Telemarketers call. I say, 'Sorry, I've got terminal cancer.' Click. But do you want to wake up in 2047 and say, 'My whole life has been one big excuse'?"

When it was over Natasha hugged Colonel Weber and was shocked by how little there was left of him. But he was still so totally there. He'd given her everything she needed to get on with it.

Jake Wood was probably his therapist's worst nightmare. He was too smart. He knew the post-traumatic stress drill backward and forward; he readily acknowledged what was happening to him. There were no sudden flashes of insight. There was no moment when the scales fell from his eyes. He'd had his moment of candor in the hotel room in Madison — and there were some things he would absolutely not concede.

He would never tolerate the idea that he *wasn't* responsible for Clay's death. He would not tolerate the idea that he would "get over it" or "put it behind him." He hated when people said that. He knew he would live with it every day, forever.

But, gradually, as 2011 emptied into 2012, he was able to sand down the sharp edges of his pain, some of it. Clay was always there somewhere, a resident demon in his brain: Jake stopped going out on Team Rubicon deployments, but he and William worked like Marine Sergeants at building the organization from within. The work now wasn't just about helping people suffering through natural disasters; it was, equally, about helping veterans to find a sense of purpose. A Team Rubicon office was opened finally, right next to LAX for easy egress; he and William were able to give themselves salaries: $30,000 per year.

As Jake gradually transformed Clay from guilt-millstone into his private motivation to make Team Rubicon stronger and better, he came to realize his relationship with Indra could be different, too. He now knew she was tough and she was steady, maybe tougher and steadier than he was. He knew that she had taken responsibility for him in a dark hour; responsibility wasn't a one-way street. He knew that she was going to be there for him and that he needed her.

Almost exactly a year after his Monday Night Football icon act, Jake bought a ring. He carried it around uncertainly for two weeks. And then there came a night when he was in the office staring into his computer, and he said: "Fuck it. This is on."

Indra was out at a concert with friends. He expected her home about nine or ten, but she didn't arrive until midnight, by which time he had drunk an entire nervous bottle of wine. He leaped up and then kneeled down and produced the ring . . . and all of a sudden his mouth could not work. He was there, on one knee, shaky, unable to say the words.

She said yes.

Eric Greitens had wrestled with political ambition for most of his life. He sensed it was radioactive, to be handled very carefully. In his Duke senior thesis, *On Courage,* he relegated the subject to an "important" footnote; indeed, it was a very long and curious footnote. In it, he attempted to tease out an ethical path between ambition and honor. It wasn't easy. He made a distinction between the need for popularity — the cheesiness at the heart of politics — and esteem. "To desire esteem," he wrote, "is not always an expression of pride . . . Rather, it often reflects a hope both that one will act correctly and a faith that others will eventually come to recognize right action."

Twenty years had passed since Greitens had written that. His "right actions" were manifest. The Mission Continues was acclaimed as something new and entirely admirable. But could you run a campaign for Governor of Missouri — as always, Eric's ambitions were not modest — based on biography and values, rather than platitudes and reflexive attacks? He wanted to run a campaign that would look and sound different. His campaign events would be service projects, to the extent that was possible. He would *show* people how he would behave in office, not just *tell* them.

Was that even vaguely possible? He needed time and space to think it through.

At The Mission Continues board meeting in the summer of 2012, Eric tried to float the idea of a three-month leave at the end of the year, after which he would become a volunteer, unpaid CEO, turning over the day-to-day leadership to Spencer Kympton.

No way, said the board. It was their first year of pushing large numbers of fellows through the system. The big funders had signed on with the assumption that they were buying Eric. Practically no one — except Eric — was confident that the organization could survive without him.

The model did need some fine-tuning. He and the staff were finding that a great many of the fellows didn't want to go back to Civilian World. They simply wanted to work, and hang around, with other veterans. That feeling actually seemed to intensify as The Mission Continues fellowship was transformed into a group experience. Nearly 30 percent of the 2012 and 2013 fellows chose to work for veterans' service organizations — and that number would have been much higher if TMC's recruiting staff hadn't pushed hard to nudge the prospective fellows into less parochial forms of community service.

It was easy to understand the tribal pull. There were 115 members of Bravo Class in 2012, and the emotion — the relief — when they gathered together in San Diego for their orientation in May was breathtaking. How could you say no to a blind Army officer who wanted to work with blind veterans? And what about those who wanted to train service dogs to provide comfort for their fellow veterans? And those who wanted to do equine therapy for veterans . . . and those who wanted to work with Student Veterans of America? Eric was prepared to make concessions: some of the Bravo Class fellows were victims of severe traumatic brain injuries who simply needed to be around others who understood the twitch and jitter of their scrambled sensibilities. Even some of the non-wounded veterans, whom The Mission Continues started to accept in 2012, just wanted to hang with their brothers and sisters.

There was no way to question the sheer human relief that the members of Bravo Class provided for one another. But Eric wanted more. He still wanted his fellows to be leaders; he wanted his generation of veterans to be remembered for what they brought to civilian life — leadership skills, moral rigor, community feeling that had atrophied in the sixty-year blaze of American affluence. It was an old-fashioned vision, and yet, he believed that people — civilians, too — were looking for a larger sense of purpose. His fellows needed to be the exemplar. He wanted civilians to look at his fellows and say, "We need to be more like them."

The fellows had been transformed into a community with the addition of orientation classes in 2012. But there was still something missing. Each individual fellow needed to be stronger when he or she rejoined civilian society. Eric decided that his last major contribution to the substance of the fellowship program would be a personal development curriculum that would directly address their feelings of fear and isolation, the lack of confidence that so many of them suffered when they wandered out their front door and tried to deal with the vast, careless fog of the nonmilitary world. He had done this individually with Mike Pereira and others; now he needed to figure out how to teach it on a larger scale.

For the next six months, Eric led a small team of colleagues and worked out the details of the program. There would be six discrete monthly challenges. Each would come with required reading and a personal essay. The lessons would start in the simplest possible way, by establishing three "smart" — that is, plausible — goals for their fellowship. And from the outset, they would deal

403

with their fears. The first month's reading was Eric's "Hell Week" chapter from *The Heart and the Fist*. The lesson was that he had overcome his fear of washing out by focusing on his men, rather than himself. The fellows would be asked to be specific, in writing, about their own fears. In the second month, the fellows would be taught how to spot allies and build friendships and business relationships — their first halting steps away from Camp Couch.

In the third month, they would be asked to identify and write about a personal role model. What made that person admirable? What qualities did they want to emulate? In the fourth month, they would assess their own strengths and weaknesses and locate their "driving force," the thing they were most passionate about. In the fifth month, they would decide what their mission in life would be. And then, at the end of the program, they would evaluate the impact their fellowship had had on them.

None of this was new, of course. It was the sort of material that had populated self-help books since Dale Carnegie. But Eric had calibrated it, synthesized it from a bunch of different sources, made it meal-sized and military for his fellows — challenging but not impossible. He unveiled it to the staff in December 2012 and told each of them to complete the curriculum themselves in time for Alpha Class. He wanted Natasha Young — Natasha, specifically, because of her utter working-class skepticism about everything tutorial — to be able to stand up in front of Alpha Class and say, "I *did* this thing — yeah, even the essays — and if I can do it, you can."

CHAPTER 3
THE BIGGEST STORMS

Team Rubicon had actually been preparing for something like Hurricane Sandy in the months before the big storm hit. Local TR volunteers, led by East Coast coordinator Matt Pelak, had been part of the city of New York's emergency planning operations for months. Team Rubicon had an official disaster relief assignment if anything terrible happened: it would provide the personnel to send "Jump Teams" into homeless shelters all over the city, do an assessment, and call for whatever help was needed.

But no one had planned for a storm as monstrous as Sandy, which hit New York harbor on the evening of October 29, 2012. The TR jump teams headed out to survey the shelters, but the enormity of the destruction beggared the city's ability to respond. There was so much more to do. Team Rubicon put out a national call for volunteers. Pelak had been working with the city's Office of Emergency Management, and now he offered to coordinate the relief efforts in Rockaway Beach, the barrier island in Queens that had taken the brunt of the storm. Dozens, then hundreds of TR volunteers started to arrive in New York from all over the country; JetBlue provided the plane tickets. A rock-climbing emporium called Brooklyn Boulders offered its facilities as a barracks for the 350 Team Rubicon volunteers who eventually showed up; the Home Depot stores provided a steady supply of equipment from shovels and gloves to earthmovers. James and Josh Eisenberg, Team Rubicon stalwarts who were local property owners, provided a Forward Operating Base (FOB) in a parking lot at Beach 124th Street in Rockaway Beach, the low-slung homeland of a fair number of New York's police and, especially, firefighters — many of whom were veterans, usually noncommissioned officers like the Team Rubicon volunteers. It was the oddest of New York neighborhoods: middle-class and working-class, almost suburban, planted on a gorgeous beach. It was an hour from downtown by subway. The A train actually ran all the way out there.

Team Rubicon became the spine of the official response in the Rockaways. Palantir, a tech company, offered the team the use of smartphone-like gizmos that TR volunteers could work to report specific house-to-house damage to FEMA and to request demolitions or repairs. Various relief organizations, including the city itself, sent civilian volunteers to the Team Rubicon Beach 124th Street FOB to be organized and deployed. For the next three weeks, 350 Team Rubicon volunteers led thousands of civilians — the estimate was ten thousand — in the cleanup. Word of the effort spread quickly; there were days when more civilians than were needed showed up at the FOB. It was, without question, the largest and most efficient Team Rubicon mission yet.

Sandy was Jake Wood's first deployment in more than a year. His role was different now; he wasn't needed on the front lines; he, McNulty, Pelak, and others spent their days making executive decisions, smoothing out logistical snafus, coordinating with the city and the federal governments. It wasn't the hands-on excitement of Haiti, but there was a certain satisfaction to watching the giant operation unfold. On the local evening news most nights, there were scenes of people wearing Team Rubicon T-shirts (usually over long-sleeved sweatshirts — it was cold and damp on the beach in November) cleaning out flooded basements and hauling trash, and testimonials from the residents to the order and good cheer that the Team Rubicon veterans had brought to their neighborhood.

There was a general exultation among the volunteers; work teams became units; units became friends for life. Vietnam veterans were joining the effort in numbers now, welcomed by the Iraq and Afghanistan vets. The widows of veterans were joining up: Clay Hunt's ex-wife, Robin Becker, flew in from California and was working in the Team Rubicon office. The parents of those who'd been killed and wounded in Fallujah and Helmand were out working in the teams.

Michael Washington, Sr. — whose son, Mike Washington, Jr., was the squad leader who had taken Jake's place and been killed by an IED in Afghanistan — was part of a Team Rubicon unit operating in Union Beach, New Jersey. Mike Sr. was an imposing, authoritative presence, a classic Master Sergeant whose rank became his name: everyone called him "Top." He took command of the toughest jobs with effortless authority and did his work while chewing on a rather complicated pipe. He was a

Marine veteran of the first Gulf War and a Seattle firefighter. He'd been a bit lost, suffering since the death of his son — but in Union Beach, Top was working with people Mike Jr.'s age, young men and women who were looking to him for leadership. One day, resting on the back fender of an ambulance in the cool sea breeze, he found himself talking to a Marine named Ryan Ribinskas who had served with Mike Jr. "You're Sergeant Washington's dad?"

"Yes," Top said, misting up a little.

"He was a great Marine."

They hugged, and later Top realized that a portion of the weight he'd been carrying had lifted; he felt closer to his son than at any time in the past few years. If he'd lived, Top was sure, Mike Jr. would have been out there with his buddies. Mike Jr. would have been one of Jake's first calls. There was a deep satisfaction — deeper even than the satisfactions of saving lives and helping people as a firefighter — to this work. A few days later, Top went to Brooklyn to find Jake. He needed to tell him personally. "Jake, thank you for this," he said. "I'm in, all the way. You need me to go anywhere, do anything, I'm there."

"Well, that's great, Top," Jake said. "We need you."

There was general acclaim for Team Rubicon after Sandy. Awards were won. Major funders came on board; a continuing partnership with Palantir was established. President Barack Obama invited Jake, William, Matt Pelak, and several of the other team leaders to the Oval Office to thank them for their work. And yet . . .

A few months after Sandy, Jake was on a panel with Barbara Van Dahlen, a psychologist who had started Give an Hour, an organization of six thousand mental health professionals, each of whom agreed to give an hour of counseling to an Iraq and Afghanistan veteran each week.

Afterward, Jake and Van Dahlen spent some time talking, and he could tell that she was not one of those dorky, shrinky sorts — she spoke English, she laughed easily, and she talked sense. She said she didn't like using the "disorder" part of post-traumatic stress disorder. She called it "post-traumatic stress." "It's a rational reaction to what you saw and did over there," she told him. "If you treat it correctly, it can be a temporary effect. But you can't just macho your way through it." She was excited about what Team Rubicon was doing, but she was wary. "In some ways, the greatest adjustment you guys have to make when you come home is being alone," she told Jake, who knew it all too well. "It's tough psychologically to leave a tight, close-knit society with intense shared values and traditions." Team Rubicon addressed that, she said, "but what happens to these kids when they come down from the high of Hurricane Sandy and they're back home, all alone again?"

Jake knew the answer to that: some of them crashed. In fact, they — actually, it was mostly McNulty — had been dealing with the psychological aftermath of Sandy for months. There were those, the natural leaders like Top Washington, who had been made stronger by the experience; but there were others, the quieter ones, the kids who had happily become grunts again, who had become *re*-addicted to being part of something with a military swagger. They were beginning to contact the Team Rubicon offices in El Segundo, lost and terrified. McNulty kept his cell phone on the pillow next to him every night, and about once a week, it rang. There were times Will would stay up all night, talking to someone with a gun to his head; it was frazzling McNulty, freaking him out. He realized he needed to go for help himself.

"Why don't we see if we can help each

other here?" Barbara Van Dahlen asked Jake.

"Absolutely," Jake said. "That's a terrific idea."

In the spring of 2013, Team Rubicon was growing rapidly, adding staff, including Eric Greitens's old friend Ken Harbaugh, who had helped to found The Mission Continues. Success piled upon success, but Jake — having been through the ordeal himself — was nagged by the problem that wasn't being addressed. The conversation with Van Dahlen had been one of those *great, let's do it* and then nothing happens sort of things. He and William squabbled about a lot, but not this: they were both terrified that someone — one of the anonymous ones, one of those they'd smiled at and hugged and slapped on the back in Rockaway Beach — would be their next Clay Hunt.

It turned out to be Neil Landsberg, a brilliant guy, a special operator who was close to Matt Pelak. Landsberg had wrapped himself in a carpet in his parents' basement, in order to prevent a mess, and shot himself. A few weeks later, on Team Rubicon's deployment to Moore, Oklahoma, after the fierce tornadoes there in late May 2013, McNulty noticed that the evening debriefs were pretty emotional — a Sergeant named Chris Dominski talked for the first time

413

about the twelve men he had lost in Baghdad, he named them, he named their wives, he named their children. He had tried suicide twice before. "But I guess I wasn't very good at it. Thank you — Team Rubicon — for saving my life," he said.

Which was a frightening responsibility. What would happen when Sergeant Dominski went home to upstate New York and was back, all alone, on Camp Couch?

On the morning of Memorial Day, beneath a scuddy mix of sun and clouds in Moore, Oklahoma, they raised the flag to half-mast above their Forward Operating Base in the Home Depot parking lot. Top Washington read aloud the Gettysburg Address: "That we here highly resolve that *these dead shall not have died in vain;* that this nation, under God, shall have a new birth of freedom; and that government of the people, by the people, for the people, shall not perish from the earth."

And then he read a list of those lost, embedded among which were . . .

Blake Howey
Nathan Windsor
Clay Hunt
Neil Landsberg
Michael Washington, Jr.

414

McNulty came home from Moore worried. He and Jake talked to Barbara Van Dahlen about it and agreed to cement their alliance. In August 2013, Van Dahlen asked a fifty-two-year-old psychiatric social worker named Dane Frost if he'd be willing to join Team Rubicon as a full-time staff therapist. Frost had an easy manner and familiarity with the military: his wife was an Army Major, a Behavioral Health Officer who had deployed to Afghanistan twice with the 101st Airborne. They had lived on Fort Campbell and other Army bases back home; Frost had done some work for the Army. He was part of the culture — and so he knew that grunts saw the shrinks as POGy dweebs. His challenge would be to overcome that.

He loved Team Rubicon from the start. The dress code at the El Segundo office was T-shirts, board shorts, flip-flops, and baseball caps turned backward; Frost could do that. He was also good for a beer and a bourbon most nights with Jake and Will. And, sure enough, about once a week there would be a crisis — someone desperate on the phone or pitched up in the offices, and

Frost would take charge, talking them down, eventually referring them to a Give an Hour therapist in their hometown. He made no structural suggestions at first; he just watched and listened and did what he was told. He defused the crises without drawing attention to himself; he was humble about his work.

On November 8, 2013 — a year and a week after Hurricane Sandy — the strongest typhoon in Asian history, with sustained winds of up to 195 miles an hour, swamped the central Philippine Islands, killing more than 6,200 people and devastating countless others. Team Rubicon immediately sent a fifteen-person Alpha Team to scout the area and prepared two twenty-five-member medical teams to follow. Jake led an executive group that would organize the relief effort from Manila; a factory building there had been donated for Team Rubicon's headquarters. "You want to come?" Jake asked Dane Frost. "We may need you out there."

Frost, by now, had a theory of the case: The best way to be Team Rubicon's official shrink was to not act like a shrink. And so, on his first real deployment, he acted like a grunt. He helped lift and sort supplies. He did errands. He would go to the airfield to pick up or drop off this or that; he would go to downtown Manila; he would go to Starbucks and bring back coffee for the team. And still, about once a week, he'd have a crisis back in the States, which he'd manage from Manila with the help of a Give an Hour therapist who had located herself temporarily in the Team Rubicon Los Angeles office.

Manila was quiet. The devastation was far to the south, in Tacloban, and most of the headquarters work was, as always, logistics. Jake — and William, from Los Angeles — tried to get USAID, which was managing the flights into the disaster area, to allow the Team Rubicon medical personnel on the planes. There were constant trips to the airfield, endless frustration dealing with the USAID bureaucrats. There was a half-empty plane ready to fly to Tacloban, and USAID wasn't allowing Team Rubicon aboard.

"When do you stop banging your head against the wall?" Frost asked Jake. "When do we go to Plan B?"

Jake just smiled. There was a Marine Sergeant in charge of the flight manifest. At the last minute, the medical team was surreptitiously ushered on board.

Frost saw the disaster area only briefly, in

the last days of his two weeks on the ground in the Philippines. His real challenge came in Manila, when the Alpha Team returned from Tacloban after an emotionally intense ten days in the field. They had seen hundreds of dead bodies; they had treated hundreds of survivors; they had buried Americans who had died in the storm in shallow graves marked for retrieval. They would find children, six and seven at a time, dead in houses that had been crushed by the winds. The experience had been overwhelming, and Frost sensed a real tension in Alpha Team as it gathered for a debrief with Jake and other TR leaders in a weirdly pleasant spot under a gazebo on the grounds of the airport hotel.

These were people Frost didn't know. They were Team Rubicon's elite. The team leaders were Matt Pelak and JC McGreehan — both of whom had been close to Neil Landsberg — and they seemed just barely able to control their anger as they described the myriad of problems they'd had on the deployment; Frost watched their men, who seemed pretty angry, too. And then Ken Harbaugh did exactly what Frost did not want anyone to do. He said, "Hey, guys, this is Dane Frost. He's our new mental health guy. Dane, why don't you say a few words . . ."

Frost tried to make it as brief and as far away from tell-me-how-you-*feel* as possible. "Look," he began, "I'm the newbie here, but if you want to . . ."

"We don't have time for that," Matt Pelak interrupted. His team needed time to decompress, clean up, and have a couple beers before they started to hash out a very difficult mission.

". . . talk about anything, either here or back home, I can . . ."

"We need to pack up — and *go,*" Pelak said. And they went to their hotel rooms, leaving Frost standing there, mouth agape, with Jake, Ken Harbaugh, and Vince Moffitt, the operations specialist. "I think," Frost said, "there's a fair amount of anger there that we're going to have to deal with."

"It's always like that after a tough deployment," Moffitt said.

"No, I think Dane's right," Jake jumped in. Matt Pelak, normally a total rock, seemed to be seething. Jake needed to get up with Matt and McGreehan about it; it probably wasn't a coincidence, he realized, that they were having problems six months after Neil Landsberg had died.

In the next few months, quietly, and for the first time, Jake sat down with Pelak and

McGreehan and told them how much of a mess he'd been after Clay's suicide and how the shit had really hit the fan after six months. He was absolutely candid — a straight Jake infusion — without being gooey. He'd been there. He'd been desperate. He'd felt useless. He understood how overwhelming the Philippine experience, on top of Landsberg's suicide, must have been. But he knew them. They'd get through it. Oh, and by the way, Dane Frost was a good guy. "You might want to get to know him better."

In the spring of 2014, Give an Hour held its annual meeting in Washington, D.C. The audience was mostly composed of mental health professionals, frustrated by the difficulties they had dealing with veterans. One of the first speakers was Jake Wood, who began simply, "My name is Jake Wood. I'm the cofounder of Team Rubicon . . . and I've been helped by counseling."

Chapter 4
Post-Traumatic Growth

Natasha Young came flying out of Alpha Class orientation in January 2012, but it was a false high. She was still facing a hysterectomy. The temptation was to retreat to Camp Couch and lowball her Mission Continues fellowship — nobody would knock her if, in this mess, she put in twelve rather than twenty hours a week at the Veterans Northeast Outreach Center. She spoke on the phone to Mark Weber almost every day, especially the bad days — somehow he was hanging on, month after month, dying without diminishing. She wasn't dying; the surgery in March was a "success" — if the loss of a womb could ever be considered successful. How could she be any less vital than Weber was? He refused to give her advice or tell her what to do. "Let me just give you my perspective," he'd say. As her fellowship was drawing to a close, she heard that The Mission Continues was hiring recruiters.

She called Tiffany Garcia. "Bitch," she said. "Why don't you hire me?"

She was put in charge of recruiting in the northeast region for The Mission Continues.

Natasha was asked to tell her story at the Bravo Class 2012 orientation in San Diego, not long after her hysterectomy. She wasn't at her strongest, but there she was — and since when had anything ever stopped her from talking? She introduced the term "Camp Couch" into TMC's lexicon. She had them laughing and cheering, especially the Marines, whom she played to shamelessly.

After the speech, she realized that she was bleeding — not badly, but leaking a little — from her wound. Tiffany Garcia found some gauze and butterfly bandages and helped put Natasha back together.

Both Tash and Tiffany — inseparable now, even if the bond most days was only electronic — kept talking to Mark Weber, almost every day. He said that he really wanted to become a full-fledged Mission Continues fellow before he died. He wanted to do his fellowship with Outward Bound, but there was a problem: he wasn't a veteran yet. He was still on active duty — desk duty — with the Minnesota National Guard. It was important for him to stay "active" as long as he could. He intended to die active. TMC fellowships were available only to veterans, which was ridiculous in this case. When Natasha raised this point with Tiffany and the others, there was no dispute. Weber became a fellow, part of Alpha Class 2013, but he struggled to complete his mission with Outward Bound. He was now, obviously, getting weaker. The fellowship, he said, was keeping him alive. He was desperate to finish it before he died.

In May 2013, Eric Greitens asked to be relieved of his day-to-day duties once again at The Mission Continues board meeting. Again he asked for a three-month leave of absence, starting in January 2014; he would return as a symbolic CEO, while he decided what he was going to do next — which everyone assumed would be a career in politics.

This time, the board said yes.

The board meeting had been timed to coincide with Bravo Class orientation, which would be held that weekend at a hotel in Brooklyn. Natasha Young would be the master of ceremonies. She was a controversial choice. "I don't want you dropping any f-bombs," her boss, Meredith Knopp, warned her. And so it was an expurgated Tash who opened the proceedings. "Well," she began, staring out at the seventy-three new fellows, spiffy in their royal blue T-shirts, "don't you all just look beautiful!"

She told them about her escape from Camp Couch. She did Spencer's bit: "Look to the left of you, look to the right of you: this is your new unit!" Eventually she introduced Eric, not knowing that he had just arranged his departure from The Mission Continues. "He saw us, our generation, he saw us for our possibilities, and he challenged us."

Eric talked about the thousands of veterans who woke up this morning and would spend all day without speaking to another human being. "They're going to go to bed tonight, after having spent the day watching TV, playing video games, doubting whether or not they were still needed. What they all need is to wake up one day and see what their fellow veterans are capable of. What this country needs is to look at this generation of veterans and to see what we are capable of."

The Mission Continues would never have a triumph equivalent to Team Rubicon's Haiti mission or Hurricane Sandy cleanup. Its victories would be more subtle and enduring. In the end, Eric realized, the best, most realistic model was Tim Smith, his first St. Louis recruit, who just never stopped growing.

Tim had gone on to graduate from Washington University with a Master's of Social Work degree. One of his first classes had been Urban Economic Development, and during a lecture about employment possibilities in downtown areas, Tim wrote down the word "cleaning." He had met more than a few veterans at the VA who went to school during the day but were looking for work at night — like his old job at the post office. He went to his father and asked, "What if we started a company where we had veterans doing cleaning work in offices at night?"

His dad not only thought it was a good idea, he also had a potential customer — a Vietnam veteran who had a real estate brokerage that needed cleaning. Tim and his dad did the job themselves, and Patriot Commercial Cleaning was born. Over time, Tim recruited veterans as nighttime janitors and gradually accumulated enough customers that he could leave his job at the VA and become the full-time president of the company.

He even came up with a slogan: "We Do Corners."

And then there was Mike Pereira, who continued his fierce, bare-knuckle fight to complete his intellectual journey. He was obsessed by his insufficiencies. He was wrestling with a joint anthropology and psychology major at Washington University. He knew exactly what he wanted now: a PhD in psychology. He had come up with an idea for his thesis: post-traumatic growth. It was the opposite of what everyone seemed to think about his fellow veterans. The experience of combat was the perfect launching pad for the hero's journey toward wisdom. That was what The Mission Continues was all about. Knowledge through suffering, right?

He was certainly suffering. He knew that he had to settle things with his father to have any pretense of being a plausible adult. He was beginning to realize that the teenage altercations with Doc were partly his fault — he was trying to piss his dad off, trying to get him to blow up, knowing that his mom would jump in on his side, which would cause Doc to go truly berserk. (He also began to understand that he had come by his own volcanic tendencies genetically.)

A childhood memory tormented Mike. He was twelve. His dad packed the family into the truck and took them to southern California, where Mike's grandfather — the monstrous grandfather who had abandoned Doc and his mother, who had beaten Doc mercilessly — was dying of cancer. And it was astonishing, embarrassing: Doc threw himself on his father's expiring body, wailing and sobbing, snot flying. Mike didn't want his final scene with Doc to look anything like that.

He had tried to reconcile with Doc several times in the past — as recently as 2012. The story was always the same. He'd go out to Bellingham, to the house in the country that his parents had been living in for the past five years. He'd work some chores with his dad — that was how they got on. No small talk, no shooting hoops or tossing a football. They might work on a car together — as always, Doc had a garage full of wrecks — or mow the property or repair a fence.

It had been a fence that last time. But within a half hour, they were screaming at each other. Mike wanted to tell his dad about the difficult patch he was going through; he and his wife, Georgia, had grown past each other. They were splitting.

It didn't seem as if Doc was listening to Mike's story at all. He was working on the fence. And Mike blew up. Doc started to walk away, and Mike followed him into the house, the two of them really getting at it now, Mike's mother trying to stop Doc — a perfect re-creation of Mike's youth, as if nothing had changed, as if he hadn't been to war, as if he wasn't the first person in the family to go to college. He slammed the door, spun his rental car out of the drive, and was gone without saying good-bye.

A year passed.

Mike still couldn't get the image of Doc wailing over his near-dead father out of his mind. One day in therapy, Mike was talking about the chopper crash in Iraq — and all of a sudden he was back, terrified, in the San Francisco earthquake, his dad swooping him up, saving his life like Superman.

He called Doc again, and a funny thing happened: they just talked. Doc actually asked a few questions about Mike's life. They talked about the old house — the wreck-yard — which Doc still owned and was renting out. He was thinking about selling it, but there was work to be done to get it ready for sale.

Mike began calling Doc more regularly; Doc even called *him* a few times. But it wasn't enough. A grand gesture was needed. "Hey, Dad, I was thinking," he said to Doc, "maybe I should come home on spring break and help you fix up the old place so you can sell it."

"Really?" Doc asked. "How long is spring break?"

"Ten days." Mike gulped. Ten days without a blowup would be a new world record.

"That would be great," Doc said. "That would be huge."

So they worked. Mike looked at his father, still an imposing man at the age of sixty-two, fit and trim, with a long gray ponytail. They didn't talk about anything but work when they were working. They did talk some about the past when they were done working. It wasn't easy. Doc was not willing to give an inch: he had always been right. Mike had been an angry kid. He was glad Mike had grown up and calmed down and started to respect his father. Mike bit his tongue a lot that week.

As the days passed, Doc loosened up and began to treat Mike as he would any construction worker. He'd yell at him angrily, when Mike wasn't doing the job to Doc's specifications. Mike tried to roll with it, but one day he couldn't take it anymore. "Could you just stop yelling at me?" Mike screamed.

"I'm trying to help."

Doc returned the scream: "You're doing it wrong!"

Mike dropped his tools and walked away, sat down on the back steps of the old house, and began to cry. This is impossible, he thought. This will never work. He had tried so hard, conceded so much — he had stopped caring, for the first time in his life, whether or not he won the argument. He just wanted peace. He was absolutely convinced that if he didn't settle things with Doc, he wouldn't fully experience the burst of creativity and purpose that came from fighting his way past post-traumatic stress to post-traumatic growth. His whole theory was on the line.

He saw Doc ambling over. Uh-oh. But the body language wasn't aggressive. His father sat down next to him on the steps and threw an arm around his son's shoulder. "Sometimes I just lose track of the sound of my voice," Doc said. "I wasn't meaning to be harsh. From now on, if it's getting hot between us, maybe we just say, 'Reset. Let's take it down a notch,' okay?"

"Okay," Mike said.

"You know I love you, son," Doc said. "And I'm grateful you came out here to help with this work."

It would never be easy with Doc, but for the third time in his life, Mike Pereira felt that he had been recruited into heaven.

On the afternoon of May 9, 2013, at Ground Zero, where the story of their generation's service began, Natasha Young and Tiffany Garcia stood arm in arm as Bravo Class took its oath of service:

We are fellows of The Mission Continues. As fellows, our personal service did not end with our military service, but has only just begun . . .

Scanning the faces of the young men and women they had recruited, Natasha was overwhelmed. She had done this; she had helped to build this class. She had spent hundreds of hours on the phone, stalking recruits as Tiffany had stalked her. She had learned their stories. She and Tiffany had a stake in them now; they were rooting hard for these kids, their brothers and sisters. Tears formed. Soon, she and Tiffany were bawling joyously.

Ground Zero was busy that day, as it is most Saturdays. The sun was setting, and new leaves were silvering in the just-planted trees. The massive, descending fountains, carved from the footprint of the towers, descending so far that the bottom was hard to see, splashed and sent a fine mist flying. Only a few of the tourists, boggled by the size and sanctity of the place, noticed the phalanx of seventy-three young people in their blue T-shirts with the compass and the slogan, "A Challenge, Not a Charity," standing in front of the North Tower abyss, reciting an oath. Some turned their heads when the oath ended with a roar and tears and hugging. A few asked, "What is this all about? Who are those people?"

And when asked, the fellows stopped and politely, respectfully — as if addressing a superior officer — explained their new mission to the civilians. They did so articulately, proudly. You could see the civilians squaring themselves up, standing taller to shake the hands of these young men and women. Slowly the crowd dispersed, and the blue shirts went off in groups of two and three, often with arms draped over one another, away from a scene of unimaginable horror and into the lifeblood of the nation.

Mark Weber kept his spirit to the end, but he didn't live to graduate from The Mission Continues with his class. He passed away and was powerfully mourned on June 13, 2013.

Soon after his death, Natasha and Tiffany

got tattoos on their wrists. Tiffany's right wrist said WEBER'S and Natasha's right wrist said PERSPECTIVES. Both Tash and Tiffany eventually left The Mission Continues to work for other veterans' organizations — but they would often look at their wrists, often when they were feeling down, and remember Weber's spirit in the face of the worst hand that God could deal. From time to time, strangers would ask Natasha what the tattoo was all about.

It was a story she loved to tell.

AFTERWORD

If I had one thing to say to my fellow veterans, it would be this: continue to serve, even though we have taken off our uniforms. No matter how great or small your service is, it is desired and needed by the world we live in today. Volunteer to mow your elderly neighbor's lawn for them. Spend a day at a soup kitchen helping feed the homeless, many of whom are veterans themselves. Work on a trail maintenance project. Start a service organization. It doesn't matter what it is; it only matters that you are continuing to put others before yourself, just like you did when you were in the military. Actions like that are the only sure ways to bring about the positive social change that our country and our world need so badly these days.

— *Clay Hunt*

ACKNOWLEDGMENTS

This book could never have happened if I hadn't seen the wars in Iraq and Afghanistan firsthand, embedded with U.S. troops who performed magnificent service under impossible circumstances. I'd especially like to thank Major Jeremiah Ellis and First Sergeant Jack Robison of Dog Company, 1st battalion/12th regiment of the Army's 4th Infantry Division, who first demonstrated the leadership skills in Afghanistan's Kandahar Province that led me to the theory of the case: that the post-9/11 military would produce civilian leaders with a genius for public service.

My greatest thanks, obviously, go to Eric Greitens, whose vision and honor provided the backbone and spirit of this book. But Jake Wood and William McNulty were absolutely essential as well, generous with their time, insights, and mockery. Also, of course, Mike Pereira, Natasha Young, Kaj

Larsen, Spencer Kympton, and all the others who let me into their lives, trusted me, spent patient hours with me, and became my friends. Thanks to the Greitens and Wood and Pereira families — and of course, to Clay's parents, Stacy Hunt and Susan Selke, who opened their hearts to me; to Sheena Greitens and Indra Petersons, who supported their guys and tried to protect them from my prying, and gave me great perspective in the process; to all the staff and fellows at The Mission Continues and Team Rubicon, who spent hours, days, weeks sharing their lives with me.

Thanks to the dozens of veterans who spent time with me, but whose remarkable stories didn't find their way into this book. I'd also thank those Team Rubicon and Mission Continues members I served with on service deployments; your devotion and cheer should be a lesson to this country. And to Barbara Van Dahlen, whose big, smart heart and her organization — Give an Hour — has provided great service to the veterans' community. I hope I've honored all of your work with this book.

Thanks, too, to General David Petraeus and his brilliant COIN-istas, who schooled me in counterinsurgency warfare, both at Fort Leavenworth and downrange. I'd especially like to thank Lt. Col. John Nagl (Ret) and Col. Derek Harvey (Ret) for their affectionate impatience with my block-headed civilian cast of mind. ("Klein, you're too lazy to tie your shoes in the morning," Nagl once said, eyeing my loafers.) I'd like to thank Paul Reickhoff of Iraq Afghanistan Veterans of America, David Gergen (who told me about Eric Greitens), Rachel Kleinfeld and Michael Breen of the Truman Project, and Paula Broadwell, all of whom introduced me to dozens of returning soldiers and Marines, spectacular young people whose stories were told in my August 2011 *Time* magazine cover story, "The New Greatest Generation." These include people who will surely help lead our democracy in the years to come — Congressman Seth Moulton, former VA Assistant Secretary Tommy Sowers, Elizabeth McNally, John Gallina and Dale Beatty of Purple Heart Homes, Nate Fick, Wes Moore, Rye Barcott, and Dr. David Callaway. Special thanks also to Admiral Mike Mullen, who has been a voice of sanity and intelligence throughout this process. And also to my *Time* magazine war buddies, Franco Pagetti and Bobby Ghosh.

I'd like to thank my editors at *Time* magazine — Jim Kelly, Rick Stengel, Nancy

Gibbs, and Michael Duffy — who allowed this old political reporter to become a war correspondent; especially Gibbs and Duffy, who gave me the time to write this book. I'd like to thank my wonderfully sharp and persistent editor at Simon & Schuster, Priscilla Painton, who simply would not let this book be any less than all it could be. And Jonathan Karp, Sophia Jimenez, and the rest of the team at S&S as well. Captain Nate Rawlings (Ret), Trish Stirling, and Alexandra Raphel were a trio of exemplary researchers, all of whom came to love the characters and premise of this work.

Thanks and cheers to my friend, Baroness and Bomb-Thrower Helena Kennedy, the principal of Mansfield College, Oxford, who made me a visiting fellow and gave me the time and space and alcohol necessary to write this book. (And her husband, Ian Hutchinson, for the medical care and laughs, when needed.) Ditto for Alex Jones of the Harvard Kennedy School's Shorenstein Center, an old friend, who allowed me to work on this book rather than write a research paper during my semester as a visiting fellow there.

My longtime friend and agent, and doppelgänger, Kathy Robbins deserves a paragraph all her own for her lifetime of . . .

well, just about everything. I could not have written the books I've written without her advice and support, brilliant editing, birthday parties, and all-around cheer.

Okay, finally: my family. Apologies. I know I get sort of obsessive when writing a book, especially one that sends me off to exotic places like Kandahar and St. Louis. These things take years to exorcise and you've lived through them more than once. Now I have not only children — Christopher, Terry, Sophie, and Teddy — to thank for their patience, but grandchildren — Zoe, Bibi, and Lucy — as well. And Lindsay Sobel, Ann Mah, and Silvia Santos, too.

Which leaves only Victoria, my love, and there is just not enough to say: You taught me how to live with joy, not just purpose. You are hilarious and beautiful, insanely creative and wicked smart. Boy, am I a lucky guy!

New Rochelle, February 2015

HOW YOU CAN HELP

The Mission Continues
1141 South 7th Street
St. Louis, MO 63104

Team Rubicon
300 N. Continental Blvd., Suite 100
El Segundo, CA 90245

Iraq and Afghanistan Veterans of America
292 Madison Avenue
New York, NY 10017

Give an Hour
P.O. Box 5918
Bethesda, MD 20824-5918

Ride2Recovery
23679 Calabasas Rd. #420
Calabasas, CA 91302

Team Red White and Blue
1110 W. Platt St.
Tampa, FL 33606

ABOUT THE AUTHOR

Joe Klein is an award-winning journalist and the author of seven books, including the #1 bestseller *Primary Colors* and most recently, *Politics Lost.* His weekly *Time* column, In the Arena, covers U.S. politics, elections, and foreign policy and has won two National Headliner Awards for best magazine column. Previously, he served as Washington correspondent for *The New Yorker* and as a political columnist for *Newsweek.* Klein is a member of the Council on Foreign Relations and a former Guggenheim fellow.

The employees of Thorndike Press hope you have enjoyed this Large Print book. All our Thorndike, Wheeler, and Kennebec Large Print titles are designed for easy reading, and all our books are made to last. Other Thorndike Press Large Print books are available at your library, through selected bookstores, or directly from us.

For information about titles, please call:
  (800) 223-1244

or visit our Web site at:
  http://gale.cengage.com/thorndike

To share your comments, please write:
  Publisher
  Thorndike Press
  10 Water St., Suite 310
  Waterville, ME 04901